USAF WARRIOR STUDIES

Richard H. Kohn and Joseph P. Harahan
General Editors

USAF Warrior Studies

Air Superiority in World War II and Korea, edited by Richard H. Kohn and Joseph P. Harahan, 1983
GPO Stock # 008-070-0489-5

The Command of the Air, by Giulio Douhet, New Imprint, 1983
GPO Stock # 008-070-0505-1

Condensed Analysis of the Ninth Air Force in the European Theater of Operations, 1984
GPO Stock # 008-070-0513-1

The Literature of Aeronautics, Astronautics, and Air Power, by Richard P. Hallion, 1984
GPO Stock # 008-070-0523-9

Over The Hump, by William H. Tunner, New Imprint, 1985
For distribution within the U.S. Air Force only

Air Interdiction in World War II, Korea, and Vietnam, edited by Richard H. Kohn and Joseph P. Harahan, 1986
GPO Stock # 008-070-00571-9

Air Leadership, edited by Wayne Thompson, 1986
GPO Stock # 008-070-00580-81

The Strategic Air War Against Germany and Japan: A Memoir, by Haywood S. Hansell, Jr., Maj. Gen., USAF, Ret., 1986
GPO Stock # 008-070-00583-2

The Organization and Lineage of the United States Air Force, by Charles Ravenstein, 1986
GPO Stock # 008-070-00570-1

Makers of the United States Air Force, edited by John L. Frisbee, 1987
GPO Stock # 008-070-00593-0

General Kenney Reports, by George C. Kenney, New Imprint, 1987
For distribution within the U.S. Air Force only

ULTRA and the Army Air Forces in World War II:

An Interview with Associate Justice of the U.S. Supreme Court Lewis F. Powell, Jr.

edited with an introduction and essay
by
Diane T. Putney

Office of Air Force History
United States Air Force
Washington, D.C., 1987

Library of Congress Cataloging-in-Publication Data

Powell, Lewis F., 1907-
ULTRA and the Army Air Forces in World War II.

(USAF warrior studies)
Bibliography: p.105
Includes index.
Supt. of Docs. D 301.96:UL8
1. World War, 1939-1945—Cryptography. 2. World War, 1939-1945—Electronic intelligence—United States. 3. United States. 4. Powell, Lewis F., 1907- —Interviews. 5. Judges—United States—Interviews. I. Putney, Diane T. (Diane Therese), 1949- II. Title. III. Series.
D810.C88P68 1987 940.54'86'73 87-600358
ISBN 0-912799-45-5 (pbk.)

Project Warrior Studies are published by the Office of Air Force History. The views expressed in this publication are those of the contributors and do not necessarily reflect the policies of the United States Air Force or the Department of Defense.

For sale by the Superintendent of Documents, U.S. Government Printing Office
Washington, D.C. 20402

Foreword

ULTRA and the Army Air Forces in World War II is part of a continuing series of historical volumes produced by the Office of Air Force History in direct support of Project Warrior. Since its beginning, in 1982, Project Warrior has captured the imagination of Air Force people around the world and reawakened a keener appreciation of our fundamental purpose as a Service: to deter war, but to fight and win should deterrence fail.

This volume is the first in the Warrior series to focus on intelligence, the collected and interpreted information about adversaries, which is the basis of wise decisionmaking in war. While intelligence is important to all military operations, it is especially significant to air forces, for the targets we choose and the ability to reach and destroy them often determine whether the speed, flexibility, and power of the aerial weapon is used to its utmost capacity to affect the outcome of combat.

Associate Justice of the U.S. Supreme Court Lewis F. Powell, Jr., was one of a small group of people specially selected to accept and integrate ULTRA, the most secret signals intelligence from intercepted and decoded German military radio transmissions, with intelligence from all other sources. From May 1944 to the end of the war in Europe, he served as the ULTRA officer on General Carl Spaatz's United States Strategic Air Forces staff. Earlier, Colonel Powell had served as an intelligence officer with the 319th Bomb Group, the Twelfth Air Force, and the Northwest African Air Forces. He finished the war as Spaatz's Chief of Operational Intelligence in addition to carrying out his ULTRA duties. The Air Force is grateful to Justice Powell for his generosity in giving his time and recollections so that his experiences can be of benefit, through the medium of history, to the Service today and in the future.

This volume will be part of an important new initiative by the Assistant Chief of Staff, Intelligence, to select and recommend books on intelligence in war to the men and women in Air Force intelligence. On this fortieth anniversary of our Service, eightieth of U.S. military air power, and two hundredth of the U.S. Constitution, it is entirely fitting for the Air Force to publish this fascinating and informative memoir by a citizen airman who helped to pioneer air intelligence in our nation's greatest aerial war.

LARRY D. WELCH, General, USAF
Chief of Staff

United States Air Force Historical Advisory Committee (As of July 1, 1987)

The Author

Dr. Diane T. Putney joined the Air Force history program in February 1982 as the historian for the 1100th Air Base Wing, Bolling Air Force Base, Washington, D.C. In September 1983, she moved to the Air Force Intelligence Service where she currently serves as the Chief of the Historical Research Office at Fort Belvoir, Virginia.

In 1984, Dr. Putney was appointed to the Advisory Councils of the Air Force Field History Program and the Historian Civilian Career Program. She holds memberships in the American Military Institute, the American Historical Association, and the Organization of American Historians. Her most recent publication is "The Canton Asylum for Insane Indians, 1902–1934" in *South Dakota History*.

Dr. Putney received her doctorate in American History from Marquette University in 1980.

Introduction

During World War II, the Americans and British intercepted and read hundreds of thousands of their enemies' secret military and diplomatic messages transmitted by radio. ULTRA was the designation for the signals intelligence derived from the radio communications which the Germans encrypted on their high-grade cipher machine called ENIGMA. The British Government Code and Cipher School at Bletchley Park, England, deciphered, analyzed, and evaluated the intercepted ENIGMA communications, produced ULTRA intelligence, and transmitted ULTRA to operational headquarters. The pay off for intelligence was in battle. Only now in the 1980s is the influence of ULTRA on Allied strategy, tactics, and victory beginning to be widely acknowledged and understood.

The Germans knew their enemies were listening to their secret radio communications, but they were confident their messages were undecipherable. The ENIGMA machine so enciphered the messages that the Germans assumed the contents could be deciphered only by duplicate ENIGMAs set according to precise and frequently changed settings. ENIGMA had been sold commercially in the 1920s, but the Germans modified it for military use, making it more complex and secure. The German navy began using ENIGMA in 1926, the German army in 1928, and the German Air Force in 1935.[1]

[1]Richard A. Woytak, "The Origins of the Ultra-Secret Code in Poland, 1937-1938," *Polish Review* 23 (1978): 79-85; Wladyslaw Kozaczuk, *Enigma: How the German Machine Cipher Was Broken, and How It Was Read by the Allies in World War Two*, trans. and ed. by Christopher Kasparek (Frederick MD, 1984), p xiii.

The Germans placed absolute trust in ENIGMA, which resembled a typewriter fitted with three revolving rotors, small light bulbs, plug board, wires, and batteries. Around the circumference of each rotor was an adjustable ring which could be set at one of twenty-six positions, corresponding to the letters of the alphabet. To encipher a plain text message, a clerk followed printed instructions sent to him periodically. He placed the three rotors into the machine in a certain order, connected plugs in a certain way, and set the rotor rings to predetermined settings. He then independently selected three letters for the rotor rings and enciphered the three letters two times, placing the six cipher letters at the start of the message. This was the message key.

The clerk next set the rotor rings to the three letters he had selected. He then typed the message a letter at a time, which sent an electric current through the wires, rotors, and plugs and by a complex electromechanical process transformed the original letter into another. The new cipher letter was revealed as the electric current lit the appropriately lettered light bulb. As one clerk typed the key strokes for the plain text message, a second clerk recorded the enciphered letters as they lit in response to the key strokes. The enciphered letters were grouped in fives, and this text became the ENIGMA message transmitted in Morse code by radio. At the receiving end, the enciphered message was typed on a similar ENIGMA machine set at the proper rotor positions, which translated the message back into plain text.[2]

As early as 1927, Polish cryptanalysts associated with the Polish General Staff's Cipher Bureau in Warsaw were trying to decipher ENIGMA intercepts using calculations derived from the branch of higher mathematics dealing with permutation groups and theory. The Poles knew some sort of machine was producing the German military ciphers, but they did not know what it looked like or how it operated. Sometime in 1932 they learned the machine was ENIGMA, and acquired an old commercial model. Then in December 1932, Capt. Gustave Bertrand, the chief of French radio intelligence, met with Polish cryptanalysts in Warsaw and shared with them documents about the German military ENIGMA. Bertrand had acquired the documents from a German traitor codenamed ASCHE. With the information from ASCHE, combined with their own mathematical analysis concentrated against the double encipherment of the three letters in the message key, Polish cryptanalysts broke ENIGMA ciphers at the end of 1932. During the 1930s, the Poles read ENIGMA messages by using Polish-made duplicates of ENIGMA.[3]

---

[2]Kozaczuk, *Enigma*, pp 247–251, 273, 288.

[3]*Ibid*, pp 12–13, 16–18, 25–49, 67, 274; F. H. Hinsley *et al, British Intelligence in the Second World War: Its Influence on Strategy and Operations*, 3 vols, Vol 1 (London, 1979) p 488.

In 1938 the Germans changed encipherment procedures and made additional modifications to the 20,000 ENIGMAs then in use. The Poles found these changes difficult to counter. At midnight on September 15, 1938, the Germans initiated the procedure whereby ENIGMA clerks independently selected an additional three letters for rotor ring settings, placed them in plain text at the start of the message, and then used them as initial ring settings for producing the message key. This modification vastly complicated the decryption effort and forced the Poles to use rapid calculating machines to test ENIGMA settings. Called BOMBAs, these rudimentary computing machines were electromechanical and based on the operation of six interconnected ENIGMAs. The Poles also began to use a series of paper sheets perforated at precise coordinates to determine at which of the twenty-six letters the rotor rings were set. These sheets resembled smaller versions of modern key punch cards. The sheets were superimposed and moved in respect to each other, and as the number of holes decreased, the solution became closer. A single remaining hole visible through all the sheets indicated the probable solution of a rotor setting.[4]

By the end of November 1938, the Poles could again read German army and air force ENIGMA messages. In December, however, the Germans added two more rotors, allowing the clerks to select the required three rotors from a group of five, adding to the number of encipherment possibilities. Then in January 1939, the Germans increased the number of ENIGMA plug connections vastly complicating the encipherment process. Now the Poles were completely shut out of ENIGMA message traffic, except for that of the *Sicherheitsdienst*, the Nazi Party's security and political intelligence organization, which had delayed in adopting the modifications for its ENIGMAs.[5]

In January and July 1939, Polish, French, and British cryptanalysts met in Paris and Warsaw to exchange cryptanalytic information. The July meeting in Warsaw was extraordinary. Because the political situation between Poland and Germany had deteriorated so badly and the progress against ENIGMA was so slow, the Poles shared all of their knowledge about ENIGMA with the British and French, including two Polish-made ENIGMAs and the design for the BOMBA. When Germany invaded Poland in September 1939, key Polish cryptanalysts escaped to France where they continued to work on German intercepts in cooperation with the British. The British then greatly expanded the magnitude of the crytanalytic effort against ENIGMA.[6]

The Government Code and Cipher School was the British organization responsible for studying the cipher communications of other countries and

---

[4]Kozaczuk, *Enigma*, pp 48–49, 52–54, 63, 267–68, 289.

[5]*Ibid*, pp 43, 52–55, 63, 265.

[6]*Ibid*, pp 56–60, 64, 96, 99.

for advising the British about the security of their own codes and ciphers. When the war started in 1939, the Government Code and Cipher School moved from London to the greater safety of Bletchley Park, an estate about fifty miles northwest of London. The challenge of cracking the ciphers of the ENIGMAs used by the German army, air force, navy, diplomats, and paramilitary units was formidable. The possible cipher solutions were astronomical: 150 quadrillion. With the assistance from the Poles and relying on their own brilliant mathematicians and cryptanalysts, who had been at work on ENIGMA intercepts since the late 1930s, the British achieved remarkable success. As early as May 1940 the British were using their own British-made calculating machines, called BOMBEs (after the Polish BOMBAs), but these machines were different in design from the Polish inventions and more powerful. Throughout the war, the British continued to build and use even faster and more complicated calculating machines. As a result, Bletchley Park produced nearly 84,000 ENIGMA decrypts per month from the end of 1943 to May 1945.[7]

Once the cryptanalysts at Bletchley Park deciphered German army and air force messages, they passed them over to the intelligence officers, who translated, emended, evaluated, and analyzed the messages to produce what the British termed ULTRA intelligence. The officers then prepared ULTRA messages for transmittal to operational commands. The British encrypted ULTRA on their TYPEX cipher machine and sent it over special radio links to Special Liaison Units at the operational command headquarters.

Across the Atlantic, the Americans were also making remarkable progress against ciphered enemy radio communications. As early as 1940, the Americans were reading high-grade Japanese diplomatic ciphers produced on the machine the Americans called PURPLE. In 1942 the U.S. Navy broke Japanese naval ciphers, and in 1943 the U.S. Army broke Japanese army ciphers. Within the War Department, the Signal Intelligence Service, located at Arlington Hall in northern Virginia, deciphered and translated Japanese messages with the help of American-made BOMBEs. The cryptanalysts at Arlington Hall then passed the decrypts to the intelligence officers in the Special Branch of the Military Intelligence Service at the Pentagon, who evaluated and disseminated the signals intelligence to the Army and Army Air Forces.

In May 1943, the American War Department and the British Government Code and Cipher School formally agreed to cooperate in their cryptologic endeavors and their exploitation of signals intelligence. Among the many points of their formal agreement was a section which required sending "liaison officers" to army and air headquarters to provide operational

[7]Hinsley, *British Intelligence in the Second World War*, Vol 1, pp 20, 487, 494 and Vol 2, pp 28, 659–61.

commanders with ULTRA intelligence. Col. Alfred McCormack of the Special Branch recruited the American liaison officers; among them was Maj. Lewis F. Powell, Jr., an intelligence officer in the Army Air Forces. The recruits who served in the European and Pacific theaters were known as Special Security Officers or Representatives. Their primary duties were to receive and safeguard ULTRA, present it to commanders and authorized recipients, and assist in fusing it with intelligence from other sources. The Special Security Officers assigned to Europe received training at Special Branch and at Bletchley Park. Major Powell was assigned to Headquarters, U.S. Strategic Air Forces in Europe.

The small band of men recruited for this duty in the European theater has been described by Stephen E. Ambrose in *Ike's Spies*: "The Army's selection process was superb. It managed to locate precisely the two dozen or so officers who were perfect for the job. . . . They had to be diplomatic enough not to offend the senior generals to whom they reported, but firm enough to make sure the generals heard what they had to say. . . . Men who are absolutely trustworthy, mentally quick, tireless, and self-effacing are few in number—but America had enough of them, and the Army found them. To a man, they did an outstanding job during the war; to a man, they kept their trust, not one of them ever revealing the ULTRA secret or his part in the war."[8]

In Europe, each Special Security Officer received a steady stream of ULTRA messages from Bletchley Park. ULTRA's unquestionable authenticity made it the basis of most Allied intelligence about German military operations. In June 1945, Lt. Col. William W. Haines, an Army Air Forces officer who served at the British Air Ministry, commented, "It is doubtful if any armed force in history ever had such thorough and timely knowledge of its enemies' capabilities, condition and intentions as 'ULTRA' has given the Allied Forces in this theater." In July 1945, Gen. Dwight D. Eisenhower wrote about ULTRA to the Chief of the British Secret Service: "The intelligence which has emanated from you before and during this campaign has been of priceless value to me. It has simplified my task as commander enormously. It has saved thousands of British and American lives and, in no small way, contributed to the speed with which the enemy was routed and eventually forced to surrender."[9]

ULTRA remained the great secret of World War II for nearly thirty years after the war. In part, this was because an ULTRA message sent on

---

[8]Stephen E. Ambrose, *Ike's Spies: Eisenhower and the Espionage Establishment* (Garden City, NY, 1981), p 56.

[9]SRH-013, "History of US Strategic Air Force[s] Europe vs. German Air Forces," p 4, RG 457, NA; Letter, General Eisenhower to Maj. Gen. Sir Stewart G. Menzies, 12 July 1945, File Folder "MELO-MEN (Misc.)," Box 77, Papers of Gen. Dwight D. Eisenhower, 1916–52, Dwight D. Eisenhower Library, Abilene, Kansas.

May 25, 1945, at the request of Prime Minister Winston Churchill, ordered each person indoctrinated in ULTRA not to divulge the fact that ENIGMA ciphers were read and that ULTRA existed.[10] In America, too, information on ULTRA and signals intelligence remained highly classified. Two books published in 1967 and 1973 in Polish and French, respectively, revealed that ENIGMA intercepts were broken and read, but the books received little notice. In 1974, Frederick W. Winterbotham, the British group captain who established the Special Liaison Units and who was responsible for ULTRA's security, published his memoir, *The Ultra Secret*, which became an instant bestseller. The book generated worldwide notice and led to televison and radio programs, magazine articles, letters to the editor, and other books on ULTRA.

The initial revelations about ULTRA led some people to speculate that reputations of some Allied commanders would have to be revised, that ULTRA was responsible for Allied victory, and that the history of World War II would have to be rewritten. Historians were willing to reexamine their conclusions in light of new evidence, but they still had to wait years until the U.S. and British governments declassified and released ULTRA documents. By the 1980s, however, some ULTRA documents had already been destroyed by individuals who had no understanding of the historic value of the material. Other ULTRA documents remained highly classified and unavailable to researchers. Nonetheless, ULTRA, and in a broader sense, intelligence and its influence on strategy and operations, has been a subject of foremost importance in World War II historiography in the last ten years. The subject requires further study, but well-founded conclusions have already been drawn about the influential role of intelligence in the Battle of Britain; the destruction of Axis shipping in the Mediterranean; the land and air campaigns to capture Sicily; the Battle of the Atlantic; the preparations for D-Day, including the successful deception plans and the destruction of German airfields near the English Channel and Normandy beaches; land battles in northern France after D-Day, including those before and during the capture of 50,000 Germans in the Argentan-Falaise pocket; and the sustained strategic bombing campaign against the most vital part of Germany's economy, the synthetic oil plants.[11]

[10]F. W. Winterbotham, *The Ultra Secret*, (New York, 1974, reprint 1982), p 15.

[11]SRH-230, Henry F. Schorreck, "The Role of COMINT in the Battle of Midway," RG 457, NA; Ralph Bennett, "Ultra and Some Command Decisions," *Journal of Contemporary History* 16 (1981): 131–51; Harold C. Deutsch, "The Historical Impact of Revealing the Ultra Secret," *Parameters, Journal of the U.S. Army War College* 8 (December 1978): 2–15; Stephen E. Ambrose, "Eisenhower and the Intelligence Community in World War II," *Journal of Contemporary History* 16 (1981): 153–66; David Kahn, "The Significance of Codebreaking and Intelligence in Allied Strategy and Tactics," *Cryptologia* 1 (July 1977): 209–22; Williamson Murray, "Ultra: Some Thoughts on Its Impact on the Second World War," *Air University Review* 35 (July-August 1984): 52–64.

INTRODUCTION

Lewis Franklin Powell, Jr., was born September 19, 1907, in Suffolk, Virginia. In 1929 Washington and Lee University awarded him the bachelor of science degree, *magna cum laude*, and in 1931 the bachelor of laws degree. He was admitted to the Virginia Bar in 1931. In 1932, he attended Harvard Law School and was graduated with a master of laws degree. That same year he began his legal practice in Richmond with the law firm Christian, Barton and Parker. In 1935 he became associated with the firm of Hunton, Williams, Anderson, Gay and Moore. Except for his military service, Powell remained with this firm, renamed Hunton, Williams, Gay, Powell and Gibson, until 1971.

He married Josephine Pierce Rucker of Richmond in 1936, and they had four children: Josephine Powell Smith, Ann Powell Carmody, Mary Powell Sumner, and Lewis Franklin Powell III.

During World War II, Powell served as a combat and staff intelligence officer with the Army Air Forces from May 1942 to February 1946, achieving the rank of colonel. From May to June 1942, he received his basic officer's training at Miami, Florida, and then was assigned for six weeks to the Army Air Forces Air Intelligence School at Harrisburg, Pennsylvania. At the conclusion of his intelligence training, he reported to the 319th Bomb Group at Harding Field, Louisiana, arriving there in early August 1942. Within a month, the 319th Bomb Group was on its way to England in preparation for Operation TORCH, the great Allied invasion of Northwest Africa. While in England, Powell received additional training by the Eighth Bomber Command and at the Royal Air Force school on the Isle of Man. In the TORCH invasion, Powell was a member of the Center Task Force and went ashore in Algeria on November 8, 1942.

In Northwest Africa, Powell briefed combat crews on the importance of targets and enemy defenses (flak and aircraft) and debriefed crews upon their return from missions. He also trained crews in aircraft, ship, and tank recognition and maintained target folders, maps, target charts, reconnaissance photographs, and flak and situation maps.

In February 1943, Powell was transferred to the Headquarters of the Twelfth Air Force, which was located first at Algiers, Algeria, and then at Constantine, Algeria. Shortly after the Germans surrendered in North Africa in May 1943, he was reassigned to the Advanced Headquarters of the Northwest African Air Forces, located at La Marsa in Tunis, Tunisia. In early September 1943, after the invasion of Sicily, Powell returned to the United States for assignment at the Army Air Forces Air Intelligence School. On one of his frequent trips to the Pentagon, he was recruited into the Special Branch and indoctrinated in ULTRA intelligence. In February and March 1944, Powell was at Bletchley Park, receiving intensive ULTRA briefings on the German Air Force. In April and May 1944, Powell toured operational air commands in the Mediterranean theater to see firsthand how ULTRA was used in combat operations. In May 1944 he assumed the duties as Special Security Representative to Headquarters, U.S. Strategic Air Forces in Europe. Three months later, he took the additional duty as Chief of Operational Intelligence of the U.S. Strategic Air Forces in Europe.

At the conclusion of the European war, Powell was transferred to the British Air Ministry, where he was the liaison officer representing the Military Intelligence Service. He ended his wartime service in February 1946 and was awarded the Legion of Merit, the Bronze Star, and the French *Croix de Guerre* with Palm.

He returned to Richmond, Virginia, after the war, resumed his law practice (including responsibilities as the General Counsel for the Colonial Williamsburg Foundation), and devoted himself to public service. From 1947 to 1948, he was chairman of the Special Commission which wrote the charter introducing the manager form of government to Richmond. From 1952 to 1961, he was chairman of the Richmond Public School Board. He then served as a member of the Virginia State Board of Education from 1961 to 1969, and as the board's president from 1968 to 1969. He served as a member of the National Commission on Law Enforcement and Administration of Justice, appointed by President Lyndon B. Johnson, from 1965 to 1967; as a member of the National Advisory Committee on Legal Services to the Poor from 1965 to 1966; and as a member of the Blue Ribbon Defense Panel, appointed by President Richard M. Nixon, from 1969 to 1970. He also served as president of the American Bar Association from 1964 to 1965, as president of the American College of Trial Lawyers from 1969 to 1970, and as president of the American Bar Foundation from 1969 to 1971.

President Richard M. Nixon nominated Powell as Associate Justice of the United States Supreme Court on October 21, 1971. He was confirmed by the U.S. Senate on December 7, 1971, and took office on January 7, 1972, serving until his retirement on June 26, 1987.

ULTRA and the Army Air Forces in World War II is basically an oral history interview with Justice Powell concerning his military service as an Army Air Forces intelligence officer in World War II. Dr. Richard H. Kohn, Chief of the Office of Air Force History, and Dr. Diane T. Putney, Chief of the Historical Research Office of the Air Force Intelligence Service, conducted the three-hour interview in the Justice's chambers at the Supreme Court Building, Washington, D.C., on September 20, 1984. The Historical Research Office of the Air Force Intelligence Service transcribed and edited the interview and sent it to Justice Powell and Dr. Kohn, both of whom had an opportunity to edit it for clarity of expression, accuracy of information, and amplification of topics. The final version of the transcript is thus best described as both a memoir and oral history interview.

While preparing the interview's explanatory footnotes and accompanying article, Dr. Putney often corresponded with Justice Powell and spoke with him on the telephone. He answered additional questions asked, sent photographs his wife had found in the attic, provided written recollections of his war experiences, and shared letters he had received from individuals mentioned in the interview. Some of these documents and photographs have been included in the volume in order to amplify the interview and to provide additional material to readers interested in ULTRA.

Special thanks are due to Justice Lewis F. Powell, Jr., and his wife Josephine for generosity with their time, memories, photographs, and documents. Current and former Assistant Chiefs of Staff, Intelligence, Maj. Gen. Schuyler Bissell, Lt. Gen. Leonard H. Perroots, and Maj. Gen. James C. Pfautz, encouraged and supported this undertaking. Kathy M. Ward, Brunetta Massey, and Patricia K. Garcia of the Air Force Intelligence Service provided typing, transcription, and editing assistance. Drs. Richard H. Kohn and Joseph P. Harahan of the Office of Air Force History led the manuscript review process and provided overall guidance. The final product benefitted considerably from the review and criticism of Dr. Eduard M. Mark, Mr. Jacob Neufeld, Col. John F. Shiner, and Mr. Herman S. Wolk of the Office of Air Force History; Mr. DeWitt S. Copp and Dr. Norman Graebner of the Air Force History Advisory Committee; Dr. J. Kenneth McDonald of the Central Intelligence Agency; and Dr. Thomas Johnson and Mr. Henry F. Schorreck of the National Security Agency. Special appreciation is due Ms. Vanessa D. Allen, who edited and prepared the manuscript for publication, including layout. Dr. Alfred Beck was the computer troubleshooter and assisted with contracting procedures.

Contents

Page

Foreword v

Introduction ix

Lewis F. Powell, Jr.: An ULTRA Memoir, *Diane T. Putney and Richard H. Kohn* 1

The U.S. Military Intelligence Service: The ULTRA Mission, *Diane T. Putney* 65

Endnotes 99

Bibliography 105

Appendices:

1. Memorandum of Activities of Intelligence Section of the 319th Bomb Group, 28 August 1943 111

2. Notes Taken at Bletchley Park, February–March 1944 116

CONTENTS

Page

3. Excerpt from Report on Visit to Operational Air Commands, 14 May 1944 168

4. Memorandum on the Operational Intelligence Section of USSTAF, 1 June 1944 172

5. Notes on Operational Intelligence Division, USSTAF, 9 June 1945 178

6. Citation for Legion of Merit 190

Index 193

Photographs:

Bletchley Park .... cover

Col. Egmont F. Koenig receives Harrisburg Academy keys 3

Capt. Lewis F. Powell, Jr.'s unit "messing" at Tafaraoui 7

Maj. Gen. Carl A. "Tooey" Spaatz and Air Chief Marshal Arthur Tedder 8

AAF intelligence officer inspecting reconnaissance photography ... 14

Capt. Lewis F. Powell, Jr. 23

Gen. Carl A. Spaatz 30

Ruins of ball bearing factory in Schweinfurt 36

Boeing B-17 38

Devastated Krupp works 45

Lt. Gen. Ira C. Eaker and Ambassador Averell Harriman 46

V-1 buzz bomb 49

	Page
Bombing of Dresden	56
Lt. Col. William W. Haines and Lt. Col. Lewis F. Powell, Jr.	60
Maj. Gen. Frederick L. Anderson and Col. Alfred A. Kessler	63
Purple Analog	69
War Department Munitions Building	72
Col. Alfred McCormack	75
Captured ENIGMA machine	79
German cipher clerks using ENIGMA machine	79
Converter M-134-C or SIGABA machine	83
Brig. Gen. Carter W. Clarke and Col. Alfred McCormack	87
Pilot debriefing after reconnaissance mission	89
Maj. Gen. Elwood R. Quesada	95

ULTRA and the Army Air Forces in World War II:

an interview with
Associate Justice of the Supreme Court
Lewis F. Powell, Jr.
conducted by
Dr. Richard H. Kohn
Chief, Office of Air Force History
and
Dr. Diane T. Putney
Chief, Air Force Intelligence Service
Historical Research Office

Lewis F. Powell, Jr.: An ULTRA Memoir

Putney: Would you explain the background and circumstances of your joining the U.S. Army Air Forces in 1942?

Powell: During the late 1930s, I was very concerned about Nazi Germany and about the isolationism that was in the United States—even in the presidential campaign of 1940. I was active in the Young Lawyers Section of the American Bar Association, and I initiated a program that was called the Public Information Program to try to make lawyers, and to some extent people in the public, appreciate the threat from Nazi Germany to western civilization and freedom. I was quite impatient for our country to come to the aid of England after the French surrendered.

Following Pearl Harbor, even though I was thirty-four years old and had a wife and two small daughters, I applied to the Navy. I had heard of a Navy intelligence school up in New England. I spent two or three months trying to memorize eye charts, because I had poor eyes. I never succeeded. They kept changing the charts, and finally the last time I took a look, they had one of those machines that projected different things on a screen. I even was presumptuous enough to write a letter to Mr. Forrestal, Secretary of the Navy, whom I had met; I had a pleasant evening with him once.[1] Some staff person wrote me the letter I deserved and said there was nothing he could do about me—or my eyes.

[1]James V. Forrestal (1892–1949) was appointed by President Franklin D. Roosevelt to the newly created Office of Undersecretary of the Navy in August 1940. When Frank [William F.] Knox died in May 1944, Forrestal succeeded him as Secretary of the Navy. In September 1947 Forrestal became the first Secretary of Defense, a position he held until March 1949.

I heard then of the Air Force Intelligence School in Harrisburg, Pennsylvania.[2] A friend of mine, a reserve officer who was sent to England to see how the British conducted combat intelligence, told me about it. I applied and was commissioned a first lieutenant. I was sent to officers' training camp at Miami Beach. I arrived in May of 1942 and spent six weeks there. I then attended the Air Force Intelligence School at Harrisburg. That, as I recall, was six weeks. There were 300 men in my class—no women—and I think we were the third class at that institution. The school was headed by an Army colonel named Koenig, who impressed me very favorably.[3] He ran the school the way a military school should be run. One of the instructors was a British squadron officer who had been in the Battle of Britain, and wounded as I recall.[4] He inspired all of us. I was among ten honor graduates in my class.

We were given opportunities at graduation to indicate our choice of what we would like to do, and I applied for service with a bomber group for the European theater. I was sent to the 319th Bomb Group, in training at Harding Field in Louisiana. I arrived there early in August of 1942. I have a letter that I wrote a few years ago to Colonel Poore, who then commanded the 319th.[5] He asked me if I would summarize briefly my recollections of the 319th's early history. In summary, I told him that the group was very poorly trained, and some first pilots had only about 125 to 150 hours of flying time. We had casualties, and before we left Harding Field, we had a midair collision. We were ordered to go to England early in September of 1942, and three squadrons undertook to fly the Atlantic by the northern route. Those three squadrons, as I recall, lost five or six airplanes just to weather and getting lost. The 319th was equipped with twin-engine B–26 bombers sometimes called the flying "coffins."

[2]The Army Air Forces (AAF) Air Intelligence School, established on the site of the Harrisburg Academy at Harrisburg, Pennsylvania, on April 13, 1942, operated until March 30, 1944. The school trained approximately 5,600 intelligence officers for service with the AAF. At first the school offered courses in photographic interpretation and combat intelligence, but soon added courses in prisoner-of-war interrogation and air base intelligence, which was an eclectic course, including map reading, report writing, base security, censorship, and counterintelligence.

[3]Army Col. Egmont F. Koenig (1892–1974) served as the first Commandant of the AAF Air Intelligence School from April 13 to September 30, 1942. He patterned the operation of the school after the Command and General Staff School at Fort Leavenworth, Kansas.

[4]Squadron Leader Herbert Priestley joined the AAF Air Intelligence School faculty as the Royal Air Force (RAF) liaison officer on April 25, 1942, ten days after the first class started. He had served as an intelligence officer during the Battle of Britain and was an authority on RAF procedures.

[5]For the letter from Justice Powell to Col. Walter H. Poore, June 30, 1980, see Lewis F. Powell, Jr., Papers, USAF Historical Research Center, Maxwell Air Force Base, AL. The center also holds the official histories of the 319th Bomb Group.

The ground echelon, which included intelligence officers, went on the Queen Mary. The living was not posh. There were seventeen thousand troops on the Queen Mary, more people than it had ever carried before or since. The 1st Infantry Division, the entire division, was aboard. I was appalled when we sailed out of New York Harbor in broad daylight. I was then a first lieutenant, and I found myself assigned as the last man to a stateroom that normally accommodated two people, and there were fifteen other people already there. They had put bunks four high. I had one up next to the ceiling.

I was the commanding officer of the ground echelon of my squadron, so I was in on the daily briefing by the captain of the ship. After we had been out about three and a half days, he told us that the Admiralty had advised—and it may have been ULTRA—that there were U-boats in the normal route. We then went all the way north of Iceland or made a big turn in that direction. We were a day and a half late getting to England. Our group ended up on a base in East Anglia. It was a temporary air base not far from Norwich. I took my wife back there four or five years later, and we could not find it at first. We finally did locate the runway. We trained there not knowing what we were going to do because we were in a twin-engine bomber group, not a four-engine group, and it seemed curious to be operating out of England against Germany with that type of aircraft. It turned out that England was just a stop for a couple of months on the way to North Africa.

Army Col. Egmont F. Koenig receives old Harrisburg Academy keys.

While I was in England, I was sent to a Royal Air Force (RAF) school on the Isle of Man. The school, I thought, wasted a lot of time teaching us how to identify airplanes, although that was a role of a combat intelligence officer, so that was helpful. We were given some general instruction in what combat intelligence officers had to do. We got a good deal of it at Harrisburg, of course, but here the instructors had been in combat themselves.

I never quite finished that course, because I was ordered back to my group. I spent less than twenty-four hours there before we were on a troop train at night going down to Bristol, where we boarded a ship that assembled later into one of the convoys that went to North Africa. We were issued, in addition to combat uniforms, some arctic equipment. Only senior officers knew our destination. Some of us thought it might be Murmansk in the Soviet Union. The invasion of North Africa was a well kept secret.[6]

The convoy that I was in was quite a large one. Incidentally, the 1st Infantry Division was in it, and we went ashore east of Oran on a wide beach called Arzeu Beach. The French had a fort there, and as they withdrew, there was fighting for about three days. They could not compete very long with the 1st Infantry Division. Admiral Darlan ordered the French to stop fighting.[7]

Kohn: Was there something about intelligence from the very beginning that attracted you? Why did you choose to go into intelligence work?

---

[6]The Allied invasion of Northwest Africa, Operation TORCH, took place on November 8, 1942. The largest amphibious invasion thus far in the history of warfare, it involved 300 warships and 370 merchant ships. The Supreme Commander of the Allied Expeditionary Force, Lt. Gen. Dwight D. Eisenhower, led the 107,000 men during three landings on the North African coast: the Western Task Force (U.S. Army units transported by the U.S. Navy) went ashore at Casablanca, Morocco; the Center Task Force, (U.S. Army units transported by the Royal Navy) landed at Oran, Algeria; and the Eastern Task Force (U.S. Army and Royal Army units transported by the Royal Navy) landed at Algiers, Algeria. See Thomas E. Griess, ed., *The Second World War: Europe and the Mediterranean*, West Point Military History Series (Wayne, NJ, 1984), pp 171–72; George F. Howe, *Northwest Africa: Seizing the Initiative in the West*, [United States Army in World War II: The Mediterranean Theater of Operations] (Washington, 1957; reprint 1970), pp 31, 89–252.

[7]TORCH landings were politically problematic, because Algeria and Morocco were French. After Germany invaded and defeated the French in June 1940, the French government in Vichy was left in control of French colonies in Northwest Africa so long as it defended them against attacks from all nations. As TORCH commenced, the official position of the Vichy government was to urge resistance against the invaders and to break diplomatic relations with the United States. The French did resist briefly at all landing areas, but in different degrees. At Algiers, invading forces arrested Adm. Jean François Darlan, the commander of all armed forces in Vichy France. On November 10, 1942, Darlan issued directives broadcast over radio, ordering French forces in North Africa, which included Tunisia, to cease resistance. The next day, all French hostilities ended. With American and British approval, on December 1, Darlan became chief of state in French North Africa, but he was assassinated in Algiers December 24, 1942. See Howe, *Northwest Africa*, pp 4–5, 22, 77, 253–73.

Powell: I was a lawyer, and I think a good many lawyers entered intelligence in the Navy, Army, and Army Air Forces. Legal training was not directly related, but it was basically good training. The British recruited a number of their combat intelligence officers from the bar. I was a little old for combat. I never had any military training. The closest military activity that had come to my family was during the Civil War. My grandfather on my mother's side was a Confederate veteran as was my great grandfather on my father's side. My father was too old to serve in World War I. I suppose a short answer is that I felt I was best qualified to be an intelligence officer.

Putney: When did you arrive in North Africa?

Powell: November 8, 1942. We in the Army Air Forces did not storm the beaches. We went in very promptly as soon as the beaches were thought to be secure. Snipers took potshots at us, and one of my people was killed the first night we were there. It was several days before we really operated from an air base called Tafaraoui. Our airplanes flew down from England, as did two B-17 groups, when this air base was made secure. This was a French base near Oran, and then we moved up to the air base that served the city of Algiers, Maison Blanche. That was almost exclusively by then a military air base. Initially, the intelligence section of my group also served the two B-17 groups.

But apart from interrogating aircrews, the intelligence section of my group really did very little in those early days in North Africa. The headquarters of the Twelfth Air Force was on the same base as we were, both at Tafaraoui and at Maison Blanche. We primarily relied on intelligence from the Twelfth Air Force. It eventually began to put out intelligence summaries. We had all had some training on the German Air Force; the initial targets were the harbors and air bases in Tunis that we knew about. Of course, the Germans came in immediately after we landed, but they did not attack our invasion forces.

It may interest both of you to know that I had an opportunity after the war to interview the German colonel who had been in charge of German Air Force intelligence in the Mediterranean, and I asked him why in the world the Germans let two enormous convoys proceed unattacked; one landed just west of Algiers, and the one I was in went in on both sides of Oran. We must have had 30 to 35 or 40 ships in our convoy. We did not see a single German airplane for several days. He said they had misappreciated our objectives and thought the African landing was a feint. They thought it would make a lot more sense for us to have gone to Sicily or, perhaps Malta, or even to reinforce the Eighth Army in the eastern desert under Montgomery.

Putney: At this time did you interrogate any prisoners of war or were you debriefing pilots?

Powell: Just pilots. In fact months passed before I even saw a PW. If you are familiar with the battle of Kasserine Pass, you know that the early months in North Africa were less than successful.[8] At the time of that battle we were on an air base not terribly far from Kasserine, called Telergma, which was southwest of Constantine. No hard surface landing strips were there; we were operating on grass runways that the French Foreign Legion had used. There were no PXs, no American supplies for a long time. We were eating C-rations and sleeping in tents and in part of an old French barracks. There was no hot water, no running water in any toilet facility; everything was outdoors. That was a memorable experience. We also had fairly heavy combat losses, primarily because we were making low-level attacks in our B-26s.

The really effective work that my group did before it was taken out of operations was skip bombing of enemy ships in the Sicilian Straits.[9] And the intelligence must have come from ULTRA. We knew nothing about ULTRA at that level, of course, but we would receive orders from the Twelfth Air Force to send our bombers out in the Sicilian Straits. Headquarters would give us some approximate coordinates and give us an approximate time for the mission, and more often than not we would find targets.[10]

Kohn: Did you ever ask yourselves, as intelligence officers, "Where are they getting the information to task us so exactly?"

---

[8]On February 14, 1943, the Germans launched an offensive against the Allies in Tunisia, seizing Sidi-bou-Zid, Sbeitla, Gafsa, and the Thelepte airfield and causing panic among the inexperienced Americans of the II Corps. The Americans stubbornly resisted at the Kasserine Pass, but on February 20, the Germans broke through the pass and entered Thala. The Allies then counterattacked, and on February 22, the Germans began an orderly retreat back through the pass to the Mareth Line, as the British Eighth Army approached from the south. The U.S. 1st Armored Division was the Allied unit hit hardest, suffering 1,401 men killed, wounded, or missing. See Howe, *Northwest Africa*, pp 438–80.

[9]Skip bombing was a tactic by which ships were attacked broadside from low altitude using bombs with delayed-action fuzes. The bombs "skipped" along the surface of the water until they struck the side of the ship, then sank below the water before detonating. The bombing was done in high-speed runs from less than 200 feet; typically, 500-pound bombs were directed at the target ships. The B-26s of the 319th Bomb Group began their attacks against Axis shipping from Sicily on January 15, 1943.

[10]See Appendix 1 for Capt. Lewis F. Powell, Jr., "Memorandum of Activities of Intelligence Section of 319th Bomb Group from June, 1942 to March, 1943," 28 August 1943.

Powell's unit "messing" at Tafaraoui air base. *Courtesy Lewis F. Powell, Jr.*

Powell: I thought this information came—as it often did—from Coastal Command reconnaissance, but I really did not know. I'll move on, and then I'll answer your question in a different way. When my group was taken out of operations, sometime in late February of 1943, rather than go back to Morocco, where the group was to rest and refit with additional planes and fresh crews, I was sent to the Twelfth Air Force headquarters and was put into its operational or combat intelligence unit. I have no idea why I was sent to headquarters, but was happy to avoid the inaction of refitting my group.

Twelfth Air Force was then headquartered in Algiers. After I was there for only a brief period, it was moved to Constantine, a fascinating city in the Atlas mountains, perhaps fifteen miles north of Telergma, where my group had been based. General Spaatz had come down from England and succeeded General Doolittle, and then General Cannon became commander of the Twelfth Air Force.[11] George McDonald was its chief intelligence

[11]Brig. Gen. James H. Doolittle (1896-) assumed command of the Twelfth Air Force (12th AF) on September 23, 1942, in England. Five months earlier, he had led sixteen B-25s on the daring raid over Japan for which he won the Medal of Honor. He was promoted to major general in November 1942, while commanding the 12th AF in North Africa.

Maj. Gen. Carl A. "Tooey" Spaatz (1891-1974) succeeded Doolittle as commander of the 12th AF on March 1, 1943; two weeks later he was promoted to lieutenant general. He also commanded the newly established Northwest African Air Forces (NWAAF), which included the 12th AF.

Maj. Gen. John K. Cannon (1892-1955) replaced Spaatz as 12th AF commander on December 21, 1943; he also commanded the Mediterranean Allied Tactical Air Command and was responsible for all air operations for the invasion of southern France in August 1944.

Maj. Gen. Carl A. "Tooey" Spaatz (left) and Air Chief Marshal Arthur Tedder.

officer.[12] Before the Germans surrendered in North Africa in early May, as I recall, the Northwest African Air Forces were formed.[13] At least for air

[12]Brig. Gen. George C. McDonald (1898–1969) became the Director of Intelligence for the 12th AF in December 1942 and subsequently assumed the same responsibility for the NWAAF. In February 1944 he was named Director of Intelligence for the U.S. Strategic Air Forces in Europe (USSTAF). During World War I, McDonald was trained as a pilot and served with the 5th Aero Squadron. His interwar service included assignments with aerial photographic units. From 1939 to 1941 he was the Assistant Military Attache for Air and the Assistant Military Attache at the American Embassy in London. During this tour, he reported on the Battle of Britain. In October 1941 he was appointed to the Military Mission, Office of the Coordination of Information (later named Office of Strategic Services). During the war, McDonald helped to establish the Allied evasion and escape system to help downed AAF personnel. After V-E day, he became Director of Intelligence for U.S. Air Forces in Europe (USAFE), and upon returning to the United States in January 1946, became Assistant Chief of Air Staff, Intelligence. In 1947, he was named Director of Intelligence for the U.S. Air Force, a forerunner post to the present day position, Assistant Chief of Staff, Intelligence. McDonald retired in 1950 as a major general.

[13]At the Casablanca Conference, January 14–23, 1943, attended by President Roosevelt, Prime Minister Winston S. Churchill, and their military advisers, the assault against Sicily, codenamed HUSKY, was agreed upon. In preparation for HUSKY, the Middle Eastern and Northwest African theaters were merged, and Air Chief Marshal Arthur Tedder became overall air commander for the Mediterranean, under General Eisenhower's Allied Force Headquarters. NWAAF were activated on February 13, 1943, commanded by General Spaatz, as one of three subordinate commands to Tedder's Mediterranean Air Command. The other two were Malta Air Command and Middle East Command. Although the 12th AF aircraft and personnel were transferred to the NWAAF, its headquarters continued to function as the administrative organization for American elements in the NWAAF. See Howe, *Northwest Africa*, pp 354–55, 486; Wesley F. Craven and James L. Cate, eds, *The Army Air Forces in World War II*, 7 vols (Chicago, 1948–58), Vol 2: *Europe: Torch to Pointblank, August 1942 to December 1943*, pp 113–14, 161.

operations, Air Marshal Tedder of the RAF was commanding officer, and Spaatz was the deputy commander.[14] An advanced headquarters was set up on a beach near Tunis—I think it was called La Marsa. The final planning and conducting of air operations for the invasion of Sicily was the responsibility of this command. I had the good fortune to be sent to this headquarters in a small combat intelligence unit under McDonald, responsible for serving Spaatz.

Group Captain Harry Humphreys was the senior RAF intelligence officer there.[15] No one in our intelligence unit knew about ULTRA; we began to wonder why we were kept segregated at critical briefings. We also wondered about the accuracy of some intelligence that we were not familiar with. We relied primarily on aerial reconnaissance, and we began to get a good many reports through the British, their agents, and also by this time from the interrogation of many prisoners. It was not our role to interrogate prisoners, but we captured about 300,000 Germans when they surrendered in North Africa. There was no way they could get out; Montgomery came from the east, and the Americans came from the west.[16] We had some successful attacks on

[14]RAF Air Chief Marshal Arthur W. Tedder (1890–1967) was named Commander in Chief of the Mediterranean Air Command when it was established in February 1943. Tedder reported directly to General Eisenhower and was responsible for all Allied air operations in the North African, Sicilian, and Italian campaigns. See Arthur W. Tedder, *With Prejudice: The War Memoirs of Marshal of the Royal Air Force Lord Tedder* (Boston, 1966).

[15]Group Capt. Robert H. Humphreys (1896–) served in World War I as a lieutenant in the Derbyshire Yeomanry (1915–1916) and as a captain in intelligence with the Royal Flying Corps and RAF (1916–1919). At the outbreak of World War II, he was granted a commission in the RAF Volunteer Reserve and posted to the RAF Headquarters, British Expeditionary Force, France. In January 1941 he was transferred to the Directorate of Intelligence (Operations) at the Air Ministry. A year later he was posted to the A.I.1(C) Section of Air Ministry and was involved with the dissemination of ULTRA. From May 1942 to August 1943, he served with the Headquarters, RAF, Middle East, the RAF 333d Group, and the Mediterranean Air Command. He then returned to the Air Ministry to serve as Deputy Director of the D.D.I.3 unit, commanding approximately 100 intelligence officers. From May 1944 to January 1945 he served with the RAF element of the Supreme Headquarters, Allied Expeditionary Forces, and the Headquarters Air Disarmament organization. He then became Chief Intelligence Officer at Fighter Command, where he served until June 1945, when he was transferred to the Second Tactical Air Force. He was released from RAF service in May 1946. For a report by Humphreys on the use of ULTRA in the Mediterranean and Northwest Africa, see SRH-037, pp 16–33, RG 457, NA.

[16]Field Marshal Bernard L. Montgomery (1887–1976), while Commander of the British Eighth Army, defeated Field Marshal Erwin Rommel's forces at El Alamein, Egypt, in October 1942. Montgomery then pursued the Germans through Libya into Tunisia, while Allied forces from the TORCH landings in North Africa squeezed the Germans from the west. Fierce fighting occurred in Tunisia in late April and early May 1943, and by May 13 all Axis forces in North Africa had surrendered. In the week before the 13th, the Allies took approximately 275,000 prisoners. Montgomery was a controversial commander; for a sympathetic portrait, see Nigel Hamilton, *Master of the Battlefield: Monty's War Years 1942–1944* (New York, 1983). See also Montgomery of Alamein, Bernard Law Montgomery, *El Alamein to the River Sangro, Normandy to the Baltic* (New York, 1974), pp 9–78; Howe, *Northwest Africa*, pp 644–68.

bases in Sicily and on shipping. The United States Army Air Forces, with considerable help from the RAF, were in control of the air in the Mediterranean, certainly in the middle to lower part of the Mediterranean, before the invasion of Sicily. The Italian Air Force was never a factor then or later.

Kohn: At that time you were on Spaatz's staff?

Powell: Yes. General McDonald was my boss, and he was Spaatz's intelligence officer.

Kohn: Through May of 1943, then, you were essentially unaware of ULTRA?

Powell: I had never heard of ULTRA. We knew where the SLU unit that received the coded messages was located.[17] It was sort of concealed. It had a camouflage netting over it located in some little trees. We knew it had something to do with wireless intercept, but we thought it was low level.

Kohn: The "Y" service intercept?[18]

Powell: Yes. What we called the "Y" service, generally covered a large spectrum of wireless intelligence. Much of it was helpful in putting information together.

Putney: Was it known as an "SLU" at that time?

Powell: I do not know. I don't think I thought of it as an SLU. It was manned by Britishers, and we got to say hello to the two or three people there, not many. They would come and go all the time. We knew they were taking and delivering messages to and from the British.

---

[17]Special Liaison Units (SLU) were units at the operational commands which used radio equipment and cipher machines mounted in vans to receive and decipher encrypted ULTRA messages sent from England over special radio links. For accounts of the role of ULTRA in TORCH preparations, the Tunisian campaign, and Axis shipping losses in the Mediterranean, see F. H. Hinsley *et al, British Intelligence in the Second World War: Its Influence on Strategy and Operations*, 3 vols (London, 1979–84) Vol 2, pp 463–505, 607–12, 729–46.

[18]The British "Y" Service consisted of men and women from the army, navy, and air force who manned intercept stations and listened for and recorded enemy voice (radio) and signal (wireless) message traffic. Most Y intercepts were messages in plain language or in medium- or low-grade cryptographic systems, consisting primarily of communications between lower echelons of command and between ground stations and aircraft in flight. During the war, the Y Service expanded considerably, encompassing much of Western Europe, North Africa, the Middle East, and the Atlantic Ocean area. The American counterpart to the Y Service was the Signal Intelligence Service. For a fascinating account of the Y Service as told by the first woman British intelligence officer, see Aileen Clayton, *The Enemy is Listening* (New York, 1980).

Putney: At this time were you aware of a successful campaign against the German convoys?

Powell: In the Mediterranean? Oh yes. I'm sure you know from many other sources, and we knew it at the time, that Rommel's supply of petrol was drying up as a result of sinking tankers. ULTRA was a primary source of intelligence in this battle of attrition. The Germans, in their usual methodical way, would advise Rommel that such and such a tanker was leaving Naples, Civitavecchia, Leghorn, or wherever, and when it was expected to arrive. They could only communicate by radio. There were messages saying that tankers were sailing for Bengasi, as far east as that, later it was Tripoli. So the problem was to protect the ULTRA source. I did not know it at the time, but the source was protected by treating the bomber crews and the lower level intelligence officers the same way we were treated when I was with the 319th. Reconnaissance aircraft—sent to the designated area—were used to locate a tanker, and the pilot would be very excited when he saw the target. He would radio back, either in the clear or in a very simple word code that the Germans knew as well as we did. Sometimes we would intercept a signal from the ship saying it had been spotted.

Putney: Was this one of the methods for the use and protection of ULTRA?

Powell: Yes.

Putney: You had to have a second or any number of other sources as "cover" before you could act on ULTRA information?

Powell: Yes. That's right. That's exactly right.

Putney: Was that an absolute rule and was it faithfully followed?

Powell: Yes, it certainly was the rule. It was fairly simple once you had access to a number of other sources. After I was taken into the ULTRA secret, I would intersperse ULTRA with other sources in briefing people who had no idea of ULTRA. That was routinely done. Then another factor that, I think, had more to do with preserving the ULTRA secret than any other single factor is that almost everyone in intelligence, or close to intelligence, or close to operations, knew that there was a spectrum of codes. It was also common knowledge that in modern wars, that is, since wireless telegraphy became known, nations undertook to read the codes of other nations around the world. Even in peacetime codes were read, even codes of friendly nations. Everyone knew that there were codes being broken and messages read.

At Bletchley, I think there were hundreds of people there, and many of them knew nothing about ULTRA. They knew that they could not enter Hut 3 or Hut 6. Hut 6 was where the cryptographers operated.[19] Hut 3 was where the messages were translated, and the intelligence work was done. One could go to lunch with people who were working on various levels of intercept, all the way from just listening to German pilots talk to each other when they were not trying to deceive people. They were just talking about family, whatever. I remember a young woman at Bletchley who said that she had become so fond of some of the German pilots, just from listening to their voices, that whenever they were in danger she was terrified for fear they would be shot down.

Putney: Such empathy. Before we leave North Africa, would you describe what the American intelligence unit did on a typical day in the Northwest African Air Forces?

Powell: The American Operational Intelligence Unit at the advanced headquarters located at La Marsa (Tunis), after the Germans in North Africa surrendered in the spring of 1943, was quite small. The unit consisted regularly of four or five officers. We ran a "watch" on a 24-hour basis, even though little happened at night. Our forces were attacking targets in Sicily and southern Italy preparatory to invasion. I previously have mentioned the sources available to our unit (primarily photographic reconnaissance, "Y" reports, and reports from the combat intelligence officers assigned to our operational bomber and fighter groups).

On a typical day, we received and collated these reports and made the information available usually to Gen. Larry Norstad, who was Spaatz's operations officer.[20] We rarely went directly to General Spaatz who was briefed with Air Marshal Tedder usually by Group Captain Humphreys. We summarized and made available to the American component of the headquarters the intelligence received from the sources mentioned.

[19]In current usage "cryptanalysis" refers to the process of analyzing and breaking codes and ciphers, and "cryptography" to the process of devising and making them. Codes and ciphers were analyzed and broken in Hut 6.

[20]Brig. Gen. Lauris Norstad (1907–) was the Assistant Chief of Staff for Operations for the NWAAF, as he had been for the 12th AF since August 1942. In December 1943 he became Director of Operations of the Mediterranean Allied Air Forces. He returned to Washington, D.C., in August 1944 to serve as Chief of Staff of the newly formed 20th AF. In October 1947 he was appointed Deputy Chief of Air Staff for Operations of the newly established U.S. Air Force. From 1950 on, he served in Europe and was promoted to general in July 1952. In November 1956, President Eisenhower appointed him Supreme Allied Commander, Europe, and Commander in Chief, U.S. European Command. He served in the former post until his retirement in 1963.

When special information came to our attention we carried it directly to Norstad. For example, when I was once on night duty, photographs came in showing two Italian cruisers at anchor in one of the Sicilian ports. I forget the names of the cruisers, but we sank them—as I recall—the next day. In view of the importance of the information, Harry Bowers and I went to General Norstad's private quarters and awakened him.[21]

Our little unit was composed of Maj. Harry Bowers, a fine National Guard officer who was later killed; Leavitt Corning, who later became A-2 of one of the tactical Air Force commands in Italy; Bill Ballard, a well-known architect from New York; and Bill Lathrop, a reserve officer from Alabama.[22] I felt that we were being underused primarily because we were in a combined headquarters that was dominated by the RAF.

I add one general observation. Even though the Army Air Forces commenced the war with *no* intelligence service worthy of the name, and few if any personnel had ever been given anything more than counterintelligence training, it was clear to me from my experience with the 319th Bomb Group and at the several headquarters in which I served, that we overstaffed intelligence, wrote more intelligence summaries, and in general did a good many things that were only marginal in utility. In short, having made the mistake of neglecting intelligence before the war, this function was overstaffed.

Putney: From North Africa were you sent back to Washington?

Powell: Yes. I don't know why I was sent back to Washington, but it was after we had occupied Sicily and were commencing the planning of the invasion of Italy. The work of my section had tapered off. We knew the strength

[21]Maj. Harry G. Bowers (1914–1943), a native of Georgia, was graduated from The Citadel, a military college in South Carolina, in 1937. He received his law degree from the University of Georgia and was admitted to the Georgia Bar. He practiced law in Americus, Georgia, until 1940 when he entered active military service with the Army and attended the Command and General Staff School at Fort Leavenworth, Kansas. Subsequently he served in England and then in North Africa. He was killed in a B-24 aircraft accident in the Mediterranean on December 21, 1943.

[22]Capt. Leavitt Corning, Jr., (1905–1972) was an AAF intelligence officer from 1942 to 1945. He served in Africa and Europe, achieving the rank of lieutenant colonel. After the war, he continued his career as a geologist in Texas.

Capt. William F. Ballard (1905–   ) served as an AAF intelligence officer in Africa and Europe from 1942 to 1945, rising to the rank of lieutenant colonel. In 1944 he was Chief of the Target Section of the Mediterranean Allied Air Forces. In 1945 he returned to his career as an architect in New York City.

Capt. William R. Lathrop (1911–   ) served with the AAF from 1941 to 1946 and achieved the rank of lieutenant colonel. In 1944 he was in the Operational Intelligence Section of the Mediterranean Allied Air Forces. After his Army discharge, he studied at the Sorbonne University in Paris in 1946 and then returned to the United States to pursue a career in the insurance business in his home state of Georgia.

An AAF intelligence officer in North Africa inspects reconnaissance photograph to detect enemy activity, 1943.

and disposition of the German Air Force and also of the German army units. Italian armed services were in total disarray.

When I arrived at the Pentagon, I was told that I was to be on temporary duty at the Army Air Forces Intelligence School to update one or more of its manuals and also to share my combat experience. I think I was perhaps the first American intelligence officer who had combat experience to come back to this country.

It is possible I was called back because I had teaching experience. (I had taught economics at the evening school at the University of Richmond for three years.) I went to the intelligence school, and I did work on the manuals. I also was sent with one of the professors at the school on a three weeks' trip to air bases in this country that were training bomber groups to go to the European theater. I shared what I had learned with the intelligence officers and the operations officers on these bases.

Again, without knowing exactly how it happened, I was asked to come to Washington. I had been going back and forth to the Pentagon regularly as there were people there who were interested in talking to me. I also always learned something there. This time I was invited to talk to Al McCormack, a full colonel in charge of Special Branch.[23] The first question he asked me after the pleasantries, was had I ever heard of ULTRA. The answer was negative. Anyway, I was asked to become an ULTRA officer. I was trained briefly there and then was returned to England to go to Bletchley.

Putney: Did Al McCormack personally train you and were you brought into the Special Branch at that time?

Powell: Yes, in other words, before I went to England, I was fully briefed on the Special Branch and its responsibilities. I was also interviewed by Col. Carter Clarke, who had ultimate responsibility for Special Branch and other sources.[24] I couldn't say how many days I was there, but I understood fully what was going on. The magnitude of ULTRA, the effectiveness of it, however, could not be understood just by hearing somebody describe it. One had to see it.

Kohn: Do you have any idea, Justice Powell, how you were selected or why? Was it the normal course of assignment; perhaps, "Here's a senior man who has combat experience; we are now going to move him into the ULTRA business?" Have you reflected on that at all?

---

[23]Col. Alfred McCormack (1901–1956) was Deputy Chief of the Special Branch of the Military Intelligence Service (MIS) from May 1942 to June 1944 and then became Chief of the Directorate of Intelligence, MIS. In January 1942, Secretary of War Henry L. Stimson appointed McCormack his Special Assistant, assigning him to study the way the War Department handled signals intelligence and to recommend improvements. McCormack had been a civilian lawyer, and he entered the Army commissioned as a lieutenant colonel and rose to the rank of colonel. It was McCormack's recommendation which led to the establishment of the Special Branch within MIS in May 1942. Special Branch was a unit staffed, in part, by lawyers and highly educated civilians who received commissions as Army officers and whose job it was to analyze, evaluate, interpret, process, and disseminate signals intelligence in a systematic manner for the War Department. Upon his discharge from the Army in 1945, McCormack worked with the State Department on intelligence matters until April 1946, when he returned to his private law practice. For an account of Colonel McCormack's wartime experiences and for his personal War Department files see SRH–185 and SRH–141, parts 1 and 2, RG 457, NA.

[24]Col. Carter W. Clarke (1896–1987) was Chief of the Special Branch of MIS, a position he held from May 1942 to June 1944. From 1918 to 1941, he had been an officer in the Army Signal Corps. In 1941 he was transferred to the Military Intelligence Division (MID) of the War Department. He then became Deputy Chief of MIS. After the war, in June 1949 he became Chief of the Army Security Agency. After two tours of duty in Japan from 1950 to 1953, he was assigned to the Central Intelligence Agency (CIA). He was promoted to brigadier general on July 20, 1949.

Powell: I think most of the people who went into ULTRA had not had any overseas experience. That is a fact. I knew by that time a high percentage of the American intelligence officers. I had known them from the Harrisburg days on. Several from Harrisburg later went into ULTRA, like Phil Graham, later the publisher of the *Washington Post*, and Lofty Becker.[25] You refresh my recollection: McCormack did say to me when I asked him "why me?" "we are selecting primarily lawyers to be ULTRA officers." McCormack was one of the leading partners of the Cravath law firm. I had never met him, but my firm had a fair amount of business with Cravath. I was in the largest law firm between Richmond and Houston, and McCormack had my resume. I had done very well in college and law school. I had been made national chairman of the Young Lawyers Section of the American Bar Association.

Putney: And McCormack himself was a lawyer from New York.

Powell: Yes, and one widely respected. He was a prominent lawyer.

Putney: Had you heard the comment, "Special Branch was the best law firm in Washington?"

Powell: No, I had not, but there were many gifted lawyers in Special Branch.

Putney: What was your rank at this time?

Powell: I was a major by the time I was taken into ULTRA. I was promoted to captain while on combat operations overseas, and I was promoted to

[25]Capt. Philip L. Graham (1915–1963) became the ULTRA Special Security Officer for the Far East Air Forces (FEAF) in the Southwest Pacific Area (SWPA). He had received his law degree from Harvard University in 1939 and for the next two years was a clerk for Justices of the Supreme Court Stanley Reed and Felix Frankfurter. In 1942 he entered the AAF as a private; the following year, he was commissioned a second lieutenant and assigned to Special Branch, MIS. He rose to the rank of major before he concluded his wartime service in 1945. In 1946 Graham became publisher of the *Washington Post* and in 1961 became its president and chief executive. He was also a trustee of the RAND Corporation. For letters describing Graham's ULTRA responsibilities at the Headquarters, FEAF, see SRH-119, pp 34–41; SRH-127, pp 146–49, and SRH-127, pp 129–31, RG 457, NA.

Capt. Loftus E. Becker (1911–1977) received his law degree from Harvard Law School in 1936 and practiced law in Hawaii and New York until 1942 when he entered the U.S. Army as a corporal. He rose in rank to major, serving in the field artillery and the MIS. From September 1944 to May 1945 he was an ULTRA Representative for the Ninth U.S. Army in Europe. From 1945 to 1946, Becker was a military adviser at the Nuremberg war crimes trials. Following his Army discharge, he returned to his law practice in New York City until he retired in 1971. In 1951, he joined the CIA and served as a Deputy for Intelligence for two years. From 1957 to 1959 he was a legal adviser to the State Department. For accounts of Becker's assignments as ULTRA Representative, see SRH-023, part 1, pp 27–30 and SRH-031, pp 53–97, RG 457, NA.

major shortly after I returned to the United States in 1943. If you were in the Army Air Forces, promotion was fairly prevalent.

Putney: In Special Branch were you aware of the extent of reading Japanese codes and MAGIC?[26]

Powell: I knew generally about reading the Japanese codes. I never had any experience with them, although I was asked to come back to the Special Branch when the European war ended and head the Japanese Section. I did not know the full extent of it, but I was quite aware that by that time, we may have had an opportunity to know exactly what the Japanese were to do at Pearl Harbor and just "blew it."[27]

Putney: Along with that idea, did McCormack explain to you how the Special Branch was set up after Pearl Harbor? Was it a direct result of Pearl Harbor and the mishandling of information?

Powell: I do not think he ever addressed that with me. My own view, and one shared by many others, is that when we entered World War II, the general perception of intelligence was that it was the least important element, even in the Army. The Navy was way ahead of the Army and the Army Air Corps. There were almost no trained intelligence officers in the Air Corps. George McDonald, who ended up a major general, had been a fighter pilot in the same unit with Tooey Spaatz in World War I. Tooey was very faithful to

[26]MAGIC was material the Americans obtained from the interception, decryption, and translation of secret Japanese diplomatic messages. Throughout the interwar period, with the exception of the period 1931-1935, the Americans read Japanese diplomatic ciphers. For a selection of the deciphered messages, see Department of Defense, *The "Magic" Background of Pearl Harbor*, 5 vols and appendices (Washington, 1977).

[27]There is as yet no consensus on why the attack on Pearl Harbor was successful, despite the Americans' having MAGIC. Wohlstetter concluded that the Americans failed to properly analyze MAGIC, allowing "noise" to obscure relevant "signals." Kahn disagreed, stating that intelligence collection, not analysis, was the problem. Layton saw the failure to disseminate intelligence as the key issue. Prange blamed everyone in the chain of command for failure to communicate with each other and failure to believe that the Japanese would dare to attack Pearl Harbor. Toland revived the unconvincing revisionist thesis that President Roosevelt and high-ranking Army and Navy officers knew of the impending attack, but deliberately ignored or suppressed evidence to force the United States into war. The Wohlstetter and Prange views will probably prevail. See Roberta Wohlstetter, *Pearl Harbor: Warning and Decision* (Stanford, CA, 1962); David Kahn, "The United States Views Germany and Japan in 1941," in *Knowing Ones's Enemies: Intelligence Assessment Before the Two World Wars*, ed. Ernest R. May (Princeton, NJ, 1984); Edwin T. Layton, Roger Pineau, and John Costello, *"And I Was There": Pearl Harbor and Midway—Breaking the Secrets* (New York, 1985); Gordon W. Prange, *At Dawn We Slept: The Untold Story of Pearl Harbor* (New York, 1981); John Toland, *Infamy: Pearl Harbor and Its Aftermath* (New York, 1982).

old friends. Many of the top people on his staff in the United States Strategic Air Forces in Europe were "retreads" as we called them. There was Everett Cook, who was head of personnel.[28] Ted Curtis was chief of staff; he was later the executive vice president for Eastman Kodak.[29] Cook and Curtis were highly intelligent and excellent officers. They knew little about intelligence. George McDonald had stayed in the Army after World War I. But there were no regular army or reserve officers trained in operational intelligence. I could not identify a single properly trained one in the then Army Air Corps. There were a few who came into operational intelligence as the war progressed, and who learned quickly—especially West Point graduates. The top operational intelligence officers throughout the war against Germany were civilians. I think in some ways that was an advantage and other ways it was a dreadful disadvantage, because none of us, or very few of us, had had any military training at all. I never learned how to salute properly.

Kohn: When you were selected and brought into Special Branch, were you given an overall briefing to show you the big picture of what was happening, or were you just told enough to go out and do the job? Could you describe that a bit?

Powell: I think it is fair to say that I was given the large picture by Al McCormack. He spent a fair amount of time with me. We had mutual friends; he was a good deal older than I was, but I liked him and admired him a great deal. I digress to say that after the war he recommended me to be the general counsel of the Marshall Plan. I had been away for four years during the war, and I had two kids, and by that time I think I had a third. My law firm, with whom I discussed it, said, "Look Powell, if you want to be a

[28]Col. Everett R. Cook (1894–1974), Commander of the 91st Aero Squadron in France from 1918 to 1919, downed five German airplanes. In the interwar period, he was a cotton merchant and exporter in Memphis, Tennessee. He joined the AAF in 1942 and served with 8th AF, 12th AF, NWAAF, and USSTAF. In 1944 he became national chairman of the Agricultural War Board. After the war he continued with his cotton export business. He was also a member of the Air Force Reserves, promoted to brigadier general in 1948; on the Board of Directors of the Falcon Foundation for the U. S. Air Force Academy, 1966; and a trustee of the Air Force Historical Foundation.

[29]Brig. Gen. Edward P. Curtis, Sr., (1897–1987) was a pilot with the 95th Aero Squadron in World War I, achieving the rank of major before he was discharged in 1919. In 1921 he joined the Eastman Kodak Company in Rochester, New York, and eventually became vice president of motion picture films. In November 1940, he took a leave of absence to join General Spaatz's staff in the Plans Division of the Army Air Corps. He served with Spaatz in North Africa and Europe and concluded his service in World War II as a major general. He returned to Eastman Kodak after the war. In 1956, at the request of President Eisenhower, he conducted a comprehensive study of American aviation and air traffic control, which led to the creation of the Federal Aviation Agency (FAA).

lawyer, why don't you stay here and practice law?'' Although I decided to stay with my law firm, I had the pleasure of an interview with the Marshall Plan administrator.

Returning to your question, Dr. Kohn, I did not understand the full scope of the ULTRA information until I went to Bletchley. I just could not believe the volume of traffic that was being intercepted and deciphered. The real heroes were the cryptographers.

Putney: The Hut 6 people.

Powell: Yes. Bletchley left a profound impression on me. For the most part the people who worked on ULTRA in Hut 6 could fairly be called geniuses. They were the best mathematicians in Great Britain. There were some physicists and even some philosophers, on the theory that you needed a sort of mixed quality of intellectual giants. Bletchley had them.

Putney: Did you know then for what position you were being trained?

Powell: Yes, I was being trained to be what they called the ULTRA representative at General Spaatz's headquarters.[30] I can't say that I had been chosen before I went to Bletchley; I do know that before I left Bletchley, I had been told that I was to go back to General Spaatz's headquarters after I did the mission to Italy. I have never known whether Spaatz asked for me or whether by the law of chance they sent me back—I was happy to go. I just did as I was told. I was glad to go back, although I had met Pete Quesada down in Africa.[31] I met him when he was commanding two or three fighter groups down there, and he was not very far from my group. Pete is a dear

[30]The U.S. Strategic Air Forces in Europe (USSTAF) were established in January 1944, and in that same month General Spaatz arrived in England from North Africa to take command of USSTAF headquarters at Bushey Park in Teddington, a London suburb. USSTAF coordinated the heavy bomber missions of the 8th AF in the United Kingdom and those of the recently established 15th AF in the Mediterranean and also had administrative control over the 8th AF and 9th AF. See Craven and Cate, *Army Air Forces in World War II*, Vol 2, pp 740–44, 751–56, and Vol 3: *Europe: Argument to V-E Day January 1944 to May 1945*, pp 6–7.

[31]Brig. Gen. Elwood R. "Pete" Quesada (1904–) assumed command of the XII Fighter Command in Africa in early 1943 and also served as Deputy Commander of the Northwest African Coastal Air Force. In October 1943 in England, he assumed leadership of the IX Fighter Command. Promoted to major general in April 1944, he then led the IX Tactical Air Command, flying missions in support of the D-Day invasion and the subsequent battles into Germany. In April 1945 he returned to the United States to become the Assistant Chief of Air Staff, Intelligence. In 1946 he was appointed the first Commander of the Tactical Air Command, achieving the rank of lieutenant general in this command, which he held until March 1948. He then worked on special projects for the newly established Joint Chiefs of Staff. He retired from active duty in October 1951. From 1958 to 1962 he served as the first Administrator of the FAA.

friend, and we have kept in touch ever since. Since I know Pete and had a personal relationship with him that was far more personal that my relationship with Spaatz, I toyed with asking if I could change my assignment. I might have done it except for the fact that another friend of mine named Jim Fellers, who was at Bletchley with me, a lawyer from Oklahoma City, was very eager to go with Quesada.[32] I talked it over with Jim, and he said, "Powell, please don't try to pull your rank and go with Pete." I was glad I went back to Spaatz, though, because I knew more about strategic bombing operations.

Putney: How long were you at Bletchley?

Powell: I have tried to reconstruct that. If I had to guess I would say three or four weeks. For the most part, those weeks were spent being briefed and studying. I thought I knew a fair amount about the German Air Force before I went, but by the time I left, I could proudly say to myself that I was an authentic expert on the German Air Force. Bletchley had the best information on the GAF. The intelligence officers in Hut 3 probably knew more about it than high ranking German officers. Bletchley had the famous card files that I am sure you have read about. They were massive. The Bletchley staff people were highly intelligent and impressive.

Putney: This is the Air Index?

Powell: Yes.

Putney: Did you use it then?

Powell: I did not directly myself. I saw it because I was concerned about what sort of records I would have to keep. But every time a message was decoded it would be scanned, and any item on it that possibly could ever be of interest was usually indexed in double, triple, or quadruple so that intelligence officers could find it. The second category of real heroes in the ULTRA operation were the intelligence officers at Bletchley, because they would interpret the messages. It was very helpful to us in the field to have their assistance, the benefit of their interpretations, that they were better able to make than we.

---

[32]Maj. James D. Fellers (1913–) practiced law in Oklahoma until he entered the Army in 1941. He rose to the rank of lieutenant colonel within MIS and served as the ULTRA Representative to IX Tactical Air Command in Europe from 1944 to May 1945. After the war, he returned to civilian life and continued to practice law. From 1974 to 1975 Fellers was president of the American Bar Association. For descriptive reports of his service as ULTRA Representative, see SRH–023, part 2, pp 57–100 and SRH–031, pp 1–20, RG 457, NA.

Putney: Did you meet Peter Calvocoressi?[33]

Powell: Yes I did. He was one of those who briefed me. Jim Rose and Peter Calvocoressi were the two primary experts on the German Air Force.[34] Harry Humphreys was at Bletchley briefly, and he was brilliant—as were all of these people. Harry did have a high opinion of himself. I rather enjoyed him, but I never developed the friendship with him that I had with Jim Rose and Peter Calvocoressi. Peter visited in our home in Richmond a few years after the war. He sent me a page proof of his book before it was published.[35]

Putney: Was Telford Taylor there at the time you were?[36]

---

[33]Flight Lt. Peter J. Calvocoressi (1912–) was an Oxford graduate and a lawyer, serving as an RAF intelligence officer from 1941 to 1945. He attained the rank of wing commander. He was stationed at Bletchley Park and was an expert on the German Air Force. In 1945 and 1946, Calvocoressi served at the Nuremberg war crimes trials. Calvocoressi then was on the staff of or a member of the Royal Institute of International Affairs (1949–1970); a reader at the University of Sussex, (1965–1971); the director of Hogarth Press (1954–1965); and publisher and chief executive of Penguin Books (1973–1976). For notes Major Powell wrote at Bletchley Park while Calvocoressi lectured on the German Air Force, see Appendix 2. Among his books are *Total War: The Story of World War II* (New York, 1972) and *Top Secret Ultra* (New York, 1981).

[34]RAF Squadron Leader E. J. B. "Jim" Rose (1909–) was Chief of the Air Section at Bletchley Park from 1941 to 1944. From January 1945 to the end of the war, Wing Commander Rose served as Deputy Director of Operational Intelligence at the British Air Ministry. He visited the United States during this time to assist with the selection of officers for work at Bletchley Park and to coordinate on matters with Col. Alfred McCormack of MIS. After the war he pursued a successful career as a journalist and publisher, including serving as director of Penguin Books, England, and Viking Press, New York (1973–1980). From 1963 to 1969 he was director of the five-year survey of race relations in Britain and produced *Colour and Citizenship* (Oxford, 1969), also known as the "Rose Report." For notes Major Powell wrote at Bletchley Park while Rose lectured on the German Air Force, see Appendix 2.

[35]Peter J. Calvocoressi's *Top Secret Ultra* (New York, 1981) is an account of the process of breaking the ENIGMA decrypts at Bletchley Park and the operational and strategic uses made of ULTRA intelligence. See also Peter Calvocoressi, "The Secrets of Enigma," pp 71–72, January 20, 1977, "When Enigma Yielded Ultra," pp 112–14, January 27, 1977, and "The Value of Enigma," pp 135–37, February 3, 1977, in *The Listener*.

[36]Col. Telford Taylor (1908–) was in charge of the London Branch of MIS, which was headquartered at the American Embassy at Grosvenor Square. He entered the Army as a major in 1942, after attending Harvard Law School and serving as a lawyer from 1933 to 1942 for federal agencies and Congressional committees. From 1945 to 1955 he served as a prosecutor in the Nuremberg war crimes trials. He was promoted to brigadier general in 1946 and remained with the Army for three more years. He later practiced law in New York City and became a professor of law at Columbia University. Among his books are *Sword and Swastika: Generals and Nazism in the Third Reich* (New York, 1952), *Nuremberg and Vietnam: An American Tragedy* (New York, 1970); *Courts of Terror: Soviet Criminal Justice and Jewish Emigration* (New York, 1976).

Powell: Telford was not at Bletchley when I was there. His headquarters were in the American Embassy in Grosvenor Square in London. Telford Taylor, a brilliant American officer, was the senior United States ULTRA officer in Europe. He was not assigned to any operational unit. Telford was my administrative "boss." I had been transferred from the Air Corps to G-2, the General Staff in Washington, when I was taken into Special Branch. General Spaatz was not my official boss, although if he spoke I listened. I came to know and admire Telford also.

Putney: Was Winterbotham there?[37]

Powell: Winterbotham was there, yes. He was the commanding officer, and he greeted us. When I say us, I include the other Americans there at that time. These included Jim Fellers and Alfred Friendly, who was not an intelligence officer, but basically a translator.[38] Jim became a nationally known lawyer and served as president of the American Bar Association. Al Friendly, another friend, became managing editor of the *Washington Post*. And there was a wonderful man named Adolph Rosengarten.[39] Have you ever heard of Adolph? He was from Philadelphia and was more military than the West Pointers. He was trained at Bletchley, and with Edward Hitchcock

[37]Group Capt. Frederick W. Winterbotham (1897-) was a member of the RAF and the senior Air Staff representative at Bletchley Park. He devised the system and security procedures for disseminating ULTRA from Bletchley Park to operational commands and was involved with assigning the name ULTRA to the signals intelligence from deciphered ENIGMA messages. His book, *The Ultra Secret*, revealed to the world in 1974 that the British were reading ENIGMA traffic in World War II.

[38]Capt. Alfred Friendly (1911-1983) had worked as a reporter for the *Washington Post* prior to joining the AAF in 1942 and being assigned to MIS. He was eventually promoted to major and stayed in the Army until 1945. He then returned to the *Washington Post*, but took a leave of absence from 1948 to 1949 to serve in Paris as the press officer for the Marshall Plan. In 1952 he became assistant managing editor of the *Washington Post*; in 1955, the managing editor; and in 1966 an associate editor and foreign correspondent. He won the Pulitzer Prize for his coverage of the 1967 Arab-Israeli war. He retired from the *Washington Post* in 1971. For his account of his wartime experience with ULTRA, see Alfred Friendly, "Confessions of a Code Breaker," *Washington Post*, October 27, 1974, pp C-1, C-3.

[39]Maj. Adolph G. Rosengarten, Jr., (1905-) practiced law in Philadelphia from 1930 until he entered the Army in 1941. He served with the 111th Infantry of the 28th Division. In 1943 he was recruited into MIS and in 1944 received training at Bletchley Park. He served as the ULTRA Representative to the First U.S. Army from May 1944 to May 1945. After the war, he returned to Pennsylvania and was associated with the Fidelity Philadelphia Trust Company, Merck and Company (a pharmaceutical firm), and Bryn Mawr Hospital. For an account of his year as an ULTRA Representative, serving in the campaigns of Normandy, North France, and Germany, see SRH-023, part 1, pp 11-18, RG 457,NA. See also Adolph G. Rosengarten, Jr., "With Ultra from Omaha Beach to Weimar, Germany—A Personal View," *Military Affairs* 42 (October 1978): 127-32.

Capt. Lewis F. Powell, Jr., in combat gear somewhere in North Africa. *Courtesy Lewis F. Powell, Jr.*

and Jim Fellers, was on our mission to Italy to see how ULTRA was used there in operations.[40] This was before the invasion of France. Jim, Ed, and "Rosey" had not seen any operations before that time. Rosengarten, I think, became the ULTRA representative for the First Army. I was asked to join the mission to Italy to observe the use of ULTRA in both strategic and tactical operations. I was impressed by the tactical operation that we observed in the heavy fighting just south of Monte Cassino.

Kohn: How were Americans being integrated into the ULTRA system? We get the impression that the British kept us rather at a distance until 1944.

Powell: That was well illustrated by the experience I have already mentioned down in Africa. I saw it again when we were in Italy. The headquarters of the Fifteenth Air Force and an Army group were at Caserta, and the chief intelligence officer there was a man named James Luard, an RAF group captain.[41] The senior American intelligence officer there was Lt. Col. Robert G. Storey; he had been the law school dean at Southern Methodist University.[42] I think Bob had been taken into ULTRA, but not through Special Branch or Bletchley. From sheer necessity the British took a number of Americans into ULTRA who had never been processed in the way Special

[40]Capt. Edward C. Hitchcock (1913–) was assigned as ULTRA Representative to the 9th AF in early 1944. He had entered the AAF in 1942, was selected for intelligence duty and received training in RAF tactical intelligence procedures and methods prior to reporting to the intelligence section of the Eighth Air Support Command in England in November 1942. He was transferred to the 9th AF in the fall of 1943. Hitchcock left the Army in 1946, having achieved the rank of major. He then worked for the U.S. State Department, and shortly thereafter he joined the new Central Intelligence Group, which became the CIA in 1947. He retired from the CIA in 1973 and from the U.S. Air Force Reserve as a colonel. For an account of how Hitchcock handled and used ULTRA at the 9th AF, see SRH-023, part 2, pp 34–52, RG 457, NA.

[41]Group Capt. James C. Luard (1908–) was commissioned as an officer in the RAF in April 1929 and qualified as a pilot. He relinquished his commission upon completion of his term of service in 1938. At the outbreak of World War II, he was commissioned as an officer in the RAF Volunteer Reserve and served with the 934th and 935th Balloon Squadrons from September 1939 to February 1940. For the three years after May 1940 he was posted as an intelligence officer to the Air Ministry; RAF Headquarters, Middle East; Washington, D.C.; and RAF Headquarters, India. In August 1943 he was sent to the the Mediterranean Air Command and in January 1944 to the Mediterranean Allied Air Force. He returned to England in August 1945 and was released from the RAF in September 1945.

[42]Lt. Col. Robert G. Storey (1893–1981) served as a lieutenant in the Army from 1918 to 1919. He was admitted to the Texas Bar in 1914 and became Assistant Attorney General of Texas for Criminal Appeals from 1921 to 1923 and Special Assistant District Attorney for Dallas, Texas, from 1924 to 1926. He then went into private law practice in Dallas, involving himself in civic and educational endeavors. He joined the AAF in World War II, rising to the rank of colonel. From 1945 to 1946 he was Executive Trial Counsel for the United States at the Nuremberg war crimes trials. From 1947 to his retirement in 1959 he was the Dean of the Southern Methodist University School of Law and involved in numerous civic affairs.

Branch contemplated. When I went to Spaatz's headquarters, of course, he knew about ULTRA, and he knew about it in Africa, and he had several officers who knew something about the source. However, they did not have anything like the understanding of it that Bletchley-trained officers did. But they used some ULTRA intelligence. That also was true in the Mediterranean. The British controlled its use at Caserta. The Americans controlled it on Spaatz's staff, of course, a purely American headquarters. We did not have a single RAF officer in our intelligence section. It was called the Directorate of Intelligence of USSTAF, but only a limited number of our personnel were in ULTRA.

To answer your question further, you asked about the extent to which there was integration of British and Americans. This varied, I am sure, at various combined headquarters. My only direct experience was with the Northwest African Air Forces. On General Eisenhower's staff, the chief intelligence officer was General Kenneth Strong, a very brilliant Britisher.[43] In some of the headquarters we visited in Africa, the only ULTRA person was a Britisher. We visited a couple of tactical Air Force commands, and I think of one in particular in which there were no American officers in ULTRA. Later, that may have changed; but the British, when they had the commanding officer, liked to have their own intelligence officers. They felt correctly that the British produced ULTRA and exploited it. Yet, as Calvocoressi says in his book, the contribution of the Americans at Bletchley, and those trained there, was quite significant. I think others have said that also. My own personal experience with the British, at and after Bletchley, could not have been better.

Putney: Did part of the training they gave you at Bletchley include going to a radio intercept station and following the whole process?

Powell: No. I never visited an intercept station. I do not recall being told where the intercept stations were located. Of course, the primary ones were in Great Britain, but there may have been others in occupied portions of western Europe in locations that were clearly secure. The intercepts, I believe,

[43]Maj. Gen. Kenneth W. Strong (1901–1982) was a British Army officer who was head of General Eisenhower's intelligence staff at Allied headquarters from February 1943 to the end of the war. He was fluent in German, Italian, and French and had been the Assistant Military Attache in Berlin before the war. From 1939 to 1941 he was head of the German Section of the War Office, and from 1942 to 1943 was the head of intelligence for the Home Forces. After the war he became the first Director General of Intelligence at the Ministry of Defence, serving from 1964 to 1966. See Major-General Sir Kenneth Strong, *Intelligence at the Top: The Recollections of an Intelligence Officer* (Garden City, NY, 1969); Major-General Sir Kenneth Strong, *Men of Intelligence: A Study of the Roles and Decisions of Chiefs of Intelligence from World War I to the Present Day* (London, 1970).

were transmitted by land lines or underwater cable whenever these were available. I did see at Bletchley, of course, the raw intercepted German messages. I saw the ENIGMA machines, and I saw the BOMBE which the British invented, a primitive early computer. You could not possibly break the ENIGMA codes just by manual mathematics.

Putney: Did you meet Alan Turing?[44]

Powell: I don't remember him by name.

Putney: One of the inventors of the BOMBE?

Powell: Oh, yes, right. I did meet him and most of the ULTRA family during the Bletchley training.

Kohn: Turing was a mathematician. . . .

Powell: Exactly. He was a don at Cambridge. The word "brilliant" fails to reflect his genius.

Kohn: Yes, I believe he was, apparently, quite an unusual, eccentric character.

Powell: There was more than one, I'll tell you.

Putney: So you saw everything there was to see at Bletchley?

Powell: I did, at least so far as I know, see everything that had to do with my future duties. I had no feeling whatever of any restraint on what we saw. Actually, Bletchley is a little crossroads between Oxford and London, and you can drive right by it without knowing you have been there. Bletchley, in the late nineteenth, maybe early twentieth century, was a country home of some rich Britisher—not a handsome building at all but it had large

[44]Dr. Alan M. Turing (1912–1954) was a British mathematician and pioneer in computer science. From 1936 to 1938 he worked at Princeton University where he made an important contribution to mathematical logic with his paper, "On Computable Numbers, With an Application to the *Entscheidungsproblem*." In this paper he described a "universal" computing machine (the "Turing Machine") capable of operating upon any sequence of zeroes and ones. In 1939 he returned to England to be a fellow at King's College, Cambridge, but his studies were interrupted by wartime service at Bletchley Park. Under intense pressure there, he designed huge calculating machines which aided in deciphering ENIGMA messages. With Turing and his colleagues at Bletchley Park, what mattered was the ability to think; of little importance were rank, age, degrees, and orderly work hours. After the war he continued his studies on mathematical theory and computers. See Andrew Hodges, *Alan Turing: The Enigma* (New York, 1983).

grounds. I have no idea how large; if I had to guess, I would say fifteen to twenty acres or more, with lots of huts scattered all over it. They had a big cafeteria in the main building, and the ULTRA people used that with the other people, and very few people wore uniforms, and rank did not make much difference at all. It was a very stimulating place to be, obviously, so much so that it gave those of us who were fortunate enough to have that training an enormous advantage.[45]

Putney: After Bletchley, however, you did not go directly to Spaatz's staff.

Powell: No, we were sent on the training mission to Italy that I mentioned. When I say "we," I'm talking now about Fellers, Rosengarten, and Hitchcock, who had gone a day or two ahead of me, and I met them in Algiers. Then we flew to Italy, and stayed briefly in Caserta and then went to the various headquarters of the United States Army and Army Air Forces. We were given an excellent briefing at Caserta, particularly in how to keep operational files. There were officers there I thought should be taken into ULTRA. Have you seen my report on that trip?[46] It has been declassified.

Putney: Yes.

Powell: Well that is the one and only thing that I wrote that was identified as ULTRA. To protect its secret, we were told never to write about it.

Putney: I do recall that with the first recommendation you made in that report you stated that ULTRA was better used or more often used by ground forces, and you advocated more use of ULTRA by persons in air intelligence. Do you recall that?

Powell: I do not specifically, but I am not surprised at what you say. The ground forces, in a way, had more need for ULTRA information on an hour-to-hour or day-to-day basis than we did. We had one big advantage, the RED code, I think it was called, which was the German Air Force ENIGMA code. This was broken very early in the war. I think the British commenced to read it in '40 or '41, and by the time I was at Bletchley, they knew as much about the German Air Force as I suppose anyone. Literally, almost everyday, every

---

[45]See Appendix 2 for Major Powell's lecture notes from Bletchley Park, February–March 1944.

[46]See Appendix 3 for the "Recommendations" section in Maj. Lewis F. Powell, Jr., "Report on Visit to Operational Air Commands in Mediterranean Theater (4 April–10 May 1944)," 14 May 1944, pp 21–47 in SRH-031, "Trip Reports Concerning Use of Ultra in the Mediterranean Theater 1943–1944," RG 457, NA.

combat unit in the German Air Force would report on the number of airplanes that were serviceable, on the number of crews who were ready and fit to fly, and, if there had been combat the day before, on the casualties, and the wins claimed. If a German Air Force unit was going to move from one base to another, they usually told us about it in advance. We would confirm the locations by aerial reconnaissance and also by DF-ing their radios.[47] Most of the time we just relied on their morning reports or daily reports. We had far better intelligence on the enemy than the ground forces, but when the ground forces received good intelligence, as they did at the Battle of the Falaise Gap, it could have a major effect on the outcome of the battle: thousands of Germans were captured or killed, and the Nazis were kept from going on to Cherbourg.[48] The ground forces had more people than we did usually working on intelligence. We had a large number of people doing economic and long-range strategic research in Washington and also in England with the RAF on possible target systems. As far as operational intelligence was concerned, I think most of the American tactical air force units had very small staffs. Ours was an exception; we had a big staff at USSTAF, probably larger than really needed.

Putney: Another recommendation you touched upon concerned bringing more Americans in as ULTRA representatives, especially where there were American commanders.

Powell: I felt that keenly, particularly upon my visit to the Mediterranean. After that I just do not recall any specific example. I stayed with the one

[47]Direction Finding (DF-ing) was the determination of the locations of enemy radio stations by measuring the angular direction of radio signals. DF units utilized radio receivers and directional antennas. DF "cuts" and "fixes" were generally merged with information from the Y Service intercept stations.

[48]On August 7, 1944, the Germans launched a counterattack at Mortain, France, to regain Avranches, which the Allies had overrun as they broke out of Normandy into Brittany, approximately two months after the great D-Day invasion of June 6, 1944. The Germans struck with full force against the American 30th Infantry Division, but they met stiff resistance, and their offensive stalled. Because the Germans attacked westward, the Allies planned an encirclement, with Gen. George S. Patton's troops swinging around Mortain and then advancing northward and Field Marshal Montgomery's forces advancing southward. By August 16, the Allied forces forming a gigantic pincers were only 15 miles apart, but this Argentan-Falaise gap was wide enough for thousands of Germans to escape eastward. When the gap closed on August 19, some Germans were still able to break out of the encirclement, but by August 20, 50,000 Germans had been taken prisoner and 10,000 had been killed in the Falaise "pocket." See Martin Blumenson, *Breakout and Pursuit*, [United States Army in World War II: The European Theater of Operations] (Washington, 1961; reprint 1970), pp 457–558. Unprecedented numbers of ENIGMA messages were intercepted and rapidly processed into ULTRA intelligence during this battle. See Ralph Bennett, *Ultra in the West: The Normandy Campaign 1942–45* (New York, 1980), pp 111–24.

headquarters. I occasionally visited some others, but basically I was with Spaatz until the end of the war.

Kohn: Could I go back and ask you when you first met General Spaatz and what your relationship was before you became his ULTRA representative? What were your impressions of General Spaatz?

Powell: I met him in North Africa, but I had no direct relations with him. He personally was briefed there by Gen. George McDonald, and we tried to keep George informed. We wrote the intelligence summaries. I think it is fair to say that I had no strong impression of Spaatz in North Africa. I did not like Spaatz being subordinated to Air Marshal Tedder after the Northwest African Air Forces were formed. The British often claimed more than I thought they were entitled to claim, even though I admired the British a great deal. I think of Montgomery as a general who sought greater authority, particularly over American operations. I should emphasize that the British were extremely generous and cooperative in the sharing of ULTRA. Of course I did get to know General Spaatz quite well at USSTAF; although if you do not know this, I think in fairness, Julian Allen should be mentioned.[49] Spaatz had an ULTRA briefing officer named Julian Allen. Has that name ever surfaced with you?

Putney: No, it has not.

Powell: I will tell you a little bit about Julian. He was ideal. He was born in the United States and had a wife from Georgia. He was the head of the Morgan bank in Paris, and had been so for a number of years. He knew Western Europe as well as I know the state of Virginia. He had a home not terribly far from the D-Day beaches and a nice house in Paris. He spoke French and German fluently. In fact, we used to say, "Julian, you know how to speak these other languages better than you do English." He had an accent when he spoke English. Julian had joined the British Army at the outset of the war. He had to leave France, of course, and he had a close call getting out. He was in the British Army when the United States entered the war. I do not recall exactly how he ended up on Spaatz's staff, but Spaatz had no Special Branch representative until I got there. One of the

[49]Col. Julian Allen (1900–1967) joined the American Field Service in World War I and was wounded while driving an ambulance in France. In 1917 he joined the British Coldstream Guards. In the interwar period, he was a banker in Paris, joining in 1933 the French firm associated with the New York banking house of J. P. Morgan. In 1942 he entered the AAF and then served on the staff of General Spaatz in both the European and Pacific theaters. After the war he continued as a successful banker in Paris.

General Spaatz. The inscription reads: "To Col. Lewis F. Powell, with greatest appreciation for his splendid work in World War II. Carl Spaatz." *Courtesy Lewis F. Powell, Jr.*

characteristics of Spaatz, that I am sure you are familiar with, is that he was basically a very private man, and the one criticism that many of us had of him was that we saw so little of him because he spent more time in his residence office than he did at the headquarters, whether they were advanced or main USSTAF. Yet I saw enough of him to feel very comfortable with him. Julian Allen had a trailer outside of Spaatz's home and usually briefed Spaatz. He briefed Spaatz more often than I did.

Kohn: Had he been chosen by Spaatz or did he come out of Special Branch, too?

Powell: No, Julian Allen had nothing to do with Special Branch. I do not think he had even heard of it until I arrived. I am not even sure I used that phrase. He knew I had been trained at Bletchley. Because Julian spent more time in Spaatz's residence than he did at headquarters, I succeeded him as Chief of Operational Intelligence. I assumed these responsibilities in August of '44.

Spaatz usually would come to the general briefing of senior officers. Maj. Gen. Frederick L. Anderson, a West Pointer who had headed the Eighth Air Force Bomber Command, was the general I worked with primarily.[50] Anderson was Spaatz's Deputy Commander for Operations (his A-3), and used ULTRA information regularly. He was a dynamic leader; he would have been, I think, Chief of the Air Staff if he had not had a health problem. In any event, I saw Fred everyday. Sometimes I would brief him privately. Everyday we gave a morning briefing to officers who sometimes were generally invited or who sometimes were very selectively invited. Spaatz fairly often, but not everyday by any means, would come to one of those. For the most part he liked to call people to come over to his residence. Julian had a little trailer with the maps, and we kept Julian fully informed, and he was always available to Spaatz. I was devoted to Julian. I don't know whether he was taken into ULTRA by Spaatz without any authority by the British, but he was in the "picture" generally.

---

[50]Maj. Gen. Frederick L. Anderson, Jr., (1905–1969) was appointed Deputy Commander for Operations when the USSTAF were formed in January 1944. He assisted General Spaatz in coordinating the strategic operations of the 8th AF in England and the 15th AF in Italy. In 1943 Anderson had commanded the VIII Bomber Command and flew with B-17 crews against Germany. After the war, he served in Washington, D.C., as Chief of Personnel on the Air Staff until his retirement in 1947. He then pursued business ventures in California. From 1952 to 1953, he served as a Representative to the North Atlantic Treaty Organization (NATO) and Deputy Special Representative to Europe, with responsibility for the Mutual Security Program. He then continued his successful business ventures and was involved in many civic affairs. In 1971 Lear Siegler, Inc., Santa Monica, California, established the Frederick L. Anderson Scholarship in his memory at the U.S. Air Force Academy.

Putney: Did he receive information directly from Bletchley?

Powell: No, we just had one SLU. Spaatz resided near our main headquarters. Spaatz's residence, when our headquarters were at St. Germain, was nearby, just a matter of fifteen or twenty minutes. Spaatz would often go to Eisenhower's briefing. Eisenhower's headquarters were at the Petit Trianon just outside of Versailles. It was not a long ways from where we were, and I sometimes went over with George McDonald to those briefings. There was no inflexible rule as to when Spaatz or other Air Force officers would attend.

When the war ended, Julian stayed in Paris and resumed his job as head of Morgan, and when I later went to France a couple of times, I always had lunch with Julian.

To digress, when Julian saw that the Germans were going to overrun France, he had the foresight to get the right people to excavate the debris from an old well somewhere on his place in Normandy that was no longer used as a well. He put all the family silver and everything else he wanted to preserve in there, and a couple of feet underneath the level of the ground, he put a cement cap, and then he concealed the hiding place by planting grass. He thought his house might be blitzed or the Germans would live in it. Julian could not wait to find out what the Germans had done to his residence. He found everything was intact. The house had been occupied by German officers, and they left him a very warm and gracious thank you note with a big stack of French counterfeit francs. That's what the Germans paid with.

Anyway that was Julian. I wanted to make the point that I was not the only person who briefed Spaatz. I kept the ULTRA records, and I was responsible for ULTRA security, and the SLU reported to me. I alone represented Special Branch.

Putney: How did you keep and use the ULTRA information? Did you try to recreate the Air Index?

Powell: When I arrived at Spaatz's headquarters, the files were reasonably adequate, but we tried not to keep things that we did not need. So we did not have anything comparable to the Bletchley card index. We also, as a result of these morning reports I mentioned, knew everyday where the German Air Force units were on the western front. They were the ones we were primarily concerned with, and if a unit moved from the eastern front we would know about it. I knew more about where the Germans were located than I did about our own Air Force units.

Putney: Did you meet with ULTRA representatives at other levels, and did you ever go back to Bletchley?

Powell: I went back to Bletchley once, but I can't pinpoint it, and I couldn't testify why I went. Yet, I do recall that I went back once, and I spent the night with Jim Rose at a pub outside of Bletchley. I remember that very well. I was very fond of Jim and recommended him for an American decoration. I think that's the last time I went to Bletchley. Things moved very fast, and we were being serviced brilliantly. I didn't feel any real need to go back.

Putney: What was a "typical day" like for you in Operational Intelligence at the United States Strategic Air Forces (USSTAF)?

Powell: As head of Operational Intelligence of USSTAF, I had two principle responsibilities: I was the only representative of Special Branch at the highest headquarters of our air forces, and also—because the organization already had been set up—I soon became Chief of all Operational Intelligence. This involved certain administrative duties. I never lost sight of the fact, however, that my primary responsibility was operational and as the ULTRA officer.

The two officers senior to me in the Directorate of Intelligence of USSTAF were Brig. Gen. George McDonald and Col. Lowell Weicker (the father of the U.S. Senator).[51] General Spaatz was the senior Air Force commander in the European and Mediterranean theaters. He had complete operational control over the strategic bombing forces of the Eighth and Fifteenth Air Forces. I believe he also had administrative and logistical responsibilities over the tactical air forces as well. In any event, at USSTAF the overall intelligence function—including, as I recall, counterintelligence—was vested in the Directorate of Intelligence of which McDonald was in charge, and Weicker was his deputy. Their responsibilities therefore were broader than mine, and they were my seniors whom I respected and tried to keep fully informed. My section, division as it was referred to in later organizational charts, was by far the largest intelligence function.

I suggest that you may find helpful information in the "Notes on Operational Intelligence Division, USSTAF," the rather informal memorandum

---

[51]Col. Lowell P. Weicker, Sr., (1903–1978) was Deputy Director of Intelligence for USSTAF. In 1944 he assisted with negotiating permission for American aircraft to land in airfields in the Soviet Union after they completed bombing missions over Nazi-occupied territory in Europe. Weicker graduated from Yale University in 1926 and then joined E. R. Squibb and Sons, the company his father, Theodore Weicker, built into a giant pharmaceutical firm. When Squibb acquired Lentheric, a French perfume company, Weicker was sent to Paris to direct it. After the war, Weicker was President of Squibb until 1953. At the request of President Eisenhower, he served as the Assistant Secretary General for Production and Logistics for NATO from 1953 to 1956. Returning to the United States, he became President of Bigelow-Sanford, Inc., a carpet manufacturing firm. His son, Lowell P. Weicker, Jr., (1931–), was elected to the U.S. Senate as a Republican from Connecticut in 1971.

I prepared for General McDonald following the end of the war.[52] This memorandum explains what normally went on in the Operational Intelligence Section. We maintained an elaborate war room, and sometimes the briefing that occurred daily was restricted to the most senior operational officers. Even then, ULTRA as such was never used. These briefings included not only information relevant to the Army Air Forces itself but also to the ground forces after the invasion as the war was being fought across Europe. I therefore was receiving from Bletchley substantial information relevant to the ground force operations in addition to the basic air force intelligence received both from Bletchley and our small unit at British Air Ministry. The ULTRA we received was rarely simply a copy of the German message. It usually was interpreted or accompanied by intelligence commentary by Jim Rose, Peter Calvocoressi, or some other competent officers. This interpretative intelligence from Bletchley was particularly helpful, as often the raw message itself would mean little. We had no time to maintain and research the sort of massive card index file available only at Bletchley.

Lt. Col. Julian Allen usually briefed General Spaatz on ULTRA, and I briefed Gen. Fred Anderson. My relationship with Fred became personal as well as professional, and his death after the war was a saddening event for me.

Whenever requested, of course, I also briefed George McDonald and Lowell Weicker on ULTRA. As a rule, both of these officers were engaged primarily in administrative duties that were considerably broader than Operational Intelligence itself. I shared a residence with General McDonald and Colonel Weicker, where we often conferred.

In addition to regularly briefing, I usually reviewed the intelligence summaries that we prepared and circulated to subordinate commands. It should be borne in mind that after the invasion, USSTAF had three headquarters: a rear one in London that worked closely with British Air Ministry, the principal one at St. Germain, and a small advanced headquarters at Rheims. I spent time at all of these. We had quality people at all of these locations.

Few of my days were "typical" in the sense that any particular routine was followed. Operating the war room, briefing the appropriate people, and seeing that all relevant intelligence was utilized and that ULTRA was duly protected, were uniform duties.

Kohn: One of the things we're interested in, generally, is the extent to which this incredible knowledge shaped the character of strategy and operations.

[52]See Appendix 4 for Maj. Lewis F. Powell, Jr., "Operational Intelligence Section at USSTAF," 1 June 1944, and Appendix 5 for Lt. Col. Lewis F. Powell, Jr., "Notes on Operational Intelligence Division of Directorate of Intelligence, USSTAF," 9 June 1945.

A commander would be able to say about the enemy, "I know where they are; I don't know what their intentions are, and how they'll use their force, but by knowing where they are, and then being able to follow how they respond to my operations, I can do all sorts of good things."

Powell: ULTRA did indeed shape the character of strategy and operations—particularly operations. In no other war have commanding generals had the quality and extent of intelligence provided by ULTRA. It was not always used intelligently, and sometimes we simply were not able to take advantage of it. The Army Air Forces, for example, chose poor targets in the early part of the strategic air war. One of the reasons was, and the primary reason perhaps, was that we did not have fighter aircraft that could escort the bombers to the targets we were most anxious to hit. After the heavy losses at Schweinfurt and Regensburg, it came as a shock to the traditional Air Force people that the B–17s flying in tight formation could not protect themselves.[53] When the P–51s came in mid-winter of 1943–1944, plus the P–47s, which were not as good escort aircraft as the 51s, but still good—when they were available to escort the bombers the whole character of the strategic air war changed. By the time I had joined Spaatz's headquarters, the target systems had become the proper ones. The single most important target category was the German synthetic oil production. Germany had no natural petroleum, and only a small percentage of its need came from the Roumanian wells. When we had the P–51s and P–47s to escort our bombers, we attacked the synthetic plants with conspicuous success.

A basic objective remained control of the air. We had it early in Italy primarily because the Germans thought that Italy was a minor theater. They were fighting the Russians when we landed in North Africa; the Germans were outside of Stalingrad. We controlled the air where we needed it down there fairly early. It was a long time before the Allied air forces, and this really means the United States Army Air Forces, controlled the air over Germany. This meant defeating the GAF and leaving us free to exploit control of the air. The primary objective, by the time Spaatz returned from Italy, was to knock out the German Air Force. Unless the Allies controlled the

---

[53]On August 17, 1943, 146 8th AF B–17s under the command of Col. Curtis E. LeMay struck at the Messerschmitt factory at Regensburg and then flew on to bases in North Africa. The same day, 230 additional B–17s bombed 5 ball bearing factories in the town of Schweinfurt and returned to England. Sixty aircraft were lost in the 2 raids and about 600 aircrew members were downed, including over 100 who were killed. A second attack against Schweinfurt on October 14, 1943, also resulted in the loss of about 60 aircraft and the downing of 600 airmen. German fighters were responsible for most of the losses, demonstrating the need for long-range fighter escorts and the limits of self-defending bomber formations. See Thomas M. Coffey, *Decision Over Schweinfurt* (New York, 1977); Martin Middlebrook, *The Schweinfurt-Regensburg Mission* (New York, 1983).

air over England and western Europe there could be no invasion. The first series of targets, as I recall, were the airframe factories. After the war, I believe Albert Speer said we should have hit the air engine plants.[54] We were still hitting aircraft factories as one of the ways to bring the German Air Force up, and bearing in mind that the primary objective was to gain control of the air, the way to do that was to knock the German Air Force out. By D-Day that had almost totally been accomplished. Very few except Air Force people ever will give the United States Army Air Forces credit for that. Our victory in the air made the land invasion possible on D-Day.

Kohn: Indeed, it was the strategic forces in effect that established air superiority, command of the air, for the tactical forces.

Powell: It is important to remember, however, that both the strategic and tactical air forces complemented and supported each other. Often—prior to

Ruins of *Kugelfischer* ball bearing factory in Schweinfurt which was hit by AAF B-17s on August 17, 1943.

[54]Albert Speer (1905–1981) was Hitler's Minister for Armaments and Munitions and in his memoirs wrote that in February 1944 the Allies ". . . bombed the enormous airframe plants of the aircraft industry rather than the engine factories, although the most important factor in airplane production was the number of engines we were able to turn out. Destruction of the plants making these would have blocked any increase in aircraft manufacture, especially since, in contrast to the airframe plants, engine factories could not be dispersed among forests and caves." See Albert Speer, *Inside the Third Reich* (New York, 1970), p 347; Williamson Murray, *Strategy for Defeat: The Luftwaffe, 1933–1945* (Maxwell Air Force Base, AL, 1983), pp 190–91.

D-Day—units of the tactical air force would provide escort for the bombers. Thus they helped defeat the GAF. But the bombers attacked the strategic targets that compelled the GAF to come up and fight. After the invasion of France, the tactical units provided direct support to our ground forces in the closest cooperation. The fighter bombers could operate without interference from the GAF by the time of D-Day, and the Germans could not move on any roads anywhere near the front in the daytime without serious risk. They had to move at night, and they had a hard time moving at night because they were short of petrol.

Putney: It was a controversial use of air power.

Powell: Always controversial. The Royal Air Force insisted that daylight bombing could not survive the losses, and if it did survive it would not be effective. But they had very different type aircraft, different type bombers, different type bombsights. One of the great credits that the commanders of our air forces deserve is that they insisted on a separate operation and insisted on daylight bombing.[55] After our bombers began to bring the German fighters up, the orders were to engage them, not simply hang around the bombers and to protect them, but engage the fighters. Also, they were to save some ammunition so that on the way back they could attack the airfields and strafe the planes on the ground, destroy the control towers. This was done in a masterful fashion, as we found out when we would get the reports from ULTRA on what had happened.

---

[55]When the Americans entered the war in December 1941, their air doctrine called for the destruction of carefully selected industrial targets by precision bombing from high altitudes in daylight. Based upon their wartime experience from 1939 to 1941, the British were opposed to the American doctrine. Heavy losses of British crews and aircraft in daylight raids had forced the British to switch to nighttime raids by May 1940. By November 1941, doubts about the accuracy of precision bombing led the British to target areas and cities instead of specifically selected targets.

At the Casablanca Conference in January 1943, the British, led by Prime Minister Churchill, pressured the Americans to abandon daylight bombing and join with the RAF in nighttime raids. Maj. Gen. Ira C. Eaker, 8th AF commander, defended American strategy. He emphasized the heavy firepower of American B-17 Flying Fortresses and their ability to defend against German daylight defenses; the accuracy of new American bombsights; the twenty-four-hour pressure the Americans and British could apply against the Germans; and the relief of congested airfields in the United Kingdom by twenty-four-hour operations. Eaker proclaimed that Americans hitting precise and vital targets would force the German Air Force to come up and fight in defense of those targets. The Casablanca Directive issued after the conference was broad enough to allow the Americans and British each to pursue their own strategy in the subsequent Combined Bomber Offensive. See Charles Webster and Noble Frankland, *The Strategic Air Offensive Against Germany, 1939–1945*, 4 vols, (London, 1961) Vol 1: *Preparation*, pp 129–30, 178, 353–63, Vol 2: *Endeavour*, pp 10–20; DeWitt S. Copp, *Forged in Fire: Strategy and Decisions in the Air War Over Europe, 1940–45* (Garden City, NY, 1982), pp 212–14, 301–02; Craven and Cate, *Army Air Forces in World War II*, Vol 2, pp 300–07.

Putney: Were your briefings and activity concerned with day-to-day issues and operational matters? Did you ever participate in writing a report, a white paper from Spaatz's office in April of 1944, critical of RAF strategy? The paper also advocated strategic bombing, as opposed to bombing attacks against rail transportation and tactical targets?

Powell: I don't think I ever wrote a paper of that kind. There were discussions often of the appropriateness of the target systems as D-Day approached, and when it was best to attack them. There were many people working on that, for the most part, back in London and in the Pentagon. Spaatz, of course, did not as a rule say today that we would hit such and such a target tomorrow. He would issue directives to the Eighth Air Force and the Fifteenth Air Force, which gave them what in effect was authority to make the day-to-day decisions as to which targets to hit within the approved categories. Spaatz reviewed, as did Fred Anderson, the reasons why they attacked one rather than the other on the basis of ULTRA and photographic evidence. The single most successful attacks were on the synthetic oil plants. As to the status of plants already damaged, judgments had to be made as to the priority of attacks on these plants. Spaatz and Anderson were in touch constantly with Doolittle at the Eighth and Eaker at the Fifteenth Air Force. We sent intelligence summaries to both of those air forces even though they had intelligence staffs of their own. We had a broader range of intelligence. For example, we received most of the ground force ULTRA from the day of invasion on. That was important for the top people in USSTAF to consider in doing their planning.

Boeing B–17.

Kohn: Did you know of this intelligence as to the German divisions at Arnhem?

Powell: No, I didn't know that combat Panzer divisions were there. Photographic intelligence, and perhaps some reports from the Dutch underground, identified a number of German tanks, but these were not thought to be in combat units. That was an intelligence failure of considerable magnitude. We did not know—when I say "we" I'm talking about Air Force intelligence—about Panzer divisions being located precisely at the drop area for the English airborne brigade.[56]

Another well-known intelligence failure was the surprise attained by the Germans in the great battle of the Ardennes in December of 1944.[57] We knew from ULTRA that several GAF units had moved to the western front. Also, several German divisions had moved from, we thought, reserves in central Germany. These were not believed to be front-line divisions. Allied intelligence thought these were defensive moves. We were planning an offensive early in 1945 to cross the Rhine. It was believed the Germans were strengthening their defenses. Weather handicapped our reconnaissance, and the Germans used land lines primarily—not radio—to communicate. The Ardennes

---

[56]Arnhem, a city on the lower Rhine River in Holland, was one of the objectives of the large Allied ground and airborne offensive called MARKET GARDEN conducted in mid-September 1944. Approximately 20,000 airborne troops from the American 82d and 101st Airborne Divisions, the British 1st Airborne Division, and the Polish 1st Independent Parachute Brigade, which was attached to the British division, were parachuted up to 60 miles into enemy territory to capture key bridges in Holland (Operation MARKET). Simultaneously, the British XXX Army Corps conducted a ground assault to link up with them (Operation GARDEN). MARKET GARDEN stalled, in part because elements of the 9th SS and 10th SS Panzer Divisions, which had earlier escaped through the Falaise gap, were in the Arnhem area and strongly attacked against the northernmost assault element, the British 1st Airborne Division. On the night of September 25, 2,200 Allied paratroops were forced to withdraw, leaving behind 7,000 men killed, wounded, or captured. Intelligence about German forces from ULTRA, photo-reconnaissance, and other sources was sufficient to convince some officers that German resistance would be stronger than previously anticipated. Senior Allied commanders, however, including Eisenhower and Montgomery, discounted this evidence for various reasons, including over-confidence based on past success and a fixed expectation of weak German resistance and disorganization. See Bennett, *Ultra in the West*, pp 149–58; Craven and Cate, *Army Air Forces in World War II*, Vol 3, pp 598–612.

[57]The Battle of the Ardennes was the last, desperate German counter-offensive in the West, which took place in the Belgian Ardennes region and in Luxembourg in December 1943 and January 1944. Also known as the Battle of the Bulge because of the bulge in American lines caused by the 29 German divisions and brigades in the attack, this was the largest single battle ever fought by the U.S. Army. The total American battle casualties reported from December 16 to January 2 were 4,138 killed, 20,231 wounded, and 16,946 missing. See Charles B. MacDonald, *A Time for Trumpets: The Untold Story of the Battle of the Bulge* (New York, 1985); Hugh M. Cole, *The Ardennes: Battle of the Bulge* [United States Army in World War II: The European Theater of Operations] (Washington, 1965), p 674.

attack was a surprise of great significance because we suffered heavy casualties.

ULTRA finally became helpful, as I recall, when we learned that the Germans were planning to do what they tried to do at Falaise, and that was to do a sweeping ground movement up to Antwerp, that would divide the Allied ground forces. When the weather cleared, our fighter bombers went into action, and so did the strategic bombers.[58]

Kohn: In any specific operations do you remember ULTRA having an impact? For example, the Big Week, February of 1944. Is there any memory on your part of planning for a special operation, using ULTRA particularly for that?[59]

Powell: No, I can't say that I have a recollection of the February coordinated attacks, as I had not rejoined Spaatz's headquarters at that time. As to the enormously successful operation against oil, we knew almost as soon as Albert Speer did that we had found the vital organ of the Germany economy in the synthetic oil plants. I forget how many of these there were, but I do not think there were more than 15 of them. They had all been located back in East Germany, so that until we had fighter escorts, it was just too dangerous

---

[58]Lewin, Winterbotham, and Rosengarten explained that there was a dearth of ULTRA about the Ardennes offensive prior to December 16, 1944. Calvocoressi disagreed, claiming ULTRA did give warnings of the offensive, and Bennett stated that ULTRA pointed "convincingly" to the impending attack. MacDonald concluded that ULTRA and other intelligence sources provided "a lot of information," but that it was improperly interpreted. See Ronald Lewin, *Ultra Goes to War: The First Account of World War II's Greatest Secret Based on Official Documents* (New York, 1978), pp 356–57; Winterbotham, *The Ultra Secret*, p 178; Rosengarten, "With Ultra From Omaha Beach to Weimar," pp 129–30; Calvocoressi, *Top Secret Ultra*, pp 45–49; Bennett, *Ultra in the West*, pp 191–92.

[59]Big Week occurred February 20–25, 1944, during a break in weather and was directed against the German Air Force in the air, on the ground, and in production at factories and assembly plants. Approximately 3,300 bombers from the 8th AF and 500 bombers from the 15th AF hit targets relating to aircraft production in central and southern Germany. The British coordinated its night attacks with the American raids, sending 2,351 bombers and 16 fighter squadrons on missions. While the 15th AF still had no long-range escort fighters, such fighters from the 8th AF and 9th AF kept American bomber losses within acceptable limits. The 8th AF lost 137 bombers, and the 15th 89, for a total average of 6 percent. Total American fighter aircraft losses were 28 of 3,673 sorties made by P-38s, P-47s, and P-51s.

Big Week attacks destroyed 75 percent of the buildings in plants accounting for 90 percent of the total German aircraft production. The German aircraft industry recuperated rapidly; Big Week delayed aircraft production by only two months. Big Week was noteworthy for the destruction it brought on the operational German Air Force. The large and fiercely fought battles over Germany mauled the German Air Force and marked the beginning of the end of the German single-engine fighter force. See Craven and Cate, *Army Air Forces in World War II*, Vol 3, pp 30–66; Webster and Frankland, *Strategic Air Offensive* Vol 3: *Victory* pp 131–32; Murray, *Strategy for Defeat*, p 243.

to attack them. We usually had damage assessment reports from ULTRA following an attack. I remember one from Leuna advising Speer that we had reduced its capacity to some 12 to 15 percent, and it would be 6 weeks before they could get production back to a significant level. The great beauty of that was that we knew when to attack again. The weather, however, had a great deal to do with planning. You could plan to go back on such and such a day, and it may be a week later before you had the right sort of weather for that part of Germany. Incidentally, ULTRA helped with weather; we would get the German weather reports and know the weather over the targets.

Putney: ULTRA was that up-to-date?

Powell: Oh, yes.

Putney: Towards the end of 1944?

Powell: Yes. We would get a report on bomb damage, usually the day after the attack. We would confirm it by aerial reconnaissance. We flew aerial reconnaissance over Germany every day, if weather permitted, and often when the weather was doubtful, hoping there would be a break, and we could photograph our principal targets. When I got up to brief people in the war room at USSTAF, I usually had intelligence from ULTRA, but I also had excellent intelligence from photographic reconnaissance and its interpretation. We had photographic interpreters with us. But anything like strategic interpretation came from the great center in England, where the British and Americans worked side by side.[60] (Incidentally, Sarah Churchill, the daughter of the Prime Minister, worked there.[61] I met her on a visit there, and years later Mrs. Powell and I gave a luncheon for Miss Churchill in our Richmond home.) Other target systems in the spring 1944, and running well through the summer and into the fall, not only included synthetic oil plants, but also communications, marshalling yards in particular, and power plants.

[60]RAF Station Medmenham, consisting of the Danesfield mansion, prefabricated huts, and spacious grounds on the banks of the Thames River near Heston Airfield and the village of Medmenham, was a large aerial photo-interpretation and analysis center. From August 1942 on, American photo intelligence officers were assigned to the station, and their numbers approximately equalled those of the RAF staff, making Medmenham a completely Allied unit. See Constance Babington-Smith, *Evidence in Camera: The Story of Photographic Intelligence in World War II*, with a Foreword by Marshal of the Royal Air Force the Lord Tedder (London, 1958), pp 107–09, 151–52; Roy M. Stanley, *World War II Photo Intelligence* (New York, 1981), pp 247–48; Webster and Frankland, *Strategic Air Offensive Against Germany*, Vol 2, p 222.

[61]Sarah Churchill (1914–1982) enlisted in the Women's Auxiliary Air Force in October 1941, specializing in photo and map interpretation. She served until the end of the war, attending the Teheran and Yalta Conferences with her father, the Prime Minister. After the war, she continued her acting career in the United States.

After the war was over I visited most of the German cities, and whether one approves of area bombing which the RAF did or not, it was effective in terms of disrupting communications, and commitment of German personnel. I stood sadly beside what was left of the cathedral at Cologne, and I walked around that great old cathedral. This was a few days after the Germans surrendered, and you could not see a single building standing in Cologne, not a single one. A person had a hard time moving about; there were just a couple of bulldozed streets. I went back to Cologne in about ten or twelve years, and the city had been rebuilt.

I also was interested in seeing the damage we had done to the Krupp works in Essen; it had been virtually destroyed.[62] Basically, from the time I joined Spaatz's headquarters, our primary objective was to destroy the German Air Force. Krupp remained a target, but we opened up target areas that had not been opened up before.

If anybody doubts the role of the Army Air Forces, as I have said frequently, the invasion of Europe would have been impossible without Allied control of the air. The public has never recognized this historic truth.

Kohn: Do you remember any use of ULTRA in the transportation campaign leading up to Normandy, when the strategic forces were, to some degree, diverted?[63]

Powell: I remember that fairly well, and in terms of there being a controversy. I heard the subject discussed frequently. Spaatz and Eisenhower were

---

[62]Krupp was the family name of a dynasty of German steelmakers known for their armaments, whose founders started as merchants in the sixteenth century in Essen in the Ruhr Valley. The Krupp works at Essen covered six million square yards of factory space, an area seven times larger than the city's center. See William Manchester, *The Arms of Krupp, 1587–1968* (Boston, 1968), p 477.

[63]In early 1944 during the planning for OVERLORD, the invasion of Normandy, General Spaatz and Air Chief Marshal Arthur T. Harris, Commander of RAF Bomber Command, objected to the diversion of bombers from striking strategic targets in Germany to attack transportation and interdiction targets in western France in order to disrupt and delay German troop movements toward the Normandy beaches. Spaatz advocated the use of the strategic forces against oil targets, which would diminish crucial German fuel supplies and bring the German Air Force up in defense of oil facilities. Among the supporters of the "transportation" plan were General Eisenhower, Supreme Commander, Allied Expeditionary Forces (AEF); Air Chief Marshal Tedder, Deputy Supreme Commander, AEF; and Air Marshal Trafford Leigh-Mallory, Commander, Allied Expeditionary Air Force.

On March 25, 1944, General Eisenhower officially decided on the transportation plan, which lasted three months. On May 12, 1944, General Spaatz was able to send bombers from the 8th AF against strategic oil targets, and after the successful Normandy invasion, oil did become a primary strategic target. ULTRA played important roles in disclosing how very effective the transportation and oil campaigns were. See Murray, *Strategy for Defeat*, pp 271–77. For a discussion of ULTRA and strategic target planning, see SRH-017, RG 457, NA.

close friends, and in the end, Spaatz, of course, would do anything Eisenhower wanted him to because he was the commanding general. But Spaatz resisted being diverted from attacks on strategic targets in Germany until the need was evident. We did attack rail communications, as I recall. The bridges over the Seine and some of the rail communications in France were important targets. Many of those were in reach of the tactical air forces. Also we then had some medium bombers in—I don't think we had any in England—but they came from Italy and bombed those bridges. We would get ULTRA damage reports and reports from the French underground that were very good on that. There was no question in anybody's mind from various sources, including and particularly ULTRA, that Allied deception plans, which created the fictitious Army group opposite Pas de Calais, had been "bought" by Hitler.[64] He had the best divisions in France stationed in that area, and when they tried to move down into Normandy, they just had a devil of a time getting there, not only because the bridges were down—they would use pontoon bridges, and they would get knocked out—but also they had to move at night to keep the troops from being destroyed on the roads. The Germans never really brought into action the full ground force capability they had at the time of the invasion. As we pushed in closer to Germany, of course, the resistance was stiffer. But again the combination of strategic and tactical bombing—and with fine help from the RAF—deprived the enemy of its best troops when needed.

Kohn: Do you remember any role for ULTRA in the shuttle bombing effort whereby we attempted to bomb Germany and land in the Soviet Union, then to bomb Germany on the return flight to Britain?

Powell: I am familiar with it and had a modest role in planning it. I will tell you a little bit about it, and what I am going to say, for the most part,

---

[64]Extensive cover and deception plans were a part of Allied preparations for the invasion of France at Normandy, which occurred June 6, 1944. The overall deception plan, codenamed JAEL and rechristened BODYGUARD, aimed to convince the Germans the invasion would come later than planned and occur almost anywhere except Normandy. FORTITUDE SOUTH was the name of the crucial subordinate deception plan, which aimed to establish the primary threat against Pas de Calais, 200 miles east of the landing site at Normandy, and to portray the actual Normandy attack as a feint and prelude to the main assault six weeks later at Pas de Calais. Deception in FORTITUDE SOUTH included use of dummy landing craft and aircraft, false radio broadcasts, bombing runs against Pas de Calais, decoy lighting schemes, fake sound devices, restricted areas, and the creation of an entirely fictitious or notional army, the First United States Army Group (FUSAG), commanded by General Patton. FORTITUDE SOUTH was successful, and divisions of the German 15th Army were held in reserve and idle at Pas de Calais well after the Normandy beachhead was established. See Charles Cruickshank, *Deception in World War II* (New York, 1980), pp 85–98, 170–89; Anthony Cave Brown, *Bodyguard of Lies* (New York, 1975), pp 473–99, 647–87.

does not specifically involve ULTRA. We wanted air bases that could be used in the Soviet Union. The United States tried to obtain those bases a long time before the Russians agreed. We had at USSTAF, at least theoretically in my section, two or three intelligence officers who specialized in air force base needs. These were people who knew how to build airfields and who knew what was needed in the way of control towers and maintenance facilities. I knew nothing about these. In any event, after the Russians finally agreed to let us use Poltava and a second base, we sent two of our people to inspect those bases. The RAF may have done the same. I just know of our people. They went to Teheran, and there they languished for two or three weeks, and finally the Soviets allowed one to enter—not both. The whole experience was what you would expect, although at that time the Soviet Union was viewed and publicized as our great and loyal ally. It was my opinion then, and I think it was shared by all of us at Spaatz's headquarters, that in the end those bases did us very little good. There were two or three missions, possibly more, that used one or both of those bases. Prior Soviet permission had to be obtained. A large number of our aircraft were destroyed by the GAF on the ground at one of these bases.[65]

What I always remember, with a great deal of bitterness, is what happened when the Polish underground forces were to assist the Russians. It had been planned that when the Soviet army reached the Vistula river and was prepared to attack, the Polish underground would rise and aid the Soviets. The Army Air Forces were to fly shuttle missions to drop arms and supplies to the Poles and land at Poltava. The underground rose up against the

[65]FRANTIC was the code word for the American project which used Russian airfields to refuel and reload munitions for shuttle bombing missions across Europe. Three airfields were eventually involved in FRANTIC operations: Poltava, Mirgorod, and Piryatin. The Americans sent the supplies and construction materials the Russians used to prepare the fields during April and May 1944. Assuming responsibility for maintenance and airfield defense, the Russians restricted the number of AAF personnel on the fields; key American officers working on the project were sometimes delayed in Teheran for days on end without explanation. USSTAF established the Eastern Command in Russia to coordinate FRANTIC operations. After disagreement between the Americans and Russians over the first set of targets, to which the Americans acquiesced, the first shuttle mission occurred June 2, involving 130 B-17s and 70 fighters from the 15th AF. The aircraft flew from Italy and attacked the rail center and marshalling yards in Debrecen, Hungary.

On June 21, the 8th AF sent 114 B-17s and 70 P-51s on the second shuttle mission against the synthetic oil plant at Ruhland, south of Berlin. The mission was effective, and the aircraft landed at the 3 Russian airfields. Shortly after midnight, however, German bombers attacked Poltava, destroying 43 B-17s and damaging 26. The next night the Germans attacked Piryatin and Mirgorod, but without much success, since they could not locate Piryatin, and the Americans had flown their aircraft away from Mirgorod. After these German attacks, American enthusiasm for shuttle missions cooled, although there were 4 more FRANTIC missions, with the last ending in Italy on September 13. See Craven and Cate, *Army Air Forces in World War II*, Vol 3, pp 308–19; Richard C. Lukas, *Eagles East: The Army Air Forces and the Soviet Union, 1941–1945* (Tallahassee, Fl, 1970), pp 192–201.

Devastated Krupp works of Essen, Germany. *Courtesy National Archives.*

Germans, as had been planned. We were prepared to fly, but the Soviets would not allow us to land at Poltava, nor would they move their own ground forces. They deliberately wanted the Polish underground wiped out, which the Germans were permitted to do.[66]

[66]On August 1, 1944, the Polish Home Army rose against the German garrison in Warsaw. The Russians were advancing towards the city, and it seemed that they would soon be in the Polish capital. Radio Moscow broadcasts had urged the Poles to rise up against the Germans. After the uprising began, however, the Russian advance towards Warsaw halted, and over the next few months, the Russians remained about six miles from the city across the Vistula River. The Russians refused the American request to use Russian airfields built for Operation FRANTIC for refueling on shuttle relief missions to the Poles. Personal appeals from President Roosevelt and Prime Minister Churchill for use of the airfields were in vain. From August 13 to 16, British and Polish volunteer crews with the RAF and volunteers from the South African Air Force attempted to supply the Poles with nighttime airdrops on exceedingly difficult round trip missions from Italy to Warsaw. The loss of crews and aircraft were heavy, and the flights were suspended, except for Polish crews who continued to fly the nearly suicidal missions. In spite of these missions, the situation for the Poles was desperate by early September.

The Allies renewed appeals for use of FRANTIC airfields for relief and resupply missions. The Soviets finally consented on September 13, and on the same day, they themselves dropped American canned food over Warsaw and publicized their assistance. They made other drops over Warsaw in September, often without using parachutes, which damaged many of the supplies and made them useless. The American shuttle mission with its large heavy bomber fleet and fighter escorts occurred on September 18. In daylight, 110 B–17s circled Warsaw, dropping 1,284 containers of ammunition, weapons, food, and medical supplies. Unfortunately fewer than 300 containers reached the Poles. At the end of September the Allies made another appeal for a shuttle mission, but the Soviets refused. In the first week of October, the Germans finally crushed the Polish insurgents, who suffered some 10,000 killed and 7,000 wounded. Ninety percent of Warsaw was destroyed. See Craven and Cate, *Army Air Forces in World War II*, Vol 3, pp 316–17; Peter J. Calvocoressi and Guy Wint, *Total War: The Story of World War II* (New York, 1972), pp 482–84; Richard C. Lukas, *The Strange Allies: The United States and Poland, 1941–1945* (Knoxville, TN, 1978), pp 61–85.

I was at Rheims on May 8, 1945, the day the Germans officially signed the surrender agreements. At a rather open-ended buffet luncheon in General Spaatz's residence, there were mixed emotions. Of course, there was deep satisfaction that the war with Nazi Germany had ended in total triumph. In the informal discussions there also were some concerns expressed. There was regret that decisions made at the Washington level had permitted the Soviet forces to occupy Berlin and a large part of West Germany. Although I cannot quote General Spaatz or any particular person, there certainly was a consensus that we had the capability to take Berlin and much of the territory that is now in East Germany. Another negative was the sobering experience we had had with the Soviet Union with respect to the use of the air bases in Russia. It was perfectly clear then that the Soviet Union was not an ally in any sense comparable to the western allies, and that Communist doctrine was antithetical to democracy.

Kohn: Did we ever share ULTRA information, to your knowledge, with the Soviet Union?

Powell: Never, as you probably know.

Kohn: Well, I raise it because it is always a question as to what degree we helped the Soviet Union. For example, there is often raised the question of whether Churchill warned the Soviets in 1941 of the coming German invasion.

Powell: He did.

Kohn: Yes, I'm just wondering where ULTRA figures in that.

Lt. Gen. Ira C. Eaker holds a bouquet presented to him by the Russians shortly after the first FRANTIC mission. Beside him is U.S. Ambassador to the Soviet Union Averell Harriman.

Powell: As a matter of fact, at Bletchley I think I asked about it. Churchill knew what the Germans were doing, in part through ULTRA, a significant part, perhaps conclusively; but he also knew through other intelligence sources. I think ULTRA told the British that the Germans were moving the major headquarters to what became the Soviet front. Then various intelligence sources, Polish as well as British, knew that major German units, including communication units, moved to the eastern front. This information was conveyed by Churchill to Stalin, but Stalin did not believe it. He was so confident that the Ribbentrop and Molotov Pact would be observed that he just ignored it.[67]

This will interest you if you do not already know it: even after we invaded France, the British would not share ULTRA with the French. They did not trust the French, many of whom had cooperated with the Nazis. When I say the French, I am obviously not condemning the entire nation, but there had been too many quislings for the British, in particular, to forget, so ULTRA was *verboten* as far as letting the French know.

Kohn: Did ULTRA contribute to our knowledge of German jet plane development?

Powell: You mean the ME-262?

---

[67]The Ribbentrop-Molotov Pact was an agreement signed in Moscow on August 23, 1939, by the foreign ministers Joachim von Ribbentrop of Germany and Vyacheslav Molotov of the Soviet Union. By the pact, effective for ten years, Germany and Russia agreed to refrain from aggressive and belligerent acts against each other, to consult about common interests, and to refrain from joining alliances directed against either party. A secret protocol provided for new boundaries in Europe for the aggrandizement of the signatories at the expense of Poland and the Baltic states.

With Operation BARBAROSSA, Germany violated the pact, invading the Soviet Union on June 22, 1941, with almost 3,200,000 men in 148 divisions. The first ULTRA confirmation that the extensive shifts of German air and ground forces eastward were preparatory to an attack against Russia came to the British at the end of March 1941. Churchill sent a warning message to Stalin on April 3. Other warnings from many sources, including American sources, followed. By the middle of May, ULTRA and non-ULTRA evidence pointed to a Russian invasion. Stalin did not make timely and effective responses to the warnings, because he dismissed some of them as "disinformation" from the West, did not want to provoke Hitler, believed Hitler would not open a second front, and was fooled by deliberate German deception.

By the middle of July 1941, ULTRA revealed that the Germans were reading some Russian air and naval signals; for security reasons, therefore, the British did not reveal to the Russians their success against ENIGMA. The British did, however, pass certain ULTRA to the Russians via the British Military Mission in Moscow and British naval liaison officers in Russia. Nonetheless, no significant collaboration developed between the British-American intelligence communities and the Russians. See Hinsley, *British Intelligence in the Second World War*, Vol 1, pp 429–83, Vol 2, pp 58–66; John Erickson, *The Road to Stalingrad: Stalin's War with Germany* (London, 1975; reprint Boulder, CO, 1984), p 98; Barton Whaley, *Codeword BARBAROSSA* (Cambridge, MA, 1974), pp 241–45; John Erickson, "Threat Identification and Strategic Appraisal by the Soviet Union, 1930–41," in *Knowing One's Enemies: Intelligence Assessment Before the Two World Wars*, ed. Ernest R. May (Princeton, NJ, 1984), pp 419–22.

Kohn: Yes—early operations, testing, that sort of thing.

Powell: Yes, my recollection is that we knew about the ME-262, in significant part through ULTRA, but we had confirmation of it from sources of the American Office of Strategic Services and British agents. I cannot say, but I would guess, we had some information from photographic reconnaissance. I do remember that the major concern was that the ME-262 would be used as fighters, and obviously they were faster than any other fighters in the world. They may not have been as maneuverable (they were twin-engine, twin-jet), but Hitler insisted on their being used as bombers. Certainly at the beginning, they were wholly ineffective, and apparently they had no bombsight of any significance. In any event they had such a small carrying capacity. So his misjudgment prevented the ME-262 from being a weapon of any significance. We were far more concerned about the ME-262 than the single engine ME-163. There is little doubt, however, that if the Germans had developed these planes earlier, and had several ME-262 fighter squadrons operational, the result could have been serious if not catastrophic. The ME-262 represented a marked advance in aviation, and we had nothing comparable.[68]

Putney: Do you recall ULTRA information pertaining to the rocket sites?

Powell: The V-1 and V-2, yes, but not much.[69] For whatever reason, perhaps because of different chains of command, most of the early intelligence we received on rocket sites came from non-ULTRA sources: primarily, the

[68]A 3,750-pound thrust rocket engine powered the Messerschmitt Me-163 *Komet*. Twin turbojet engines propelled the Me-262 *Sturmvogel*. In May 1944, Hitler ordered the Me-262 redesigned as a fighter-bomber to counter Allied invasion forces, but by October 1944, when the aircraft were starting to be available in quantity, the decision had been rescinded. The Germans formed the first Me-262 fighter group in November 1944. Ethell and Price have estimated that Hitler's decision delayed the deployment of this group by less than six weeks. See Jeffrey L. Ethell and Alfred Price, *The German Jets in Combat* (London, 1979), p 58. See also Murray, *Strategy for Defeat*, pp 252-53. For intelligence on Germany's new aircraft, see Hinsley, *British Intelligence in the Second World War*, Vol 3, part 1, pp 329-53.

[69]V originally stood for *Versuchsmuster* (experimental type), but after Allied air attacks against German cities, Nazi propagandists publicized the weapons as *Vergeltungswaffe* (vengeance weapons).

The German Air Force developed the V-1 as a pilotless aircraft powered by a pulse-jet. The V-1 was essentially an aerial torpedo with wings and was dubbed the "buzz bomb" or "flying bomb." The German army developed the V-2, a liquid fueled rocket designed by Wernher von Braun.

CROSSBOW was the code word for the Anglo-American air operations against all phases of the V-weapons program: research, testing, manufacture, construction of launch sites, transportation, and destruction of missiles in flight. See Craven and Cate, *Army Air Forces in World War II*, Vol 3, pp 84-106.

underground. Then photographic reconnaissance began to pick them up when the sites were created or built on the coast. At Bletchley I saw photographs of these launching sites, and there was some speculation then as to what type of V-weapon would be launched. It could not be a rocket by the way these sites were constructed. It was soon realized that it would be the buzz bombs. You know, of course, that Peenemünde was blitzed very successfully by the RAF, and the intelligence on which that opportunity became available developed before I arrived at Bletchley. Again my understanding is that the first tip that the British had about Peenemünde was from a Norwegian who had worked either at or near Peenemünde and had gone back to Norway, and through the underground up there, tipped the British. Even though most of Peenemünde was covered with camouflage netting (apart from the runways), the British used agents plus ULTRA plus reconnaissance to make sure that that was the main base. Then the mission, as I recall, involved a lot of deception in itself, so I think the Germans thought we were going to bomb Berlin or some other major target. That set the V-weapon program back six to nine months, perhaps longer.[70]

The V-weapons would have been devastating against the invasion forces that were crowded in southern England. I went down there with George

A V-1 Buzz Bomb still intact except for a wing and motor which were probably lost upon impact with the ground. *Courtesy National Archives.*

[70]The British originally learned about V-weapons from informants, agents, prisoners of war, and photographic reconnaissance. ENIGMA intercepts confirmed that both types of V weapons were under development. See Hinsley, *British Intelligence in the Second World War*, Vol 1, pp 99–100, 508–12, Vol 3, part 1, pp 357–455.

V-1 and V-2 weapons were developed, built, and tested at Peenemünde on the Isle of Usedom in the Baltic Sea. After deception about their planned target, 597 aircraft of the British Bomber Command attacked Peenemünde the night of August 17–18, 1943. After the devastating raid, the Germans dispersed, but continued, V-weapons development. The scientific officer on the staff of the Air Ministry estimated that the Peenemünde attack delayed V-weapons development by about two months. See David Irving, *The Mare's Nest* (Boston, 1965), pp 93–146; R. V. Jones, *The Wizard War: British Scientific Intelligence, 1939–1945* (New York, 1978), pp 412–61.

McDonald several times, and the V-weapons could have caused heavy casualties.

I did not have many close calls in the war, but a buzz bomb exploded very near the house I was billeted in outside of Bushey Park, where the headquarters of USSTAF then were located. General Eisenhower's headquarters were at Bushey Park and so were ours until well after the invasion. A buzz bomb blew the windows out of my bedroom. I heard it coming, and I had done this before: I got under the bed. So while there was flying glass all over my room, I was not hurt. Basically the buzz bombs caused a lot of damage and killed a good many people, particularly in the London area. But they had no real effect on the outcome of the war, nor did the rockets used later.[71]

Putney: Was ULTRA becoming eclipsed by other forms of intelligence towards the end of the war?

Powell: Certainly no other form of intelligence was as dramatic as ULTRA in terms of shaping strategy, resulting in saving tens of thousands of lives. I think, even if there had been no ULTRA, that with aerial reconnaissance, primarily, plus the work of scholars and economists, we would have identified target systems in Germany. It may have taken us longer—in fact, I know it would have taken us much longer—but in the end we would have destroyed the German economy, because we had things they did not have. We had a bomber that was by far the best in the world; the German bombers were inferior. We ended up with the best fighters. We also had a strategic position being in England protected by the water, and by the highly competent RAF. The Germans lost control of the air over England following the Battle of Britain. The only other intelligence threat in Great Britain were agents, and what happened to those I know you know. Literally 99 percent of them were caught shortly in time and "turned." It was a very simple formula; it always worked. "We will shoot you tomorrow unless you broadcast only what we tell you, and you can't broadcast unless one of our people is present."[72]

[71]By the end of the war in Europe, Germany had fired more than 16,000 V-1s and 3,000 V-2s against England and continental targets. See Gregory P. Kennedy, *Vengeance Weapon 2: The V-2 Guided Missile* (Washington, 1983), p 4; Craven and Cate, *Army Air Forces in World War II*, Vol 3, p 84.

[72]The British caught over 100 German spies in England and made them betray or "double-cross" the *Abwehr*, the German Secret Service. These "double agents" were under the control of a subsection of M.I.5, the British internal security agency. See J. C. Masterman, *The Double-Cross System in the War of 1939 to 1945* (New Haven, 1972).

Kohn: Did you know that at the time?

Powell: Yes, oh yes.

Kohn: Those of you in the intelligence business knew that.

Powell: Yes. The ULTRA officers were totally frank with us, I thought. They told us things that I don't think Americans would have told us.

Kohn: The ULTRA officers?

Powell: At Bletchley.

Kohn: I see. In other words, you learned about other intelligence activities and sources. The double-cross system was really a different source, a different system.

Powell: Yes it was. Of course, we had nothing to do with that, but as intelligence officers we were interested in the extent to which the Germans would be able to take photographs of the buildup for the invasion. We knew that the RAF had control of the air over England, but still if the V-weapons had come into operation sooner, and agents in Great Britain had been able to pinpoint the proper targets, it could have been a very different situation. The invasion probably would have been delayed; it might have been aborted. No one has a higher opinion of the value of ULTRA than I do. It alone was a most dramatic and significant intelligence source, but the other sources of intelligence were also good.

Kohn: One other question occurs to me, as you talk about German intelligence. Did you know at the time or did you suspect that the Germans were succeeding to any extent in doing what we had done, that is, break some of the codes, read some of the ciphers?

Powell: I did not know specifically about this. I cannot tell you when I learned that the Germans had been reading a code used by the military attaches in Cairo.[73] This was before we went into North Africa and when Rommel was

[73]From the autumn of 1941 to July 1942, the Germans read the enciphered code system used by the American Military Attache in Cairo, Egypt, Col. Bonner F. Fellers. ENIGMA and ULTRA revealed the compromise to the British, who informed the Americans. See Hinsley, *British Intelligence in the Second World War*, Vol 2, pp 331, 361, 640; Wladyslaw Kozaczuk, *Enigma: How the German Machine Cipher Was Broken, and How It Was Read by the Allies in World War Two*, trans. and ed. by Christopher Kasparek (Frederick MD, 1984) p 171; SRH-002, pp 192–97, RG 457, NA.

receiving excellent intelligence on what the British Eighth Army was doing. I do not know how we learned that that code was being compromised, but we did know about it. Everybody in intelligence did—that the Germans were reading some of our codes. But we had no reason to believe, and people were very concerned with the possibility, that they might be reading the very codes that transmitted ULTRA to the SLUs. The Germans were so confident that the codes produced on the ENIGMA machine were unbreakable. They became suspicious at times. The British were very clever in so many ways. Whenever the British had the opportunity, as long as the Italians were in the war, they would plant in some way or other a story that we got the intelligence from the Italians. The Germans readily believed that.

Putney: As ULTRA representative, were you concerned with communications with Bletchley or transmitting ULTRA information? Were you using SIGABA machinery or TYPEX?[74]

Powell: I had no responsibility in this respect. The British maintained and safeguarded the transmission of ULTRA both from the intercept stations to Bletchley and from Bletchley to the operational commands. I do not identify SIGABA or TYPEX specifically. When we were in England, I believe land lines were used exclusively and perhaps these were extended by underwater cables when we were in France. I do know that the British were extremely careful to safeguard these transmissions.

Kohn: Could I ask a semi-personal question, Mr. Justice Powell? How has it been to live with the secret about ULTRA for thirty years after the war?

Powell: Well, my wife wondered about that also. I never told her. In fact, I never told anybody. I think I indicated earlier that the basic reason that the secret never leaked out is that everyone knows there was some code breaking. The spectrum of codes is large. The heart of the ULTRA secret is that we were reading Germany's most secret codes on a scale wholly unprecedented. This is what we never disclosed.

I was looking through papers last night trying to prepare myself to talk to you. I came across the citation for my Legion of Merit, and it referred in the citation to the fact that I had provided "top secret special intelligence"

[74]American SIGABA and British TYPEX were cipher machines the Allies used to encipher their most secret communications and ULTRA messages. These machines were more complicated and secure than ENIGMA. SIGABA, also known as Converter M-134-C, was jointly designed by the Army and the Navy. See SRH-359, RG 457, NA.

to the commanding general.[75] I thought that was a little indiscreet. But it was a War Department citation, because I was assigned to the Special Branch of the War Department.

Kohn: It's a fascinating thing, because as far as we know to this point, the great secret of the war, kept so long, has been ULTRA. It will undoubtedly spawn many legends.

Powell: I'll ask you a question: was the secret deliberately preserved to the extent our government could preserve it, in the hope we would have the same success with Soviet codes?

Kohn: I have no personal knowledge of that and would only be speculating.

Powell: I think one could speculate, that quite apart from Soviet codes, most of the countries in the world with any sort of resources try to read other peoples' codes, so that the fact that we had penetrated a code of that complexity and at that level I'm sure would put other nations on guard.[76]

Kohn: I think so, and I think also that the dominance of radio intelligence that early, as opposed to the other forms, was not well-known. It just impresses me that it is the nature of the business to say as little as possible for as long as possible.

Powell: Yes. Even newsmen who knew about ULTRA did not disclose it. Al Friendly is my best example, because I knew Al very well. He was the managing editor of the *Washington Post* after he came back from the war. He had been at Bletchley.

---

[75]See Appendix 6 for the Legion of Merit Citation for Lt. Col. Lewis F. Powell, Jr.

[76]Even before the end of the war, Americans were thinking about postwar uses of signals intelligence. Assistant Secretary of War John J. McCloy and Colonel McCormack of MIS believed that a continual and extensive intercept service was essential to maintain American national security and to support American postwar objectives. As late as 1946 MIS was daily publishing an ULTRA "Black Book." See SRH-141, part 2, p 314; SRH-116, p 38; and SRH-146, pp 1-7, RG 457, NA.

The first book to reveal that ENIGMA had been broken was in Polish by Wladyslaw Kozaczuk, *The Battle of Secrets: The Intelligence Services of Poland and the German Reich, 1922-1939* (Warsaw, 1967), but it received little notice. Six years later, Gustave Bertrand published in French, *Enigma: The Greatest Enigma of the War of 1939-1945*, (Paris, 1973), but it too was generally overlooked. The following year, F. W. Winterbotham published *The Ultra Secret* (New York, 1974), which became a best-seller and revealed to the world the best kept secret of World War II. For a survey of the literature on ULTRA, see David Syrett, "The Secret War and the Historians," *Armed Forces and Society* 9 (Winter 1983): 293 328.

Kohn: And then a professor of journalism in his later years.

Powell: The press ordinarily will print anything about intelligence that it can lay its hands on.

Putney: Could we go back to this question that you had originally posed to the Justice, but he had bounced back to you? What exactly are you saying in terms of how you lived with this secret? In your own mind, are you assuming that the United States is continuing the process of reading codes and ciphers and by talking about reading the codes and ciphers of World War II, there will be a tip-off as to what was going on in 1954 and 1964 and 1974 and 1984?

Powell: Yes. Of course with satellite photography and electronic intelligence, code breaking is no longer quite as important, but it still has to be important. Another reason for the secret, the real secret being kept, is that even the ULTRA officers who had never been to Bletchley had no idea of the full extent of the reading of the German codes. As I recall, there were fewer than thirty American officers, ground *and* air force, trained at Bletchley for the entire European and Mediterranean theaters, and wherever you were, you were sent only messages that pertained to your responsibility. I happened to be at the top command in the Air Force, so I saw more ULTRA intelligence than officers at lower levels. But I knew little, for example, about the success of ULTRA against U-boats. I began to hear vaguely about it. It was generally known by mid-43, maybe late 1943, that the Allied tonnage sunk was beginning for the first time to go down rather than up. ULTRA was primarily responsible for that. Without ULTRA, we could have lost the war to the German U-boats.

I learned, I guess when I was at Bletchley, that ULTRA had been a major factor in the sinking of the *Bismarck*.[77] I think the British Admiralty had guessed or reasoned that the *Bismarck* was headed for Brest rather than for the middle Atlantic. The *Bismarck* itself sent a message confirming that it was headed for Brest, which the Admiralty people at Bletchley read. If you pick specific instances like that, they are very dramatic, but basically the Admiralty was reading the messages from the German Admiralty to the submarine packs in the Atlantic, directing them where to go. We were able to

[77]On May 24, 1941, the German Battleship *Bismarck* sank the *Hood* and badly damaged the *Prince of Wales*. The *Bismarck* itself was damaged by the *Prince of Wales* and by a torpedo from an aircraft from the *Victorious*. As the *Bismarck* headed for Brest on the west coast of France, aircraft from the *Royal Ark* hit and jammed the battleship's rudder. On May 27, the *Bismarck* was encircled by British vessels and destroyed. For the role of deciphered ENIGMA traffic and other sources of intelligence in the sinking of the *Bismarck*, see Hinsley, *British Intelligence in the Second World War*, Vol 1, pp 339–46.

route our convoys accordingly and to determine the extent to which the particular convoys needed escort vessels. But I rarely saw an Admiralty ULTRA message.

Kohn: You mentioned some special topics that might be of interest.

Powell: Yes; one concerns Oranienburg. Fred Anderson came into my office, not long before the end of the war and said, "Lewis, we have orders to bomb a heavy water plant in Oranienburg." I vaguely knew that that had something to do with atomic weapons.

Kohn: Did you know about atomic weapons?

Powell: No, I did not. I knew that several nations were trying to develop atomic weapons. I did not have any idea that we had reached the point where we were even close, but we knew the Germans were working toward that end. They had great scientists. Anyway, we laid on a mission, and nobody knew exactly what we were attacking. We did not have any target maps. I did obtain a city map of Oranienburg by a hectic flight to London at night and going to the British War Office there.[78]

Kohn: Do you remember when that was, sir?

Powell: I would say it was March or April, probably April of '45.

Kohn: You also mentioned Dresden.

Powell: I have been much concerned about the Soviet propaganda with respect to Dresden. The first and most devastating attacks occurred, as I recall, in February of 1945. General Anderson, Deputy Commander of USSTAF (and, as I have noted, Spaatz's operations officer with whom I regularly worked closely) told me that a plan had been approved for back-to-back attacks on

---

[78]In December 1943 the Americans sent the ALSOS mission to Europe to follow Allied armies and discover how far the Germans had progressed with atomic energy research. In November 1944 ALSOS representatives questioned German atomic scientists and examined documents at the University of Strasbourg, which confirmed earlier reports by German POWs that Oranienburg, a town eighteen miles north of Berlin, was the site of a processing plant for thorium and other ores related to the production of atomic energy. The plant was in the projected Russian zone of occupation and could not be investigated by ALSOS. Maj. Gen. Leslie R. Groves, the head of the MANHATTAN Project, requested through the Army Chief of Staff that the Oranienburg facilities be destroyed. On March 15, 1945, 8th AF aircraft dropped nearly 1,300 tons of high explosive and incendiary bombs on the complex at Oranienburg, completely destroying all aboveground parts. See Vincent C. Jones, *Manhattan: The Army and the Atomic Bomb*, [United States Army in World War II: Special Studies] (Washington, 1985), pp 287–88; Leslie R. Groves, *Now It Can Be Told: The Story of the Manhattan Project* (New York, 1962), p 231.

Heavy incendiary bombs from 8th AF fall on Dresden, February 14, 1945.

Dresden by the RAF and the American Army Air Forces. He asked if we had target information or maps on Dresden, and particularly the marshalling yards. I responded that we did not, and that I had understood that Dresden was off-limits so far as any objectives of the American Army Air Forces were concerned. General Anderson agreed fully, and said that this was the uniform view of senior American commanders. He stated that the Soviet Union, as early as at Yalta—and thereafter—had urged the Allies to attack Dresden. The argument was that the Germans were using the Dresden marshalling yards for the assembly by the Germans of reinforcements and supplies for the eastern front, a front on which the Soviets were mounting a wide-ranging offensive.

We all have read, I suppose, that Winston Churchill and British Bomber Command thought that attacking Dresden would somehow shorten the war. But the prevailing view at our headquarters was that the Soviet Union—probably by request from Stalin to Churchill or to Roosevelt—urged these attacks. Of course, it is true that after the Germans had blitzed English cities by indiscriminate fire bombing at night, the British felt free to retaliate in the same way. British Bomber Command, with a large fleet of bombers capable of operating only at night, did destroy large portions of most of the major German cities. It was not the policy of the Army Air Forces to bomb cities indiscriminately. We sought to attack military targets in the daytime, and were, with some exceptions, highly successful in pursuing this policy.

I have a correspondence file on Dresden, containing letters from some Americans who were in positions to know about the attacks: General Eaker, Robert Lovett, and John McCloy.[79] All of these understood that the Allies

[79]During the bombing of Dresden in February 1945, Lt. Gen. Ira C. Eaker (1896–1987) was Commander of the Mediterranean Allied Air Forces, Robert A. Lovett (1895–1986) was the Assistant Secretary of War for Air, and John J. McCloy (1895–) was Assistant Secretary of War. For their correspondence with Powell concerning Dresden, see Powell Papers, USAF Historical Research Center, Maxwell Air Force Base, AL.

simply bowed to persistent Soviet pressure. In theory, I suppose it also was argued that whatever aided the Soviets at that time indirectly aided us. Yet knowing senior American air commanders as I did, I am confident that Spaatz, Fred Anderson, and Eaker—and indeed other senior operational air commanders—would never have attacked Dresden on their own initiative. We would not have sacrificed the lives of young Americans and our aircraft against a target of limited military significance to the major responsibility of the American Air Force.[80]

Kohn: I think sometimes that we government historians fail to compete in the public estimation with a David Irving or Kurt Vonnegut.[81] It's very difficult. We have good scholarship on Dresden, we know what happened from various interpretations, yet amongst the more objective historians. . .

---

[80]Dresden was a lovely city known as the "Florence on the Elbe." Since its beginnings as a commercial town in the Middle Ages, Dresden's strategic position involved it in many military campaigns. On the night of February 13–14, 1945, the British RAF Bomber Command used approximately 770 bomber aircraft in two attacks against Dresden. In two separate daylight attacks on February 14 and 15, the American 8th AF used a total of 527 bomber aircraft. For accounts of these Allied Dresden attacks concerning the number of casualties, the vast marshalling yards as American targets (including discussion of inaccurate bombing), and the extent of Soviet influences on the Allied decision to bomb Dresden, see Webster and Frankland, *Strategic Air Offensive Against Germany*, Vol 3, pp 95–119; Joseph W. Angell, "Historical Analysis of the 14–15 February 1945 Bombing of Dresden," USAF Historical Division, Air University, 1953, K239.046-38 in USAF Historical Research Center, Maxwell Air Force Base, AL; Melden E. Smith, Jr., "The Bombing of Dresden Reconsidered: A Study in Wartime Decision Making," Dissertation from Boston University Graduate School, 1971; Mark A. Clodfelter, "Culmination Dresden: 1945," *Aerospace Historian* 26 (September 1979): 134–47. None of these accounts provided any evidence that Stalin asked specifically for the Dresden bombing. The Russians did know of the impending attack and raised no objections.

[81]In *The Destruction of Dresden* (New York, 1964), David Irving claimed that the best evidence disclosed that approximately 135,000 people were killed in the attack on Dresden February 13–14, 1945; however, in a letter to *The Times* of London on July 7, 1966, Irving stated that he had made a mistake with the mortality statistics, and new evidence, a report of the area police chief, written one month after the attack, revealed casualty figures as follows: 18,375 dead, 2,212 seriously injured, and 13,918 slightly injured. The chief's report listed 35,000 people as "missing" and estimated that the total death toll was expected to reach 25,000. For a critique of other incorrect assertions in *The Destruction of Dresden* see Melden E. Smith, Jr., "Dresden Revisited: New Perspectives on a Lingering Controversy," a paper presented at the 1978 Missouri Valley History Conference, located in Powell Papers, USAF Historical Research Center, Maxwell Air Force Base, AL.

Kurt Vonnegut's *Slaughterhouse-Five* was a novel made into a movie and was based partly on Vonnegut's experience as an American prisoner of war in Dresden. In the editors' introduction to the Franklin Library edition of the book in 1978, the figure of 135,000 fatalities was described as "conservative" and the attack as a "ghastly atrocity."

For a discussion of sensational press reporting, Nazi wartime propaganda, and postwar propaganda about Dresden, see Smith, "Bombing of Dresden Reconsidered," pp 248–81. Smith concluded that the final Dresden death toll was approximately 35,000.

Powell: A great exaggeration of the casualties, also.

Kohn: Yes, very much. I think the last figure I saw was 30,000.

Powell: The East Germans claim, I think, that casualties exceeded 100,000. Of course there is nothing I can do about it now, but I was outraged by the acceptance of Soviet propaganda by the western press, and perhaps, by some scholars. Let me share with you one of my pet peeves about one scholar. You of course have read the Strategic Bombing Survey Report.

Kohn: Parts of it, and, of course, the overall portions and the summary.

Powell: It is an informed and responsible summary of the great success of strategic bombing.[82] The survey team arrived at Spaatz's headquarters a few weeks before the end of the war. Initially, I was annoyed by their presence because they were very nosey. But the survey staff was competent and thorough.

Kohn: Who on the survey showed up, sir?

Powell: Henry Alexander, a first-rate American, was the deputy head of it; D'Olier as I recall, was the head of it.[83] It was a strong commission. One member of the Strategic Bombing Survey, who did not dissent from the report, later wrote an article published in the magazine section of the *New*

[82]Responding to proposals originating with AAF leaders, President Roosevelt in November 1944 directed that the United States Strategic Bombing Survey be established to evaluate the American bombing offensive in the European Theater of Operations. Since the American strategic bombing campaign against Germany was enormous and complex, the survey was authorized 350 officers, 500 enlisted personnel, and 300 civilians, who examined the offensive in 4 major areas: overall, military, economic, and civilian. The survey also examined the strategic bombing campaign against Japan after the surrender in September 1945. Relying heavily on interrogations and captured documents, the survey teams produced over 300 European and Pacific war reports and nearly 1,000 cubic feet of documentation, the latter of which were deposited in the National Archives in late 1946. See David MacIsaac, *Strategic Bombing in World War Two: The Story of the United States Strategic Bombing Survey* (New York, 1976).

[83]Franklin D'Olier (1877–1953), the president of the Prudential Insurance Company and head of the committee promoting the government's war bond drives in New Jersey, was chosen as chairman of the Strategic Bombing Survey. He served in the Quartermaster Corps in World War I, achieving the rank of lieutenant colonel.

Henry C. Alexander (1902–1969), a lawyer, banker, and vice president of J. P. Morgan and Company, was chosen as vice-chairman of the survey.

York Times in which he severely criticized strategic bombing as a failure that may have prolonged the war. But he was dead wrong.[84]

Kohn: Yalta was the third special topic.

Powell: The United States was very anxious to convince the Soviet Union that it had not won the war alone. General Spaatz was invited to go to the Yalta Conference to brief President Roosevelt and whomever else probably should have been briefed on the role of the United States Army Air Forces. Well, you asked me earlier about Tooey Spaatz as a person. He was basically very shy—not in terms of performing the role of commanding general. He was a 100 percent soldier, with one exception: he would have fought the Navy of the United States as well as the Nazi Germans. He did not like the Navy (for understandable reasons). Anyway, Tooey Spaatz asked Fred Anderson to go to Yalta in his place. Fred asked me if I would write a position paper, which Bill Haines and I did.[85] I don't have a copy of it. It must be somewhere in USSTAF papers, as Bill and I received letters of commendation from Fred on our paper.

When Fred Anderson came back from Yalta, he was very depressed. He said that no one was interested at all in what the American air forces had done. He was not asked to brief anybody. Although Fred did not get to talk to Roosevelt, he saw him. He said that Roosevelt clearly was a sick man. I thought that you might find this an interesting bit of history.[86]

---

[84]John Kenneth Galbraith (1908-), professor of economics at Harvard University and former ambassador to India, criticized the value of American strategic bombing in World War II in his review of Albert Speer's *Inside the Third Reich*. As the director of the Overall Economics Effects Division of the United States Strategic Bombing Survey, Galbraith had participated in the interrogation of Speer in May of 1945 near Flensburg, Germany. See John Kenneth Galbraith, "Albert Speer Was the Man to See," *The New York Times Book Review*, January 10, 1971, Section 7, pp 2-3, 30, 32. Walt W. Rostow, a professor of political economy at the University of Texas who had served during the war with the Enemy Objectives Unit of the Economic Warfare Division of the U.S. Embassy in London, wrote a letter challenging Galbraith's assessment about strategic bombing, and that letter with Galbraith's reply were subsequently published. See *The New York Times Book Review*, 4 April 1971, Section 7, pp 20, 22, 24; John Kenneth Galbraith, *A Life In Our Times: Memoirs* (Boston, 1981), pp 192-227.

[85]Lt. Col. William W. Haines (1908-) had been a freelance writer before he joined the AAF in 1942. In the 1930s, he published two books and wrote five screenplays for Warner Brothers and Paramount. When his wartime service ended in 1945, he continued his writing career in California, producing books, screenplays, and stories for magazines. His postwar novel of 1947, *Command Decision*, about a B-17 bomber group based in England, was produced as a film and Broadway play.

[86]The Yalta Conference was held in the Crimea February 4-11, 1945, and attended by President Roosevelt, Prime Minister Churchill, Premier Stalin, and their top military and diplomatic advisers. Two months later on April 12, 1945, President Roosevelt died of a cerebral hemorrhage at Warm Springs, Georgia.

Kohn: My last question has to do with the history on ULTRA (Haines Report) that we gave you that was written at the end of the war. Perhaps you can give us some background on that report.

Powell: Yes. Let me tell you about the little unit at the British Air Ministry, because it was composed of very able people. When I reached Bletchley, I learned that we had, I think, four officers at the British Air Ministry, all of whom had been indoctrinated in ULTRA by the British. The senior of those was Kingman Douglass; he later became Deputy Director of the CIA.[87] He had been a partner in Dillon, Read, one of the major investment banking firms in New York. Then there were Bill Haines, Stewart McClintic, and Ken Beeson—all able.[88]

Lt. Col. William W. Haines (left) and Lt. Col. Lewis F. Powell, Jr. *Courtesy Lewis F. Powell, Jr.*

[87]Col. Kingman Douglass, Sr., (1896–1971) had served as a pilot in the Army Air Service in World War I. With America's entry into World War II, he joined the AAF, serving in the European theater with the 8th AF and as liaison officer with the RAF, and in the Pacific theater as the Chief of the Allied intelligence section group which selected targets for Allied bombardment. After the war, he helped to establish the Central Intelligence Group, the forerunner to the CIA, and in March 1946, became its Deputy Director, holding that post until the end of the year. From 1950 to 1952 he served as Assistant Director of the CIA. He then joined Dillon, Read and Company, investment bankers, and continued his career as a financier.

[88]Lt. Col. Stewart McClintic (1904–1982) was a graduate of Sheffield Scientific School of Yale and was employed by the Mellon Bank and Trust Company of Pittsburgh, Pennsylvania, prior to his joining the AAF in early 1942. By the summer of that year he was in England assigned to the U.S. VIII Bomber Command. He was later assigned to USSTAF, and in December 1944 remained in England in charge of Rear Headquarters of the Directorate of Intelligence when the Main Headquarters moved to St. Germain, France. He subsequently was assigned to USSTAF's Intelligence Division at the British Air Ministry. After the war, he returned to Pittsburgh and the Mellon Bank.

Lt. Col. John K. Beeson (1907–1980) received his basic AAF officers training at Miami, Florida, and was assigned to Craig Field, Selma, Alabama, before being sent to England. He was assigned to the British Air Ministry, where after January 1944 he represented USSTAF on the Oil Committee. After the war he became president of the Gage and Supply Company in Pittsburgh, a wholesale supply house servicing steel companies.

Putney: Haines is listed as the author of the ULTRA Report.

Powell: Yes, he was the author. He was a Hollywood scriptwriter before the war. He writes brilliantly. He was one of our officers in the little ULTRA unit which worked as a team with the British ULTRA people at the British Air Ministry. These were Spaatz's people—not Special Branch. As the war was ending, Spaatz asked McDonald to have the ULTRA report written. We previously had instructed everybody not to mention the word ULTRA in any report and not to write any reports. McDonald talked to me, and we went to Bill Haines. I reviewed the report, and I think Bill wrote 98 percent of it. Although I have not reread all of the report since it was declassified and sent to me, it does not overstate the role of ULTRA.[89]

Kohn: What was the exact purpose of it? Just for the record, to know exactly what had happened, why, and how ULTRA was used?

Powell: Yes. It was written for history. Bill Haines knew as much about ULTRA generally as any American. He had been working in it longer, and with the British. He probably saw a broader picture than I. Bill had the Air Ministry records, as well as our reports. His report is excellent, and merits the respect of historians. Bill did not, however, work directly on operations.

Putney: As scholars are using the records being released from the National Security Agency, they are coming to that report, and they are using it. It is working its way into the histories.

I see that at the British Air Ministry you also worked on a manual on the Soviet Union.

Powell: As the war was ending, we learned—from what source I do not recall—that the Germans had moved most of their General Staff down to the Berchtesgaden area in Bavaria. General McDonald, Lowell Weicker, and I flew down there on an intelligence mission. I think we may have arrived before May 8th; it was very close to the German surrender. The 101st Airborne Division had occupied the Berchtesgaden area, and the Royal Air Force had just blitzed the chalets of Hitler and the other senior officers. These chalets were halfway up a beautiful mountain. We were given the location of the component of the German General Staff which specialized in the Soviet Air Force. With some 101st Airborne troops to look out for us, we went

[89]For the original study and a critique of the Haines report see SRH-013, "Ultra History of U. S. Strategic Air Force[s] Europe vs. German Air Force," RG 457, NA. For a published edition of the report, see U. S. Army Air Forces, *Ultra and the History of the United States Strategic Air Force[s] in Europe vs. the German Air Force* (Frederick, MD, 1980).

to the school where this segment of the General Staff was billeted. They were happy to go to England, as we asked them to do. They were afraid of what the Russians would do to them. The agreement, as I recall, was that if they would go to England and share their intelligence on the Soviet air force with us, we had authority or would obtain it, to send them back to Germany within a year. It was fascinating to work with these German intelligence officers. We put them up in a house outside of London. They had brought some of their records with them and were fully cooperative. I have never seen the end product. I was out of the Army Air Forces before it was completed. We did a lot of work on it, although I doubted the utility of the project.

Putney: Essentially, then, at the Air Ministry you worked on that project.

Powell: I worked on the Soviet manual, on trying to develop information derived primarily from the German officers who were experts on the Soviet air force. The Germans had fairly good information, but it was not of vast importance to us. The Soviets did not have a strategic bomber force. They had fighter bombers that were fairly good. The basic organization of the Soviet air force was what we focused on primarily, as I recall.[90]

At Air Ministry, I was promoted to full colonel and became the Special Branch representative of A-2 of the General Staff in Washington. This was primarily a liaison function. I conferred regularly on the entire scope of intelligence with the RAF Chief of Intelligence, Air Vice Marshal Inglis (a splendid officer), and his successor Air Vice Marshal Elmhirst.[91] Until the end of the Japanese war we shared intelligence on it, and there were a number of studies other than the one on the Soviet air force. As I recall, RAF personnel carried the primary burden of that study. There was a project General McDonald had ordered that we called the Coffin Project. This was to be a history of USSTAF operations. It was still in its early stages when I came

[90]In 1960 the USAF Historical Division of the Research Studies Institute at Air University printed Generalleutnant a. D. Walter Schwabedissen, *The Russian Air Force in the Eyes of German Commanders*. This was one of a series of studies written by, or based on information supplied by, key officials of the German Air Force. Other sources for this study were captured *Luftwaffe* records, documents from the British Air Ministry, and donated material from private collections. The series was part of the USAF's German Air Force Historical Project. See Generalleutnant a. D. Walter Schwabedissen, *The Russian Air Force in the Eyes of German Commanders*, with an Introduction by Telford Taylor (USAF Historical Study, Maxwell AFB, AL, 1960; reprint New York, 1968).

[91]Air Vice Marshal Francis F. Inglis (1899–1969) was the Assistant Chief of the RAF Air Staff, Intelligence, from 1942 to 1945. Air Vice Marshal Thomas W. Elmhirst (1895–1982) served in the same position from 1945 to 1947.

back to Washington in the late fall. If it was ever concluded, I have never seen it.[92]

Putney: We started off with your entering active service in 1942. Were you still active until February 1946?

Powell: When the war ended in Europe, Special Branch asked me to return to Washington and become the chief Japanese Air Force specialist of Special Branch. General Spaatz also had asked me to go with him to the Pacific, but I had been away from my family for nearly three years. I was given the third alternative by Special Branch of going to the British Air Ministry as its senior representative there. I chose that alternative on the understanding that I would not have to stay at Air Ministry more than five or six months. I was promoted to full colonel. I thought I had made a good choice. I was avoiding going to the Pacific or being tied up in Special Branch as chief of

Maj. Gen. Frederick L. Anderson, Deputy Commander of USSTAF (right), chats with Col. Alfred A. Kessler, Jr., Deputy Commander of Eastern Command, USSTAF, during an inspection tour of U.S. bases in Russia.

[92]The "Coffin Report" was prepared at the request of General Spaatz and under the direction of Lt. Col. Caleb Coffin. See Assistant Chief of Staff, A-2, Headquarters, United States Air Forces in Europe, "The Contribution of Air Power to the Defeat of Germany," 3 vols and appendices, 7 August 1945 in USAF Historical Research Center, Maxwell Air Force Base, AL, control no. 519.601c. See also MacIsaac, *Strategic Bombing in World War Two*, pp 97–98, 201.

Japanese air intelligence for two or three years. Then the war suddenly ended against Japan in August, and I did not get home until November.

I had accumulated leave that enabled me to have credit for, I guess a month and a half, January and part of February. I may have come to the Pentagon once or twice then, and when Spaatz became the Chief of the Air Staff, I spent parts of two summers there at his request.[93] I did not take an active reserve commission. I took the inactive commission just because I was interested in the Air Force. General Spaatz asked me if I would do what I could to encourage Congress to authorize a separate Air Force, and I did work with Virginia Senators on that.[94]

I have wandered afield, but it's been fun to make me think again about these things. I could be wide of the mark with respect to some of it but not the general outline. Memory is a fragile thing.

Kohn: I am not an expert on the individual details, but it all squares with what I know, and I have learned much, and I think other people will learn, too.

Powell: Yes. If one lives through experiences which I was fortunate enough to have, you don't forget the broad outlines.

I may well have made my role and contribution seem more important than they actually were. As Chief of Operational Intelligence, I had the support of a staff of dedicated officers and enlisted men. There were many gifted people who contributed a great deal—civilians like myself and professional members of the United States Army Air Forces. I was particularly impressed by the West Point graduates. But myself quite aside, what I have said about our Air Force and its essential contribution to the victory over Germany is substantially correct.

[93]In 1946 when Gen. Henry H. Arnold retired as Commanding General of the AAF, General Spaatz succeeded him. In September 1947, President Truman appointed Spaatz the first Chief of Staff of the newly established U.S. Air Force. He retired from the Air Force in July 1948. In retirement, Spaatz served on the Committee of Senior Advisors to the Chief of Staff, USAF, from 1952 to his death in 1974. He was also president and member of the Board of Directors of the Air Force Association; a president and member of the Board of Trustees of the Air Force Historical Foundation; and chairman of the U.S. Air Force Academy Site Selection Board. See Alfred Goldberg, "Spaatz," in *The War Lords: Military Commanders in the Twentieth Century*, ed. Sir Michael Carver (Boston, 1976), pp 568–81; David R. Mets, "Carl Spaatz: A Model for Leadership?" and I. B. Holly, "General Carl Spaatz and the Art of Command," in *Air Leadership: Proceedings of a Conference at Bolling Air Force Base, April 13–14*, 1984, USAF Warrior Studies, ed. Wayne Thompson (Washington, 1986), pp 3–14, 15–37.

[94]The effective date for establishment of the Department of the Air Force was September 18, 1947, the day W. Stuart Symington was sworn in as the first Secretary of the Air Force. See Herman S. Wolk, *Planning and Organizing the Postwar Air Force, 1943–1947* (Washington, 1984).

The U.S. Military Intelligence Service: The ULTRA Mission

by
Diane T. Putney

During World War II, the United States and Great Britain cooperated in the most significant intelligence enterprise in the history of warfare. The Allies intercepted, deciphered, and translated hundreds of thousands of Japanese and German messages sent by radio in high-grade code and cipher, including messages from Adolf Hitler to his top commanders. These messages produced valuable signals intelligence known as ULTRA, which commanders in the field sometimes used with deadly effectiveness. The organization which evaluated and distributed this special intelligence in the U.S. War Department for the Army Air Forces and Army Ground Forces was the Military Intelligence Service (MIS). After the attack on Pearl Harbor, reforms in the War Department to establish better procedures for processing and disseminating signals intelligence directly affected the growth and operations of MIS. In May of 1943, as a result of an agreement between the U.S. War Department and the British Government Code and Cipher School at Bletchley Park, England, the Americans established a branch of MIS in London. The story of how MIS fulfilled America's obligations under this agreement and handled—and sometimes mishandled—ULTRA is an important segment of the history of World War II which explains, in part, how the Allies destroyed the Axis war machine.

On December 7, 1941, the Japanese successfully attacked the U.S. Pacific Fleet at Pearl Harbor and Army air bases on Oahu in the Hawaiian Islands, killing 2,400 American soldiers, sailors, and civilians, sinking or disabling 19 ships, and destroying 150 airplanes. The Japanese also attacked U.S. bases in the Philippines, Guam, and Midway, and British bases in Hong Kong and the Malay Peninsula. At the time of the attacks, the Army's intelligence function was represented on the War Department's General Staff as Military Intelligence (G-2), one of five staff divisions. Brig. Gen. Sherman Miles, the Acting Assistant Chief of Staff, Intelligence was the head of the Military Intelligence Division (MID), which included over 400 people in Washington, D.C. The heart of the division, the Intelligence Branch, comprised these sections: Administration, Dissemination, Situation, Contact, Air, and the geographic sections: Western Europe, Southern Europe, Central Europe, British Empire, Latin America, and Far East.[1]

Col. Rufus S. Bratton, Chief of the Far East Section, and General Miles were regular recipients of highly classified intercepts known as MAGIC. This material was obtained from the interception, decryption, and translation of secret Japanese diplomatic messages. As it was evaluated and interpreted, MAGIC became signals intelligence.[2]

The Army's Signal Intelligence Service (SIS) and the Navy's Op-20-G of the Office of Naval Communications intercepted, deciphered, decoded, and translated the MAGIC intercepts. In September 1940, a full year before the Pearl Harbor attack, SIS had broken, with extraordinary skill and patience, the high-grade ciphers produced by the machine the Americans called PURPLE, which the Japanese used to prepare signals transmitted to and from their diplomats worldwide. American cryptanalysts also understood the operation of the RED machine and other codes and ciphers used for Japanese diplomatic traffic; throughout the interwar period, with the exception of the period 1931 to 1935, the Americans read Japanese diplomatic ciphers. Through a network of Army and Navy monitoring stations in North America, the Panama Canal Zone, Hawaii, and the Philippine Islands, the Americans eavesdropped on Tokyo Foreign Office communications to and from Washington, Honolulu, Berlin, London, Moscow, Mexico City, and Buenos Aires, to name just a few locations. Most MAGIC intercepts were radio transmissions, but a few were cables photocopied at the commercial companies which dispatched them.[3]

In addition to MAGIC, other sources of intelligence about Japan included officials in the American Embassy in Tokyo, reporting through the State Department; military attaches; observers of allied missions in Washington; and G-2 officers in theater commands. At this time MID had no secret agents or spies in place.[4]

Because MAGIC was special and compartmented intelligence within MID, strict security was essential so the Japanese would not learn about their compromised equipment and codes and shun their use, thus stopping the flow of translatable messages. Gen. George C. Marshall, Army Chief of Staff, limited the designated recipients of MAGIC to only a handful of people:

the President, the Secretary of State, the Secretary of War, the Secretary of the Navy, the Army Chief of Staff, the Chief of the War Plans Division (WPD), the Assistant Chief of Staff, Intelligence, the Chief of the Far East Section, the Chief of Naval Operations, the Chief of the Navy's WPD, and the Director of Naval Intelligence.[5]

Each day, an officer from SIS personally delivered MAGIC intercepts to Colonel Bratton. The colonel read all the material, screened out the important intercepts, and burned the rest. Those with intelligence value he sorted for the Chief of Staff, the Secretary of War, the Assistant Chief of Staff, Intelligence, the Chief of WPD, and the Secretary of State. The SIS sent multiple copies of each item to ease the administrative burden on Bratton's section, although certain trusted clerical aides and officers assisted with the paperwork. The colonel then placed each batch of material into a folder; locked each folder in a leather pouch; and delivered a pouch to each authorized recipient, each of whom had a key for his own delivery. Next Bratton collected the previous day's intercepts, returned to his office, accounted for all items, and destroyed them. Colonel Bratton's Navy counterpart followed a similar procedure, which included the delivery for the White House. One master copy of MAGIC was retained by each service. Sometimes Bratton included memoranda to various MAGIC recipients that provided his evaluation of one or more intercepts; still, most intercepts were passed on raw and uninterpreted.[6]

Some of the thousands of intercepted and deciphered signals before December 7, 1941, disclosed that the Japanese wanted to know the numbers and locations of American naval vessels. One message sent from the Foreign Office in Tokyo to the Japanese Consulate in Hawaii on September 24, 1941, requested detailed information about ships in Pearl Harbor according to their placement within five distinct and precise areas. Battleships and aircraft carriers were to be identified as to which were anchored separately or tied up at wharves and buoys and in docks; types and classes were to be reported, as well as two or more vessels tied up at the same wharf. This was just one of many messages inquiring about ship movements and locations. Between August 1 and December 6, 1941, the number of such messages totaled twenty for Pearl Harbor, twenty-three for the Panama Canal, and fifty-nine for the Philippines. At the time, however, messages about the fleet at Pearl Harbor set off no alarm bells.[7]

MAGIC intercepts did not make intelligence officers and policymakers omniscient. They did not disclose precise war plans and decisions, because the Japanese did not use diplomatic channels to transmit this type of information. In December 1941, the Americans could not read high-grade encipherment systems used for Japanese army and naval communications; furthermore, when the Japanese maintained radio silence to achieve surprise, there were no signals to intercept. Even Japanese naval intelligence officers were ignorant about the attack on Pearl Harbor in the final war plan of the Imperial Japanese Navy. Also, MAGIC was not centrally, thoroughly, and systematically analyzed, evaluated, and interpreted to separate its meaningful messages from extraneous ones. A Japanese attack on Pearl Harbor seemed to the Americans too bold to be rational or probable. On December 5, 1941, General Miles reported, "The most probable line of action for Japan is the occupation of Thailand."[8]

In the wake of the Pearl Harbor disaster, President Franklin D. Roosevelt appointed Associate Justice of the U.S. Supreme Court Owen J. Roberts to head a commission to examine the causes of the unpreparedness of American forces in the Pacific. The commission convened from December 18, 1941, to January 23, 1942. On its final day, the commission published its conclusions, but kept its proceedings and evidence secret. The Roberts Commission decided that the Secretaries of State, War, and Navy, the Army Chief of Staff, and the Chief of Naval Operations had properly discharged their duties. It severely censured, on the other hand, the Army and Navy commanders in Hawaii, Lt. Gen. Walter C. Short and Adm. Husband E. Kimmel, for their failure to take appropriate defensive and preparatory actions. These commanders had not been regular and designated recipients of MAGIC, and believed that they had, indeed, responded appropriately to general and nonspecific warnings, the same type of which had been sent to commanders in the Caribbean Command, the Western Defense Command, and the Philippines.[9]

The Roberts Commission discussed MAGIC, but not in detail, and no MAGIC intercepts were introduced as evidence. The commission took no focused testimony about how intelligence in Washington was received, evaluated, and disseminated; some testimony went unsworn and unrecorded. The commission passed judgment and assigned blame within a narrow scope of inquiry, without considering the full range of evidence. The Roberts Commission concluded its work swiftly, because the MAGIC secret had to be maintained and the morale of the nation kept high, while the policymakers and commanders caught up in the Pearl Harbor disaster still had to direct and fight the nation's war.[10]

In January of 1942, the same month the Roberts Commission completed its inquiry, Secretary of War Henry L. Stimson directed that a "special" unit be established within the Far East Section of the MID to process MAGIC. He concluded that MAGIC had not been studied closely enough prior to December 7th, and while the airwaves had not been saturated with messages about Pearl Harbor, the attack was "foreshadowed in the Japanese diplomatic traffic of 1941."[11] Hundreds of intercepts had not even been deciphered and remained untranslated until after the attack.[12]

Secretary Stimson believed that the War Department needed to improve its handling of MAGIC and that the best qualified person to introduce reforms would be a lawyer, who had experience with organizing and synthesizing numerous facts and complicated issues associated with major law cases. (As a young man, Stimson attended Harvard Law School and established a law partnership.) He discussed candidates with Assistant Secretary of War John J. McCloy, who recommended Mr. Alfred McCormack, a

Purple Analog, 1944.

former law partner from the Cravath, deGersdorff, Swaine, and Wood law firm in New York City.[13]

Secretary Stimson appointed McCormack as his special assistant to study the way MAGIC and cryptanalytic materials were being handled within the War Department. McCormack's job was to determine how to expand cryptanalytic operations to meet the requirements of war, while developing methods for correlating, assessing, and disseminating signals intelligence. Fortunately for the Allies, the Japanese continued to use the PURPLE machine in 1942 and throughout the war. For two months, McCormack studied MAGIC material, visited production units, and conferred with Assistant Secretary of War McCloy, Brig. Gen. Raymond E. Lee, the new Assistant Chief of Staff, Intelligence, and Lt. Col. Carter W. Clarke, the head of the Safeguarding Military Information Section of MID.[14]

McCormack observed the recently established "special" unit within the Far East Section and disapproved of what he saw. First, he thought the analytical skills of the personnel were not of a high caliber, and second, he faulted the manner in which intercepted material was being reported. The unit simply paraphrased what looked interesting and passed it on, without checking it for accuracy, evaluating it, and supplementing it with collateral intelligence. "It seemed to me," McCormack stated, "that the Secretary, the Chief of Staff and the others to whom reports were made were entitled to have every item carefully checked, evaluated and supplemented by all possible sources of intelligence, and that their time should not be wasted in reading odd and unchecked bits of information not related to attendant circumstances and given their proper value. Further, it appeared to me that the daily reporting of current messages was only one part of the job, and that the real job was to dig into the material, study it in the light of outside information, follow up leads that it gave, and bring out of it the intelligence that did not appear on the surface." McCormack believed that for "total war," the Army needed "total intelligence."[15]

While McCormack was conducting his study, MID underwent a major reorganization on March 9, 1942. This was part of a fundamental reorganization of the entire War Department ordered by President Roosevelt to create a more efficient Army command structure to direct the conduct of the war. Accordingly, within the War Department, three separate commands were established under the Army Chief of Staff: Army Ground Forces, Army Service Forces, and Army Air Forces. The War Department General Staff was reduced to a small number of officers who assisted the Chief of Staff in strategic planning and coordinating the activities of the three new commands. Under the organizational changes, the General Staff was to be a planning unit, not an operational one.[16]

The Army Chief of Staff issued Circular No. 59 on March 2, 1942, to implement the War Department reorganization. The circular directed the establishment of MIS which was to be the "operations" function of the G-2, while MID was to be the "staff" function. All personnel assigned to MIS, except certain commissioned officers, were transferred from MID.[17]

Two months after the establishment of MIS, Maj. Gen. George V. Strong became the Assistant Chief of Staff, Intelligence, replacing General Lee, who was ill. Calling the distinctions between MIS and MID "unfortunate," General Strong immediately began restructuring them to merge "operating" and "staff" functions. He could not, however, unilaterally abolish MIS, because it had been established by order of the Chief of Staff. By the end of 1942, MIS was organized into four groups: Administration, Intelligence, Training, and Security. The chief of MIS was the Deputy Assistant Chief of Staff, Intelligence. MIS was attached to, although not part of, the War Department General Staff.[18]

As a result of Alfred McCormack's study of the War Department's handling of cryptanalytic material, the Special Service Branch, shortly renamed Special Branch, was established within MIS on May 15, 1942. The branch was built around the "special" unit in the Far East Section established by Secretary Stimson in January. Following McCormack's recommendation, Special Branch supervised the signals intelligence operations of the War Department and managed the handling and dissemination of special intelligence material. It reported directly to General Strong. The recently promoted Colonel Clarke, one of the individuals who had worked closely with McCormack, became the Chief of Special Branch, and McCormack who was commissioned a lieutenant colonel, became the deputy chief. Colonel Clarke also became the G-2 liaison officer with the Departments of State and Navy, the Federal Bureau of Investigation, the Federal Communications Commission, the Office of the Coordination of Information, and the Office of Facts and Figures.[19]

During the first months of Special Branch's operation, Colonel Clarke focused on expanding the work of the Signal Intelligence Service (SIS) and its intercepting, deciphering, and translating functions. As a result of the War Department reorganization, SIS had remained a part of the Signal Corps, which was placed under the authority of the commanding general of the Army Service Forces. General Strong had recommended to the Chief of Staff that SIS be transferred to MIS, but initially the proposal was not accepted. Operational control of SIS, which underwent growth and name changes during the war, eventually did pass to the Assistant Chief of Staff, Intelligence, in December 1944; nine months later he assumed complete control of the organization.[20]

Since SIS and Special Branch were both located on the second floor of the Munitions Building in Washington, D.C., it was convenient for Colonel Clarke to hold frequent discussions with officials from SIS about plans for expanding intercept stations and overcoming cryptanalytic problems. During these meetings, Clarke encouraged the Signal Corps to acquire and develop Arlington Hall, a women's junior college in Arlington, Virginia, to be the new headquarters for SIS; to establish at Vint Hill, Virginia, one of the largest intercept stations in the world; to expand facilities at Two Rock Ranch, Petaluma, California, and elsewhere; and to organize a personnel program adapted to the requirements of war. SIS also installed and used more teletype lines to speed transmissions from intercept stations, instead of relying on slower cable and airmail communications. By June 1942, SIS was sending about 165 special intelligence items to the Special Branch every day. SIS had, however, some 350,000 items of back material, and of these, 100,000 had

Before moving to the Pentagon in 1942, the Special Branch, MIS, was headquartered in the War Department Munitions Building. *Courtesy National Archives.*

never been processed to any extent. Both to relieve this backlog and process new material, the staff of SIS was increased, and in the fall of 1942, it moved to Arlington Hall. At the same time, the Special Branch relocated to offices on the ground floor of the "E" ring of the new Pentagon building.[21]

While Colonel Clarke worked with SIS, Colonel McCormack concentrated on recruiting a suitable staff for the Special Branch and on acquiring and disseminating "intelligence" from the mass of intercepted "information" flowing to the branch. Using "Cravath" hiring methods, McCormack recruited and hired many lawyers from prestigious law firms.[22]

McCormack's attempts to acquire well-educated, talented men for intelligence work met with considerable resistance. He constantly faced denials that intelligence work required the sharpest and most talented individuals; a lack of appreciation for intelligence on the part of the War Department General Staff; a drive by Congress to keep the number of officers in Washington to a minimum; the Army's "heavy-handed" methods for handling personnel; and the "stupidity" of the Civil Service system, as McCormack characterized it. McCormack described the type of intelligence officer he sought: "To do the work well, a man must have not only a broad education and background of information, but he must have more than his share of astuteness, skepticism and desire to solve puzzling problems and he must have a capacity for laborious detail work that very few people have."[23]

The brightest Army officers, believing that intelligence positions were incompatible with achieving the highest ranks and positions of command, rarely chose careers in intelligence. For example, Dwight D. Eisenhower and Omar N. Bradley viewed intelligence assignments as dead-end tracks and avoided them deliberately and diligently. It was plain for all to see: the Assistant Chief of Staff, Intelligence, seldom moved to higher command, and his counterparts at regimental and battalion levels held one rank below that of the plans and operations officers. McCormack stated, "In the upper echelons of G–2 there were some able officers, but most of the regular ones knew that their futures depended on their getting assignments in the field, and of those who were willing to remain, because they realized the importance of good intelligence work, many became discouraged and obtained overseas jobs."[24]

Although there were no official procedures for assigning qualified enlisted men to Special Branch, an informal arrangement allowed the branch to acquire some of them from the Counter Intelligence Corps. Women officers and enlisted personnel from the Women's Army Corps were also assigned to Special Branch. By June 1944, the branch's roster included:[25]

Officers	—	140	(including 33 WACS)
Enlisted men	—	25	
Enlisted women	—	75	
Civilians	—	142	
Total		382	

Overall, General Strong supported McCormack's recruitment efforts. Strong was not contemptuous of McCormack's becoming a lieutenant colonel overnight, nor irritated by his bias toward recruiting civilian lawyers as intelligence officers. Strong himself was a cavalryman turned military lawyer, who had served as a professor of law at West Point. His health, however, was not good, and he persisted in following a policy which undermined McCormack's initiative. The general believed that an officer must accomplish his mission with the personnel assigned him—and make no effort to acquire more people to carry out expanded missions.[26]

McCormack encountered less difficulty with establishing systems for checking, evaluating, indexing, filing, and reporting intelligence than he did with recruitment. By the end of 1942, Special Branch was producing a daily publication, the "Magic Summary," which covered both important spot intelligence gleaned from each day's batch of messages, with necessary background evaluation, and conclusions arrived at from long-range studies of intercepted traffic. The summaries were delivered in locked leather pouches to the Secretary of War, the Chief of Staff, the Chief of WPD, the Assistant Chief of Staff, Intelligence, the Secretary of the Navy, the Secretary of State, and the Assistant Secretary of State.[27]

Special Branch drew its collateral information from the Intelligence Group, MIS, which was divided on a geographic basis. It covered some of the same ground as the geographic units of the group, but always worked with the deciphered and decoded intercepts, which were not shared with the geographic units. Thus, Special Branch's conclusions were considered more accurate than those of the other units, because MAGIC was considered more authoritative than other sources of intelligence.[28]

Within a few months after its establishment, the Special Branch was receiving a steady flow of material concerning the war in the Pacific; yet, it had little or no dependable and current intelligence about the war in Europe. The military attache in London, whose numerous reports were a voluminous source of information about that war, was not privy to highly classified British material; thus his reports disclosed little more than what could be read in newspapers. Neither did the two American liaison officers assigned to duty at the War Office and Air Ministry in London obtain essential information on German army and air force order of battle.[29]

As early as the spring of 1942, a deputation from Britain visited the United States and briefed authorities on the British success against German codes and ciphers, but the visit resulted in no working liaison and no flow of German intercepts to the War Department. SIS at Arlington Hall, even with its powerful listening stations on the North American continent, was unable to intercept German military traffic of sufficient quality and quantity for systematic analysis and decryption; it depended on British intercepts.[30]

In April 1943, a small American delegation from the War Department traveled to England to inspect the installation and activities of the Government Code and Cipher School at Bletchley Park, an organization established in 1919 and responsible for deciphering and exploiting signals intelligence for the British. The delegation included Colonel McCormack, recently promoted and the representative of the Assistant Chief of Staff, Intelligence; Maj. Telford Taylor, a lawyer from the Federal Communications Commission who had been recruited into Special Branch by McCormack; and Mr. William F. Friedman of Arlington Hall, one of America's greatest cryptologists. Just before this trip, the Army achieved its first success against Japanese military cryptographic systems, which would result in opening up new channels of highly classified information to Special Branch. Earlier, the Navy had cracked Japanese naval ciphers and had produced intelligence which played a spectacular role in the American victory at the Battle of Midway. PURPLE was still producing excellent Japanese diplomatic traffic, especially from the Japanese ambassador to Germany, Hiroshi Oshima, an army officer who sent a constant stream of reports from Berlin to Tokyo. The three Americans traveled to England confident and knowledgeable about brilliant American achievements in signals intelligence warfare.[31]

Nevertheless, the magnitude of the operation of the Government Code and Cipher School, the efficiency of the people who worked in it, and the timeliness and quality of the intelligence they produced greatly impressed McCormack, Taylor, and Friedman. McCormack in particular noted that in Britain, intelligence was given a high priority and the intelligence service had a first call on talented military and civilian personnel.[32]

The Government Code and Cipher School was headquartered at "Station X," which was Bletchley Park, a Victorian Tudor-Gothic mansion and a few acres of grounds located about fifty miles northwest of London, outside the railroad junction of Bletchley in Buckinghamshire. In addition to the large red brick mansion and stables, there were one-story huts of various shapes and sizes built to accommodate the thousands of men and women who worked there around the clock. The workers were billeted in a fifteen-mile radius of Bletchley Park, or "BP" as it was often called. Members of the Royal Air Force (RAF) guarded the fenced perimeter of the grounds.[33]

Col. Alfred McCormack. The inscription reads: "To Bill Friedman, to whom Military Intelligence owes a great debt. Alfred McCormack, Col. GSC."

By early 1943, four major communications intercept stations in England were flooding Bletchley Park with enciphered messages sent in Morse code by enemy countries. Sometimes the intercepted messages were from as far as Africa, the Balkans, and the Russian front. The reception of these signals from such great distances was possible because strong shortwave transmissions bounced back and forth between the ground and upper atmosphere several times. British intercept stations were also located in the Middle East, Malta, Gibraltar, and Egypt. The Bletchley Park staff depended entirely on the monitoring stations, and they faithfully produced thousands of messages every day.[34]

The Germans knew their enemies were listening to their radio transmissions, but they were confident that their messages were undecipherable because the ENIGMA produced them. The ENIGMA was an electromechanical machine resembling a typewriter with plug board, wires, lettered light bulbs, wheels, and batteries. The German army, navy, and air force used variations of the ENIGMA, and each had its own key settings. Four people produced an ENIGMA message: the originator who prepared the message in clear German text with proper addresses and time of origin; the keyboard operator who typed the message on the ENIGMA so that the clear text became cipher text; the clerk who recorded the enciphered message letter by letter in groups of five as ENIGMA lit the lettered bulbs corresponding to the typed keys; and the radio operator who transmitted the enciphered message in manually keyed Morse code. The recipient keyboard operator had to have an ENIGMA identical to that of the message's sender. The recipient then typed the ciphered text on his ENIGMA, and the machine lit up letters that spelled out the clear text once again.[35]

The Germans considered the ENIGMA impregnable, even if captured by the enemy, because the machine had movable parts, each with numerous possible settings. The selections and sequence of the wheels placed in the machine, the setting of the rings around the wheels, and the plug connections all complicated the ciphering process so that the chance of an enemy finding the correct settings on a captured or reproduced ENIGMA was sometimes as high as 1 in 160 trillion. Also, the parts of the machine were changed frequently, some every 48 hours, some daily, and some with each message. The breaking of the ENIGMA was not a one-time feat, but an extraordinary, continuous process.[36]

At Bletchley Park, the ingenious, complicated, and painstaking task of cracking the ciphers fell to the cryptanalysts, who had to determine the key settings of the originating ENIGMA. Sometimes they discovered "cribs," which were clues that messages contained repetitive words, such as those in weather reports, or by spotting the re-encryptions into an ENIGMA cipher of a message transmitted earlier in a known lower-grade cipher. Other complex techniques were used as well, each with the objective of revealing the ENIGMA settings. Each ENIGMA cipher was given a name. "Red," for example, was the general purpose cipher of the German Air Force (GAF). "Garlic" was the GAF weather key, and "Mustard" was the GAF radio intercept service key. The intercepted German army and air force ciphers were cracked in Hut 6, the intercepted German naval traffic in Hut 8. By the summer of 1942, Bletchley Park was solving the daily settings of approximately 26 army and air force keys of about 50 in use. From the end of 1943 to May 1945, Bletchley Park produced nearly 84,000 ENIGMA decrypts per month.[37]

A machine produced the ENIGMA ciphers, and a machine helped to crack them. In the spring of 1940, cryptanalysts, mathematicians, and engineers in England built a six-foot-high calculating machine to assist with determining which of the millions of possible ENIGMA settings produced enciphered messages. A "primitive" computer, this machine operated on electromechanical rather than electronic principles and had no memory. Shortly before the German invasion of Poland in September 1939, the Poles gave the French and British each a model of an ENIGMA and plans for the construction of a giant calculating machine, nicknamed after a popular Polish ice cream dessert "Bomba." Throughout the war, the British built more complex machines or BOMBES and used them in scattered locations in the countryside around Bletchley Park, operated by members of the Women's Royal Naval Service. These machines responded to the increased complexity of ENIGMA variations and procedures as designed and implemented by German cryptologists.[38]

One machine eventually used at Bletchley Park, the COLOSSUS, was more advanced than the BOMBES. A "pioneer programmable electronic digital computer," its reading speed of approximately "25,000 bits per second" made it comparable to the electronic computers of the early 1950s. COLOSSUS was first used at Bletchley Park in February 1944, and by the end of the war there were ten COLOSSI in service.[39]

ENIGMA material deciphered in Hut 6 was then sent to Hut 3, where it was translated, emended, analyzed, and interpreted. There it became ULTRA intelligence. The functional sections of Hut 3 consisted of the Watch, army intelligence (3–M), and air intelligence (3–A). The Watch translated the messages into English, including the precise rendering of obscure military and technical terms, and designated their priority. The army intelligence section analyzed the reports from the enemy ground forces.[40] The air intelligence section of Hut 3 housed a detailed Air Index comprising hundreds of thousands of five- by nine-inch cards with information about GAF personnel, units, locations, weapons, equipment, code words, scientific terms, special topics such as oil, and even unknown words and phrases. Because of its value, from time to time the entire set of handwritten cards would be photographed and stored beneath the Bodleian Library in Oxford. Air advisors would constantly consult the index and produce intelligence about the enemy's air strength, location, supplies, fuels, ammunition, movements, and orders.[41]

From Bletchley Park, ULTRA was sent to several groups. The heads of the Air Ministry, War Office, and Admiralty in London usually received their material by courier, with the urgent items being sent by teleprinter. The Secret Intelligence Service headquarters also received ULTRA by teleprinter and courier and passed appropriate items to Prime Minister Winston Churchill, who had visited Bletchley Park and referred to ULTRA as "our precious secret." Finally, the combat field commanders received ULTRA over special radio links which operated according to rigid security regulations.[42]

Group Captain Fred W. Winterbotham of the RAF established and regulated the procedures for securing the dissemination of ULTRA over the special radio links. Each field command receiving ULTRA was assigned a Special Liaison Unit (SLU), which consisted of two sections. One was the Special Communications Unit (SCU) which from a van operated the radio equipment for the reception and dispatch of messages. The second section, also referred to as the SLU, operated from a van and was responsible for deciphering, physically controlling, and destroying ULTRA material. The SLU officers revealed ULTRA to only a small number of persons at each command who were indoctrinated in and authorized to receive signals intelligence. The British SLU system was more controlled and centralized than any procedures the Americans used for disseminating intelligence to the field.[43]

While McCormack, Taylor, and Friedman were in England being briefed on the British ULTRA operation, complex and lengthy negotiations were underway in Washington between Colonel Clarke of Special Branch and Royal Navy Capt. Edward D. Hastings, representing the head of British intelligence. The Americans wanted to exploit European signals intelligence at Arlington Hall and Special Branch at a capacity comparable to the Bletchley Park operation. The British wanted to maintain Bletchley Park's monopoly on signals intelligence for security reasons, and possibly, to minimize their loss of control over the intelligence process once the Americans became involved, given their tremendous resources and capacity.[44]

The Americans felt they could not allow the British an absolute monopoly with signals intelligence for a number of reasons. Primarily, they believed they could make significant contributions to the decryption effort. Furthermore, the Americans thought that the Germans could target and destroy equipment and people at Bletchley Park. Finally, some messages from

A captured German ENIGMA machine. *Courtesy National Archives.*

German cipher clerks using an ENIGMA machine. *Courtesy National Archives.*

Japanese military attaches indicated that the Japanese were considering the use of ENIGMA machines. The Americans believed they had the resource potential to work on both European and Pacific cryptographic systems. Indeed, American engineers and mathematicians with the Army and Navy and in American industries and universities were independently from the British developing the forerunners of computers. The Americans, in fact, were creating the technological revolution of the new computer age, as they designed and built huge, sophisticated calculating machines to solve mathematical problems associated with cryptography, the Manhattan atomic bomb project, and ballistic artillery.[45]

In the cryptanalytic intelligence war, the Americans at Arlington Hall used two types of machines similar to the BOMBES and COLOSSI at Bletchley Park. The first types were "standard" or "modified standard" tabulating machines, the use of which involved the recording of data on keypunched cards and the processing of the cards. The second types were "rapid analytical machines" (RAM), which operated by vacuum tubes, relays, electronic circuits, and photoelectrical principles. One of these machines was "basically homologous to an automatic telephone exchange, capable of serving a city of about 18,000 subscribers." Arlington Hall had two RAMs, which performed the equivalent operations of 200,000 people doing calculations by hand. A similar machine was estimated to have performed the equivalent work of 6,000 cryptanalysts.[46]

Although the Americans had the capacity and willingness to assume responsibility for a major part of Bletchley Park's operation, the British were reluctant to open up and share on a grand scale with the Americans, primarily because the Americans were thought to be prone to security violations and to information leaks. The War Department, unfortunately, did have a flawed security record. A major compromise of security involving the American military attache in Cairo, Col. Bonner F. Fellers, affected the lives of British combatants from the autumn of 1941 to July 1942. Colonel Fellers was a conscientious and hardworking individual, whose messages to Washington about British operations against the Germans in North Africa were voluminous and accurate. German cryptanalysts, however, read the "Black" enciphered code system Fellers used to send his reports to MID in Washington. Subsequently, German intelligence officers passed all of Fellers's reports to Field Marshal Erwin Rommel, who used them to good advantage against his enemies. The British learned of the compromise from ENIGMA. Fellers was called home, and the code and cipher system was changed.[47]

Then in June 1942, the *Chicago Tribune*, the *New York Daily News*, and the *Washington Times-Herald* published stories about the Battle of Midway, which disclosed that the United States had precise information about the composition of the Japanese strike force in the Pacific. The newspapers did not state that the United States had broken Japanese codes and ciphers to acquire such precise data, but that was exactly how the Americans did come to possess it, and to an experienced observer it was obvious that that type of information could only have come from deciphered messages. The public revelation of this valuable intelligence dismayed and angered officials involved with signals intelligence, both in the United States and Britain. London sent a protest to Washington. All waited anxiously for the Japanese to learn of the newspaper stories, draw the obvious conclusions, and wreck the signals intelligence operation. Nothing happened.[48]

A month after the initial news stories, Walter Winchell's newspaper column in the *New York Daily Mirror* reported that the story in the *Chicago Tribune* about the Battle of Midway had disclosed that the U.S. Navy was decoding secret Japanese messages. The following month, newspapers throughout the country reported that a federal grand jury was investigating circumstances surrounding the *Chicago Tribune* story. Such was the case, but no indictments were rendered against the paper's editors and reporters. Within a few weeks after this publicity relating to the Battle of Midway, the Japanese began to change their naval codes and ciphers. It was unclear whether these changes stemmed from routine procedures, the originally published news stories, or the subsequent publicity about signal intercepts and compromised sources. The alterations prevented Americans from reading the codes and ciphers throughout the autumn of 1942, while the battle for the Solomon Islands was underway.[49]

The certainty of the Allied victory in North Africa alleviated the British mistrust of American security. An agreement of May 17, 1943, between the War Department and the Government Code and Cipher School inaugurated a remarkably cooperative venture in intelligence warfare. Col. W. Preston Corderman, the commanding officer at Arlington Hall, signed for the Americans, and Edward W. Travis, the director of Bletchley Park, signed for the British. The American Secretary of War approved it on June 15, 1943.[50]

The document clarified terms used by both countries to describe the types of intelligence covered by the agreement:

AMERICAN	*BRITISH*
Special Intelligence A	Special Intelligence
Special Intelligence B	Y Intelligence
TA Intelligence	Y Inference

The first category referred to intelligence from enemy high-grade codes and ciphers, such as ULTRA. The second category included intelligence derived from the solution of lower-grade codes and ciphers and from plain text, and this consisted largely of radio messages between lower echelons of command and between ground stations and aircraft in flight. The British referred to this as "Y" intelligence, because it was intercepted by their Y (Yorker) Service, which operated signal intercept stations. Y intelligence also included information from "direction finding," which was the locating of enemy radio stations by measuring the angles of radio beams. The third category referred to intelligence from "traffic analysis." This pertained to inferences drawn from the study of the volume, direction, and patterns of messages, without actually deciphering and reading the texts of such traffic.[51]

Under the agreement, both the United States and Britain agreed to exchange intelligence about the Axis powers, including the secret services, such as the German *Abwehr*. The United States concentrated on reading Japanese army and air codes and ciphers, while the British focused on the German and Italian.[52] They agreed to apply special security regulations to signals intelligence, distribution of which was to be restricted to the minimum number of persons who required it for the proper discharge of their duties.[53]

Both countries agreed to use their most secure codes and ciphers for the transmission of decodes of enemy signals and of technical cryptanalytic data. Although unstated in the agreement, for the United States, this meant using the Converter M-134-C or SIGABA machine, jointly designed by the Army and Navy, and manufactured by the Teletype Corporation, Chicago, Illinois. By the summer of 1942, the SIGABA was in widespread use in the Army, and throughout the war it was the most secure electromechanical cryptographic machine in use by any nation. The British, on the other hand, used the TYPEX machine. More complicated than ENIGMA, both SIGABA and TYPEX were a generation ahead. These Allied machines were also developed in secrecy, the Army at work on SIGABA since the 1930s. In contrast, commercial versions of ENIGMA were sold in the 1920s, disclosing their fundamental operating principles. SIGABA was considered so secure that it was used for the secret communications between President Roosevelt and Prime Minister Churchill over the special Washington-London circuit known as POTUS-PRIME (President of the United States-Prime Minister).[54]

Because SIGABA was relatively slow in operation, allowing a maximum operating speed of only forty-five to fifty words a minute, the Army introduced the M-228 or SIGCUM in 1943. SIGCUM, an on-line teletype system, permitted the preparation of plain text on a keyboard; the automatic encipherment and transmission of the text; and then the reception, decipherment, and printing of the plain text by a receiving SIGCUM.[55]

The agreement further stipulated that liaison officers be appointed to provide U.S. and British ground and air commanders-in-chief with all special intelligence necessary for them to conduct their operations. These officers were to be given full access to all decodes. Also, the two Allies were bound to notify each other immediately if either had information from any source indicating the compromise of any code or cipher used by the other. Corrective action was to be carefully considered to prevent the compromise of the source of the information, and if possible, mutual agreement sought before action taken.[56]

Finally, special intelligence from enemy high-grade ciphers was not to be intermingled in reports with general intelligence from other sources. If it was necessary to do so, the whole report was to be treated as special intelligence, and given the same strictly limited distribution. Under no circumstances was it permissible to pass such intelligence in a code or cipher which could be read by other than the authorized recipients. Because intelligence from enemy lower-grade ciphers was closely related to special intelligence, a high degree of secrecy had to be maintained in handling and acting upon the former.[57]

Two appendices, "Special Provisions Regarding Work on German Machine Cyphers" and "British Security Regulations for Special Intelligence" were included. All recipients of intelligence from enemy high-grade ciphers, whether American or British, were bound by the regulations from the second appendix, which were currently in force in the theaters of war where British forces were operating.[58]

The Converter M-134-C or SIGABA machine.

For the War Department there were immediate, significant results of the agreement. First, the SIS at Arlington Hall, now known as the Signal Security Agency, began regularly to receive operational jobs from the Government Code and Cipher School for solution on American BOMBES, which were faster than those in England. Special communication channels connected England with the small unit at Arlington Hall that worked on German decrypts. Known as PROJECT YELLOW, this unit functioned as an operational subsection of the Government Code and Cipher School. From July 1943 to January 1945, Bletchley Park sent 1,375 jobs to Arlington Hall, which solved 413 of them.[59]

Another result of the agreement was the establishment of an American unit in England which handled special intelligence and was known as the Military Intelligence Service, War Department, London Branch (MIS, WD, London). Telford Taylor was promoted to lieutenant colonel and stayed in England to head this unit, while Colonel McCormack and Mr. Friedman returned to the United States at the conclusion of their tour at Bletchley Park and signals intelligence facilities in England.[60]

At first, Colonel Taylor in England confined himself almost exclusively to examining and passing diplomatic traffic to Washington. In August, Maj. Samuel McKee, formerly a professor of history at Columbia University, arrived at Bletchley Park to be Taylor's deputy. On August 27, 1943, they sent the first high-grade German military intercept to Washington, a message announcing that German Army Group B under Rommel was taking command of German forces in upper Italy. The flow of ULTRA material from Bletchley Park to Washington then steadily increased to the point that the messages overloaded the British secure communications circuits, and the number had to be decreased. By September 1943, a dozen or so members of Special Branch had arrived in England to work in MIS, WD, London, but they still faced a reluctance on the part of the British to share ULTRA with Washington.[61]

In early September 1943, General Strong visited England with Colonel Taylor and met with the commander and other officials of the Government Code and Cipher School. After much strained negotiation and false starts, Strong and British authorities reached agreement September 25th. As a result, Colonel Taylor assumed responsibility for selecting material to be passed to Washington, while simultaneously keeping the British War Office and Air Ministry informed of all items passed. Appropriate British ministries were responsible for comments or notes made on the material.[62]

From September through December 1943, Taylor worked out a number of problems concerning the form the Washington cables would take, the route they would be sent, and the markings by which the various categories of intercepts would be recognized. The Americans sent the most important items from Bletchley Park to Washington by cable. The rest went by pouch on a steamship. In June 1944, a thrice-weekly airlift service delivered them. In September, copies of all teleprints and reports, instead of just certain selected items, were sent to MIS. The requirement for reporting each item to British offices and ministries was eliminated. Priority items were still transmitted by cable.[63]

Back in Washington within Special Branch, a Section C was established to receive and process the German military traffic. Section A handled diplomatic, clandestine, and commercial material, and Section B handled Japanese military intercepts. Section C, initially consisting of two officers and known as "Bunker Hill," was responsible for publishing a "Military and Naval Supplement" to the "Magic Summary," based primarily on ULTRA. As the information to Section C increased, the section grew—acquiring intelligence officers, writers, and editors—and maintained indexes and maps.[64]

Because the agreement of May 1943 required the United States to provide "liaison officers" to brief the American ground and air commanders in the field, Colonel McCormack intensified his recruitment efforts to acquire these officers, designated "Special Security Officers." Colonel Clarke welcomed the opportunity for the United States to establish an ULTRA field dissemination system manned by Americans. He reported that he had "heard considerably more than 100 American officers, from Majors to full Generals, rail against the British for preempting the field of intelligence as their exclusive province."[65]

Special Branch recruited and trained the Special Security Officers assigned to both the European and Pacific theaters of war, designating the senior officers as "Special Security Representatives." In addition, the personnel assigned to Europe received training and security indoctrination at Bletchley Park. A few of these officers visited commands in the Mediterranean theater to see firsthand how ULTRA was used operationally, prior to reporting to permanent posts.[66]

On March 15, 1944, in preparation for D-Day, General Marshall, Army Chief of Staff, wrote a letter to Gen. Dwight D. Eisenhower at Supreme Headquarters, Allied Expeditionary Forces, London, explaining the basis for making ULTRA available to American field commands. Marshall informed Eisenhower that the War Department had issued security regulations governing the dissemination and handling of ULTRA within the European and Mediterranean theaters, effective April 1, 1944. Marshall stated, "When operational action is taken on the basis of ULTRA intelligence, the utmost care must be taken, by means of proper cover, to insure that the action does not reveal or in any way suggest that this source of intelligence is at our disposal." The regulations were to be "meticulously observed." ULTRA was transmitted to the field commands and discussed orally only with authorized ULTRA recipients at the field commands. The letter also indicated the primary duties of the Special Security Officers. They were to evaluate ULTRA intelligence, present it in useable form to commanders and authorized recipients, assist in "fusing" it with intelligence derived from other sources, and give advice for making operational use of ULTRA so that the security of the source was not compromised.[67]

By the end of 1944 and six months after the D-Day invasion of Normandy, MIS, WD, London, had grown to five units. The first included about a dozen air and ground advisers in Hut 3 at Bletchley Park who examined incoming messages, selected those for transmittal to field commanders, and drafted the necessary signals to be sent to the Special Security Officers. ULTRA signals were marked with from one to five Zs to show their priority; the more letters the higher the priority. An example of a "ZZZ" message was a German appraisal of a bridge bombing attack in winter, when heavy cloud cover made aerial photography impossible. The second unit also worked in Hut 3 and consisted of two officers who prepared material for transmittal to MIS in Washington. Known as "3-US," the Americans in Hut 3 worked alongside the British and were represented on the Western Front Committee and the Black Sea and Aegean Study Group.[68]

The third unit of MIS, WD, London, comprised Special Security Officers and Representatives in the European and Mediterranean theaters who were stationed at and attached to field commands. The fourth unit had only one officer who worked on diplomatic traffic in London, sending significant items primarily to Washington. This material included not only the communications of nations whose cipher systems were not read in Washington, but also a large amount of traffic passing over cables outside the United States. The fifth unit consisted of one officer who worked at Ryder Street in London where counterintelligence material was produced.[69]

In addition to the 3-US unit, other Americans from the War Department worked at Bletchley Park. They formed the 6813th Signal Security Detachment, a unit representing Arlington Hall and the Signal Security Agency. In the winter of 1943 to 1944, there were about fifty officers and enlisted men in the detachment, involved primarily in cryptanalysis and some translation work. Because of information compartmentation, different work schedules, and various living quarters, there was little interaction between the intelligence officers in 3-US and the cryptanalysts in the 6813th.[70]

While the five units served as the basic structure of MIS, WD, London, throughout the remainder of the war, in Washington, MIS was substantially restructured. In February 1944, Maj. Gen. Clayton L. Bissell, Army Air Forces, replaced General Strong as the Assistant Chief of Staff, Intelligence. Unlike General Strong, he believed that a clearly defined and functioning

MID and MIS structure was needed to organize his command effectively. Within the next few months, a succession of committees studied the responsibilities, organization, and personnel needs of MID and MIS.[71]

The recommendations of the various committees culminated in a radical reorganization of MIS in June 1944. Re-established as the larger component of MID, the service was the latter's operating agency. MIS was divided into three directorates: Intelligence, Information, and Administration. The staff of Special Branch was drastically reduced and its personnel and functions assigned to the Intelligence and Information Directorates. In effect, the reorganization ended the rigid compartmentation of Special Branch, allowing ULTRA and MAGIC (which was now also referred to as ULTRA) to be fused with intelligence from other sources and used by more people whose geographic and functional expertise could effectively exploit signals intelligence. The new MIS structure remained essentially unchanged to the end of the war.[72]

The reorganization brought changes in the leadership of MIS. Brig. Gen. Russ Osmun of the Quartermaster Corps was appointed Chief, only to be replaced a few months later by Brig. Gen. Paul E. Peabody, who had returned from service as the military attache in London. Colonel Clarke was appointed his Deputy Chief and the MIS Special Security Officer. Colonel McCormack became the head of the Directorate of Intelligence.[73]

In 1945, Brig. Gen. Carter W. Clarke (left) presented the Distinguished Service Cross to Col. Alfred McCormack. *Courtesy National Archives.*

Most of the personnel from the old Special Branch ended up in Colonel McCormack's Directorate of Intelligence, as did most of the MIS personnel who were cleared to use ULTRA. The directorate consisted of a Research Unit, a Reports Unit, and a number of Specialists. The Research Unit was further divided into seven functional branches which McCormack called "unworkable": Military, Political, Economic, Sociological, Topographic, Scientific, and Who's Who and Library. McCormack eventually consolidated Japanese intelligence within the Economic Branch and German intelligence within the Political Branch. The Reports Unit and its main component, the German Military Reports Branch, produced the daily intelligence report, "European Magic Summary." ULTRA formed about 90 percent of its content, while the other 10 percent was based on information from prisoner-of-war reports, operational cables, photographic reconnaissance, agent reports, Allied and enemy radio broadcasts, and newspaper reports.[74]

Personnel in the Directorate of Intelligence, as well as Special Security Officers in the field, constantly used ULTRA as a guide in selecting items to be used in reports issued under lower security classifications than ULTRA. This ULTRA "censorship" process was widespread. One Special Security Officer reported, "It was important for the representative to give non-recipients at his own and subordinated commands as much of the situation in the light of ULTRA as could be accomplished with appropriate cover, and to kill, so far as possible, items of information known, through ULTRA, to be in error." Another individual stated, "The skillful Special Security Officer can often guide tactical intelligence officers to those open sources which will reveal information identical to that contained in Communications Intelligence." Yet another officer noted, "ULTRA was a guide and a censor to conclusions arrived at by means of other evidence, especially Y evidence. Conversely, Y was a most excellent cover in which ULTRA intelligence of [order of battle], dispositions, and tactics could be meshed and disseminated." ULTRA was used to select accurate information from prisoner-of-war, agent, and reconnaissance reports.[75]

The Specialists within the Directorate of Intelligence were primarily experts on geographic areas whose knowledge complemented that of officers who were organized functionally. There were four German and four Japanese Specialists, with one in each group specializing in air intelligence. Few of these officers had been cleared to use special intelligence prior to the reorganization. Most had been branch or section chiefs of the old MIS; consequently, relations between McCormack and the Specialists were always strained. McCormack bluntly if not objectively stated, "They disliked the idea of losing their staffs and were not happy at being put under a civilian officer. One of them . . . used to regale dinner parties with a biographical sketch of himself, starting with his birth as the son of a general officer and

A pilot is debriefed on his return from a reconnaissance mission over North Africa, 1943.

carrying through his career, including his service as Military Attache in Berlin and as G–2 of General Patton's army in North Africa . . . and ending up with a punch line that brought down the house: 'And now I am serving under the command of a Wall Street lawyer.' " McCormack was satisfied with the arrangement whereby the Specialists gave the daily intelligence briefing for the Assistant Chief of Staff, Intelligence, because McCormack disliked the general's fondness for elaborately staged briefings and was glad to have the Specialists shoulder the responsibility for the fancy color-coded graphs, charts, and maps required for each briefing.[76]

Among the German Specialists was Col. T. G. Lanphier who was responsible for all intelligence on the GAF and for the preparation and delivery of the daily morning air presentation to General Bissell. Lanphier maintained continuous contact with the Army Air Forces. Within the German Military Reports Branch, an air force desk published a weekly estimate of the capabilities of the GAF for Gen. Henry H. "Hap" Arnold, the Commanding General of the Army Air Forces, and also received, reviewed, and republished a weekly estimate of GAF order of battle, issued by the British Air Ministry.[77]

In June 1944, the little remnant of the old Special Branch was partially responsible for administering the Special Security Officer system, although responsibility for the system was also vested with McCormack as head of the Directorate of Intelligence and with Clarke, the Deputy Chief of MIS. The arrangement was not satisfactory, and in February 1945 Clarke assumed complete responsibility for the administration of the system.[78]

As of July 1944, MIS had sixty-three Special Security Officers on duty in the European and Pacific theaters. Under the 1943 agreement with the British, the Americans were primarily responsible for the security and dissemination of ULTRA in the Pacific, and they generally followed the British system of limited distribution through SLUs.[79]

There were some striking differences, however, in the way the Army Special Security Officers operated in the Pacific in comparison with their counterparts in Europe. The sources of ULTRA dissemination were more varied in the Pacific. In Europe, the dissemination was through a centralized system: Bletchley Park sent ULTRA to the Special Security Officers. In the Pacific, the following sources distributed ULTRA: MIS, Washington; Bletchley Park, England; Central Bureau, Brisbane, Australia; British and American SLUs in New Delhi, India; U.S. Army SLU at Fort Shafter, Hawaii; and Joint Intelligence Center, Pacific Ocean Area (JICPOA), Hawaii, a naval liaison operation with the Army.[80]

By far the largest of these units—a Pacific Bletchley—was the Central Bureau in Brisbane. This was Gen. Douglas MacArthur's theater agency for the Southwest Pacific Area (SWPA) and was first established with the Royal Australian Army in the spring of 1942 when the headquarters of SWPA were organized. The Central Bureau was thus activated one month prior to the establishment of Special Branch in Washington, with General MacArthur's chief signals officer, Brig. Gen. S. B. Atkin, as its director. In 1943 approximately 1,000 men and women worked there; by May 1945, its total strength was over 4,000. In contrast, the next largest unit, JICPOA, had 500 officers and 800 enlisted, excluding a group from Special Branch working on Japanese army intercepts.[81]

The Central Bureau first concentrated on traffic analysis and low-grade Japanese ciphers, but eventually, over mild protests from the War Department, it extended its activity to include the solution and translation of high-level Japanese army systems. Linked directly to Arlington Hall, the bureau was involved with some important cryptanalysis when the Australians recovered the entire cryptographic library of the 20th Japanese Division in 1944. SWPA crytanalysts also worked with 147 captured Japanese cryptographic worksheets and a complete text-key book.[82]

The Central Bureau provided General MacArthur with signal intercepts which produced intelligence reported in his SWPA daily "Special Intelligence Bulletin." MacArthur did not easily relinquish control of the evaluation and dissemination of ULTRA to the Special Security Officers in MIS even though War Department regulations required this. One of the officers reported, "We have troubles in SWPA, who consider us as interlopers." SWPA commanders believed they should assume direct and complete control over the officers and not allow them to communicate directly with Washington.[83]

In January 1945, SWPA authorities grudgingly authorized the Special Security Officers to form a "filter group" in downtown Brisbane, a few miles from the Central Bureau. Four times a day the bureau sent intercepts to the group. These were often at once detailed, fragmentary, garbled, and redundant with other material Washington had sent. The group maintained "cable indexes," however, which kept to a minimum its dissemination of duplicate radio transmissions.[84]

There was a second significant difference between the operation of the Special Security Officers in the Pacific and those in Europe. In the Pacific, the officers were responsible for deciphering and enciphering all ULTRA messages received and sent from their units; hence, the officers directly operated or supervised the operation of the American SIGABA machines. In Europe, however, where the British TYPEX enciphering machine was used, British officers and enlisted personnel operated the equipment. In SWPA in particular, the Special Security Officers had to assert themselves as intelligence officers, whose duty it was to interpret ULTRA, in order to avoid being categorized as mere "Sigaba jockeys," whose only jobs were to operate machines. "The only function which the Special Security Officer now performs," confessed one such officer, "is enciphering, deciphering, typing and delivery. . . . Honesty compels me to admit that efficiency would be vastly improved by the substitution of someone who can better my three fingered performance on the Sigaba and the typewriter."[85]

A third difference between Pacific and European operations was that until the spring of 1944, the distribution of ULTRA in the Pacific was limited to three headquarters: SWPA, China-Burma-India (CBI), and Pacific Ocean Area (POA). Upon recommendations of the Special Security Officers, regulations were revised to allow ULTRA to be sent to the level of army or equivalent air force headquarters and to corps level when the corps was operating independently, as was done in Europe.[86]

Finally, in the Pacific, the Army officers from the MIS worked more closely with personnel from the U.S. Navy than did their counterparts in Europe. Although interservice traditions and rivalry prevented a thorough and efficient integration of Army and Navy signals intelligence operations, in December 1943 Special Branch sent Capt. Edwin H. Huddleson to Hawaii to provide the Army commander with ULTRA intelligence and to establish liaison with these units and personnel: JICPOA; Capt. Edwin Layton, Fleet Intelligence Officer; Combat Intelligence Center, Pearl Harbor; and Fleet Radio Unit, Pacific, Pearl Harbor. Huddleson's mission resulted in the assignment of three officers from Special Branch to the Combat Intelligence Center and the assignment of Special Security Officers to major Army and Army Air Forces operational commands in the Central Pacific, who used the Navy's special security channels to transmit ULTRA. A special communications link at the Fleet Radio Unit connecting Special Branch with the Combat Intelligence Center was established. Ironically, MIS personnel achieved more cooperation with naval personnel under the command of Adm. Chester W. Nimitz in the Central Pacific Area than with Army personnel under General MacArthur in SWPA.[87]

Throughout the war in the Pacific or in Europe, the security of special intelligence was paramount, and while lapses in security did occur, they were relatively infrequent. The preservation of the ULTRA secret was a remarkable accomplishment. In the field, the Special Security Officers had to be ever vigilant to caution commanders from acting on ULTRA without "cover," which was information about the enemy from a source other than signal intercepts in high-grade code and cipher. The cover was necessary because the Allies presumed that the enemy would become suspicious and conduct security investigations of its own personnel and procedures when the Allies deployed men and materiel with exceptional timeliness and effectiveness. This ensured that during the course of the investigation, the enemy would, indeed, find a genuine security compromise—the cover—and evidence of how the Allies had advance knowledge of an operation. Thus the cover would sidetrack investigators from the trail of the ENIGMA or PURPLE machine as the source of the compromised information. One American regulation stated: "Any action based upon ULTRA must be so camouflaged that the action itself cannot lead the enemy to conclusions that it is based upon ULTRA. Momentary tactical advantage is not sufficient ground for taking any risk of compromising the source. No action may be taken against specific sea or land targets revealed by ULTRA unless appropriate airplane reconnaissance or other suitable camouflage measures have also been undertaken." One Special Security Officer reported that the idea of cover was the source of "the greatest misunderstanding." He stated, "Recipients were inclined to believe that cover was an invention; the idea of cover as an indication from an actual but open source was alien to all but a few recipients."[88]

Although few in number, security incidents did occur. The British were involved in one such incident in March 1943, just before McCormack, Taylor, and Friedman visited Bletchley Park. The violation centered on the British acting directly in response to high-grade signal intercepts without having cover. British naval and air forces attacked and sank two German merchant vessels and a tanker in the Mediterranean without having obtained air sightings of the ships on their way to Tunisia. ENIGMA intercepts after the attack revealed German suspicions that the British had had precise foreknowledge about the convoy. The implications were alarming. Prime Minister Churchill sent a reprimand to the British commander-in-chief in the Mediterranean threatening to withhold ULTRA from him and directing him to act on ULTRA "only on great occasions or when thoroughly camouflaged." The Germans, however, failed to follow through on their suspicions with a thorough investigation, including a study of compromised enciphering machines.[89]

In April 1943 the Americans acted directly on information from signal intercepts without real cover, in one of the war's most dramatic episodes—the killing of Adm. Isoroku Yamamoto, the mastermind of the Pearl Harbor attack and the highest ranking officer of the Japanese navy. Decoded signals revealed the exact itinerary of Admiral Yamamoto's inspection trip to the South Pacific. With precise timing, sixteen Army Air Forces P-38 fighters intercepted and attacked his aircraft and Zero escort fighters. Immediately after Yamamoto's death, the Japanese changed their naval codes, which resulted in four months of silence before the new codes were broken and read. The British, whose national existence depended on reading enemy air force and U-boat signals, protested the daring mission against Yamamoto, but the Americans believed that cover was less important than the death of the famous Japanese warrior and its blow to Japanese morale.[90]

As a security precaution during the war, recipients of ULTRA were restricted regarding where and how they could travel, always with the concern that they should avoid situations with high risk of capture. For the commander of the IX Tactical Air Command, Maj. Gen. Elwood R. Quesada, the restrictions were unwelcome. His Special Security Officer reported, "While General Quesada was exceedingly resentful of the flying instructions imposed on him, he was strongly aware of the necessity of not compromising ULTRA and the importance of preserving same from an operational point of view."[91]

In contrast with Quesada, the British Air Commodore Ronald Ivelaw-Chapman, who was knowledgeable about ULTRA, unnecessarily risked capture when he flew a British aircraft over enemy occupied France in May 1944. Flak hit and disabled the plane, and Ivelaw-Chapman bailed out before the Lancaster crashed and burned. Members of the French underground initially rescued him, but later the *Gestapo* captured him. He was, fortunately, able to keep the ULTRA secret from his captors.[92]

The Americans, too, had their airmen who could not suppress the desire to fly and by example inspire the men under their command. On June 27, 1944, Brig. Gen. Arthur W. Vanaman flew on a B-17 bombing mission over France. He flew with the approval of Maj. Gen. James "Jimmy" Doolittle, who, like Maj. Gen. George S. Patton, occasionally disregarded regulations about high risk situations. General Vanaman was forced to bail out, was captured by the Germans, and was imprisoned in Stalag Luft III. His constant anxiety, and that of the British and American authorities, was that he would disclose the ULTRA secret. The Germans, however, did not grill him, and he did preserve the vital information.[93]

Ten months after Vanaman's flight, a Special Security Officer, Col. Robert S. Allen, was wounded and captured while on a mission to investigate abandoned German installations. He was hospitalized, but then rescued by advancing American troops. The Germans, who were one month from surrendering, had no opportunity to interrogate him.[94]

Along with the problems of cover and risk of capture, the telephone was the source of many potential and real security compromises. A brigadier general reported, "It was forbidden to discuss ULTRA on the telephone overseas. The rule was daily and hourly disobeyed." A Special Security Officer noted, "The telephone is perhaps the greatest threat to ULTRA security, particularly if it masks its dangers under the green color of the scrambler phone. It is far easier to pick up the telephone on one's desk than to prepare a message and get it to the SLU. This ease has in most commands been confused with operational necessity, although in point of fact the occasions are very rare, when an hour or a half-hour's delay in intelligence are important to operations. . . ."[95]

Americans and British both listened to their own communications to identify security violations. Colonel McCormack called this "protective monitoring," but the practice did not produce 100 percent compliance with regulations. To heighten security awareness in his unit, the Sixth Army Group, one Special Security Officer rewrote the regulations and distilled them into five cardinal rules which he displayed on a poster board:

1. Don't mention ULTRA within hearing of those not on the list.
2. Don't discuss or hint at ULTRA over the telephone.
3. Don't take any ULTRA papers out of the Headquarters.
4. Don't issue orders which could give the enemy or those not on the list any notion of the nature of the intelligence.
5. Don't leave Headquarters without being de-briefed.

Commenting on security at the IX Tactical Air Command, the Special Security Officer observed, "Greatest success and least concern resulted from a stiff initial briefing followed by regular local cautions and frequent blasts from higher up. Periodic security signals from Winterbotham, Eisenhower, Combined Chiefs of Staff, etc. were a great help in maintaining security as they provided an outside excuse for reviewing the question. More would have made the job easier."[96]

In the Pacific at the Headquarters of the Far East Air Forces (FEAF), which was activated in August 1944, ULTRA material arrived before ULTRA regulations and Special Security Officers. When the officers did arrive, one reported the following in November 1944: "Security here is very much a laughing stock because of the much over-late arrival of anything authoritative such as the current regulations. It is fairly patent that security here, where matters can quickly (and actually have) been bounced around in clear radio or low-grade codes, is somewhat more vital than all the lavish preparations in the Pentagon. Everybody walks in and out of ULTRA workshops at GHQ, FEAF etc; there are no separate working rooms; there are myriad private arrangements for passing to odd individuals, made on a personal basis over the years; there is great naivete about the meaning of ULTRA and the impression is general that matters can be fairly freely discussed as long as the dendai numbers and frequencies are not mentioned, etc. With this background it is reasonably apparent that the Nip is overwhelmingly likely to get a first hand account of our operation with ULTRA."[97]

The Special Security Officers at FEAF did implement ULTRA regulations and by the end of December 1944 could report that security was "not so bad." Their job, however, was not an easy one as revealed in the following admission: "It is pretty difficult for Capt. Graham to tell Col. Cain or Gen. Sutherland that they must hustle around and build some special buildings and also knock some heads together. We know it is difficult because we have tried, picked ourselves up out of the dust in the street, gone back in and tried again."[98]

In the Pacific, Special Security Officers had closer relations with U.S. Navy personnel and procedures, and throughout the war, according to one naval intelligence officer, the Navy "vacillated between dangerous exposure of ULTRA and overrestrictive distribution of it." More than one Army Special Security Officer observed lax naval security. After his trip to Leyte

Maj. Gen. Elwood R. Quesada.

in the Philippines, one officer remarked, "I carried no classified material other than a black handbag filled with cryptographic material. This material I kept stored in a locked closet in the ship's captain cabin. This seemed the most secure procedure aboard a vessel whose Commanding Officer kept 18 quarts of bourbon whiskey in his ship's safe, and kept his top secret battle plans for several operations on top of the desk in his sleeping quarters."[99]

From the perspective of Special Security Officers, part of the problem of lax naval security was that the U.S. Navy did not use ULTRA as a secret code word, but merely as a security classification. Hence, the Navy sent furniture or mess bills to the Army addressed "the ULTRA section," Navy couriers carried packages clearly stamped "ULTRA," and Navy signs over the entrances to certain offices proclaimed "ULTRA Personnel Only."[100]

Not only was there always the danger of ULTRA intelligence being mishandled, but there was the constant risk of losing the SIGABA and TYPEX machines which transmitted ULTRA. In late autumn 1944, an intelligence report about the Japanese capturing SIGABA shocked and disheartened readers until they learned that the "SIGABA" in question was a village in New Guinea. In February 1945, however, a real SIGABA cipher machine, with instructional documents, combined key lists, rotors, and other cipher equipment, disappeared in Colmar, France, a city recently captured from the Germans. Investigators interviewed the men of the 28th Infantry Division who lost the SIGABA and the truck and trailer with it, to obtain clues, gather evidence for court martial, and develop procedures to prevent a recurrence. The Army launched a massive search, which included road blocks and checks, as well as searches of barns, sheds, and houses, and even air reconnaissance. General Eisenhower was personally involved in the effort, which went on for over a month, during which time use of all SIGABA systems in the theater was suspended; authorites acted as if SIGABA had fallen into enemy hands. On March 12th, a French search party found portions of the SIGABA equipment partially submerged in a river. The SIGABA itself was still in its locked safe, and investigators determined that it had not been in enemy hands.[101]

If ULTRA was in jeopardy of disclosure on the field of battle, it was in greater danger of being revealed on the front pages of America's newspapers. During the presidential campaign of 1944, Franklin Roosevelt was running on the Democratic ticket for a fourth term against the Republican Governor of New York, Thomas E. Dewey. Dewey had learned about MAGIC and was going to reveal it in the campaign to demonstrate the Roosevelt administration's culpability for the surprise attack on Pearl Harbor. Dewey believed that MAGIC had given Roosevelt advance warning of the attack, and because of American unpreparedness, the President deserved impeachment rather than reelection.[102] Learning of Dewey's intention, General

Marshall, Army Chief of Staff, acted on his own initiative and sent Colonel Clarke of MIS to Dewey with a personal letter requesting that signals intelligence not be openly discussed, because public scrutiny of intelligence operations would destroy their effectiveness. After a telephone conversation with Marshall, a second letter from him, and a second meeting with Colonel Clarke, Dewey withheld information about MAGIC from the electorate. He lost the election by three and a half million votes, but preserved one of the greatest secrets of the war.[103]

Overall, the ULTRA security lapses and near lapses among the Allies paled in comparison with those of the enemy, especially those charged with communications security. Consistent enforcement of all security measures could have seriously damaged the Allied decryption effort. One of the intelligence officers at Bletchley Park mused, "The more widely Enigma was used, the greater the number of careless operators and the greater the proliferation of human error." The Germans' use of standard phrases and double encipherment; their loss of ENIGMA machines, parts, and keys; their lack of an effective "protective monitoring" program; and their unshakeable—even arrogant—confidence in ENIGMA were serious and fatal mistakes. Japanese miscalculations about America's code-breaking abilities were just as deadly for Japanese soldiers, sailors, airmen, and civilians. By the end of 1944, Japanese authorities thought that the Allied military successes were the result of espionage activity, not decryption.[104]

Americans in MIS played a crucial role in the worldwide distribution of ULTRA intelligence, and particularly in its operational use. This unique source—protected with admirable fidelity—contributed significantly to the defeat of the Axis powers. The gifted men and women of MIS were involved in the most remarkable intelligence enterprise the world has ever seen— or is likely to ever see again.

Endnotes

NOTE: All Special Research Histories (SRH), Special Research Summaries (SRS), and Discrete Records of Historical Cryptologic Impact Originated by the U.S. Army (SRMA) are in Record Group (RG) 457, Records of the National Security Agency/Central Security Service, National Archives (NA). RG 319 and RG 407 contain the Records of the Army Staff (1947-) and Records of the Adjutant General (1917-), respectively.

1. Hearings before the Joint Committee on the Investigation of the Pearl Harbor Attack, U.S. Congress Joint Committee, *Proceedings of Clarke Investigation*, 79th Congress, 1st session (Washington, 1946; reprint New York, 1972), part 34, pp 48, 143; "A History of the Military Intelligence Division, 7 December 1941-2 September 1945," Army Center for Military History Manuscript, RG 319, NA, pp 6-7; Roberta Wohlstetter, *Pearl Harbor: Warning and Decision* (Stanford, CA, 1962), pp 281-82; Mark Skinner Watson, *Chief of Staff: Prewar Plans and Preparations*, [U.S. Army in World War II: The War Department] (Washington, 1950), pp 72-74.

2. Pearl Harbor Attack, part 34, *Proceedings of Clarke Investigation*, pp 10-14, 45, 48-49; Department of Defense, *The "Magic" Background of Pearl Harbor*, 5 vols and appendices (Washington, 1977) 1: preface.

3. SRH-035, "History of the Special Branch, MIS, War Department," pp 3-5; SRH-159, "Preliminary Historical Report on the Solution of the 'B' Machine"; SRH-349, "The Achievements of the Signal Security Agency in World War II," pp 13-14, 19; SRH-361, "History of the Signal Security Agency," vol 2, pp 32-47; Ronald Lewin, *The American Magic: Codes, Ciphers and the Defeat of Japan* (New York, 1983), p 57; Ladislas Farago, *The Broken Seal* (New York, 1967), pp 99-100, 103-104, 161-62; D. M. Horner, "Special Intelligence in the South-West Pacific Area in World War II," *Australian Outlook: Journal of the Australian Institute of International Affairs*, 32 (December 1978): 310-13.

4. Wohlstetter, *Pearl Harbor*, pp 281-86.

5. Pearl Harbor Attack, part 34, *Proceedings of Clarke Investigation*, p 13; Lewin, *American Magic*, p 67.

6. SRH-035, pp. 4-5; Pearl Harbor Attack, part 34, *Proceedings of Clarke Investigation*, pp 11-14; Wohlstetter, *Pearl Harbor*, p 180.

7. Msg, Tokyo (Toyoda) to Honolulu, 24 September 1941, *"Magic" Background of Pearl Harbor*, vol 3 appendix, no 356; Lewin, *American Magic*, pp 57-59; David Kahn, "The United States Views Germany and Japan in 1941," in Ernest R. May, ed., *Knowing One's Enemies: Intelligence Assessment Before the Two World Wars*, (Princeton, 1984), p 499.

8. Wohlstetter, *Pearl Harbor*, pp 3, 55-56, 387; Watson, *Chief of Staff*, pp 497-99; Edwin T. Layton, Roger Pineau, and John Costello, *"And I Was There"* (New York, 1985), p 503;

Miles quote in Kahn, "United States Views," p 500, see also pp 483-85, 497; Michael A. Barnhart, "Japanese Intelligence Before the Second World War: 'Best Case' Analysis," in *Knowing One's Enemies*, p 446.

9. Watson, *Chief of Staff*, pp 497-98; Pearl Harbor Attack, part 1, *Hearings 15-17, 19-21, 1945*, introduction, pp 1-2 and part 39, *Reports, Findings and Conclusions of Roberts Commission*, pp 1-21; Lewin, *American Magic*, p 69 fn 77; Wohlstetter, *Pearl Harbor*, pp 187-226; Gordon W. Prange, *At Dawn We Slept* (New York, 1981), pp 402-13; Husband E. Kimmel, *Admiral Kimmel's Story* (Chicago, 1955), pp 55-59.

10. Pearl Harbor Attack, part 1, *Hearings 15-17, 19-21, 1945*, introduction, p 2; Lewin, *American Magic*, p 69; Watson, *Chief of Staff*, pp 497-98; Layton, *"And I Was There,"* pp 511-12; Kimmel, *Admiral Kimmel's Story*, pp 139-40. See also SRH-115, "U.S. Army Investigations Into the Handling of Certain Communications Prior to the Attack on Pearl Harbor, 1944-1945," and SRH-118, "Incidental Exhibits Re Pearl Harbor Investigation (MIS WDGS)."

11. SRH-035, p 5.

12. SRH-012, "The Role of Radio Intelligence in the American-Japanese Naval War," vol 1, pp 1-23, 120-35; SRH-141, "Papers from the Personal Files of Alfred McCormack," part 1, p 72; SRH-116, "Origin, Functions and Problems of the Special Branch, M.I.S.," pp 4-6; Lewin, *American Magic*, p 62; Wohlstetter, *Pearl Harbor*, pp 187, 226; SRH-125, William F. Friedman, "Certain Aspects of 'MAGIC' in the Cryptologic Background of the Various Official Investigations into the Pearl Harbor Attack." In SRH-125 Friedman refuted the charges that President Franklin Roosevelt and high ranking Army and Navy personnel deliberately allowed the Japanese to attack the fleet at Pearl Harbor in order to bring the United States into the war.

13. SRH-269, Robert L. Benson, "U.S. Army Comint Policy: Pearl Harbor to Summer 1942," pp 9-10; SRH-116, pp 6-7; SRH-035, pp 5-6; Thomas Parrish, *The Ultra Americans* (New York, 1986), p 82; William Gardner Bell, *Secretaries of War and Secretaries of the Army* (Washington, 1981), pp 108, 126.

14. SRH-035, p 6; SRH-116, pp 7-11; SRH-269, p 10.

15. SRH-141, part 1, p 17; SRH-116, p 9.

16. John D. Millett, *The Organization and Role of the Army Service Forces*, [United States Army in World War II] (Washington, 1954), pp 23, 36-37.

17. Circular No. 59, "War Department Reorganization," War Department, Mar 2, 1942, RG 407, NA; "History of MID, 7 Dec 41-2 Sep 45," pp 12-16.

18. "History of MID, 7 Dec 41-2 Sep 45," pp 11-45; SRH-005, "Use of (CX/MSS ULTRA) by the United States War Department 1943-1945," p 5; SRH-269, p 12.

19. SRH-141, part 1, pp 71-74, 76; SRH-269, p 12; "History of MID, 7 Dec 41-2 Sep 45," p 21; George F. Howe, *et al*, "American Signal Intelligence in Northwest Africa and Western Europe," series IV, *World War II*, vol 1, [United States Cryptologic History] (National Security Agency, 1980), p 6. For a discussion of signals intelligence coordinating activity among military and civilian agencies, see SRH-012, vol 2, pp 375-419.

20. SRH-035, p 8; SRH-269, p 13; SRH-349, pp 8-9; SRH-276, "Centralized Control of U.S. Army Signal Intelligence Activities, 30 January 1939-16 April 1945," pp 111, 113.

21. SRH-141, part 1, pp 71-74; SRH-116, p 10; SRH-035, p 8; SRH-349, p 14; SRH-362, "History of the Signal Security Agency," vol 3, "The Japanese Army Problems: Cryptanalysis, 1942-1945," p 22; SRH-117, "History of Special Branch M.I.S., June 1944-September 1945," p 8; Parrish, *Ultra Americans*, p 180.

22. SRH-035, pp 8-9, 13; SRH-185, "War Experience of Alfred McCormack," pp 3-4, 14.

23. SRH-185, p 17; SRH-116, p 23.

24. SRH-185, p 16; Charles B. MacDonald, *A Time for Trumpets: The Untold Story of the Battle of the Bulge* (New York, 1984) p 53; Ronald Lewin, *Ultra Goes to War: The First Account of World War II's Greatest Secret Based on Official Documents* (New York, 1978), pp 251-52.

25. SRH-035, pp 12, 35, 60.

26. SRH-185, p 22; Anthony Cave Brown, *Wild Bill Donovan: The Last Hero* (New York, 1982), p 305.

27. SRH-132, "History of the Special Distribution Branch, MIS, WDGS," p 3; SRH-005,

p 6. For the early MAGIC Summaries see SRS-549 to SRS-823, " 'MAGIC' Summaries, Asst. C/S, G-2, 20 March 1942-31 December 1942," RG 457, NA.

28. SRH-005, p 5.

29. SRH-185, p 5; Howe, "American Signal Intelligence," p 124.

30. SRH-185, p 9; SRH-033, "History of the Operations of Special Security Officers Attached to Field Commands, 1943-1945," p 2; F. H. Hinsley *et al, British Intelligence in the Second World War: Its Influence on Strategy and Operations*, 3 vols (London, 1979, 1981, 1984), vol 2, p 56. For a discussion of early wartime contacts between the Government Code and Cipher School and the Signal Intelligence Service see SRH-361, pp 17-19.

31. SRH-110, F. W. Hilles, "Operations of the Military Intelligence Service, War Department, London," p 10; SRH-107, "Problems of the SSO System World War II," pp 1-2; SRH-349, p 26; SRH-362; SRH-035, pp 30-33; Layton, *"And I Was There,"* pp 418-48; Ronald Clark, *The Man Who Broke Purple* (Boston, 1977), pp 161, 181-82, 199.

32. Howe, "American Signal Intelligence," p 126; SRH-035, pp 20-24; SRH-185, p 10.

33. Peter Calvocoressi, *Top Secret Ultra* (New York, 1981), pp 43-46; Aileen Clayton, *The Enemy Is Listening* (New York, 1980), pp 17-18; MacDonald, *Time for Trumpets*, p 58.

34. Calvocoressi, *Top Secret Ultra*, pp 44-45; MacDonald, *Time for Trumpets,* p 59; Clayton, *Enemy is Listening*, pp 145-82.

35. Calvocoressi, *Top Secret Ultra*, pp 25, 30; Patrick Beesly, *Very Special Intelligence: The Story of the Admiralty's Operational Intelligence Centre, 1939-1945* (Garden City, NY, 1978), p 64; Clark, *Man Who Broke Purple*, pp 96-97; Jozef Garlinski, *The Enigma War* (New York, 1979), p 32; Andrew Hodges, *Alan Turing: The Enigma* (New York, 1983), pp 166-170.

36. SRH-016, "The Need for New Legislation Against Unauthorized Disclosure of Communication Intelligence Activities, 9 June 1944," p 11; Beesly, *Very Special Intelligence*, pp 66, 133-34; Hinsley, *et al, British Intelligence*, vol 1 (London, 1979-1984), p 487; Garlinski, *Enigma War*, pp 20-23; Lewin, *Ultra Goes to War*, p 33; Wladyslaw Kozaczuk, *Enigma: How the German Machine Cipher Was Broken and How It Was Read by the Allies in World War Two*, trans. and ed. Christopher Kasparek (Frederick, MD, 1984), p 23.

37. Calvocoressi, *Top Secret Ultra*, pp 54, 77-78; Hinsley, *British Intelligence*, vol 2, pp 28, 659-61.

38. Calvocoressi, *Top Secret Ultra*, p 57; MacDonald, *Time for Trumpets*, p 58; Kozaczuk, *Enigma*, p 63; Hinsley, *British Intelligence*, vol 1, pp 487-95; Lewin, *Ultra Goes to War*, pp 29-50; Hodges, *Alan Turing*, p 191.

39. I. J. Good, "Early Work on Computers at Bletchley," *Cryptologia* 3 (April 1979): 74; Hinsley, *British Intelligence*, vol 3, part 1, pp 479-80; Garlinski, *Enigma War*, pp 146-48; Lewin, *Ultra Goes to War*, p 131.

40. Calvocoressi, *Top Secret Ultra*, pp 18, 60-65; Clayton, *Enemy Is Listening*, p 17; Ralph Bennett, *Ultra in the West: The Normandy Campaign 1944-45* (New York, 1980), pp 12-13.

41. Calvocoressi, *Top Secret Ultra*, pp 60, 68-70, 124-25.

42. Howe, "American Signal Intelligence," p 126; Hinsley, *British Intelligence*, vol 2, p 647.

43. F. W. Winterbotham, *The Ultra Secret* (New York, 1974; reprint ed., New York, 1982), pp 40-43, 132-33; Hinsley, *British Intelligence*, vol 1, p 572; Lewin, *Ultra Goes to War*, pp 139-43.

44. SRH-107, pp 2-3; Hinsley, *British Intelligence*, vol 2, p 56; Parrish, *Ultra Americans*, pp 97-98.

45. SRH-349, p 31; Hodges, *Alan Turing*, pp 235-36, 243, 299-301; SRH-361, p 275.

46. SRH-349, pp 18, 32.

47. Hodges, *Alan Turing*, p 222; SRH-125, p 73; SRH-141, part 2, p 196; SRH-002, William F. Flicke, "War Secrets in the Ether," pp 192-97; David Kahn, *Hitler's Spies: German Military Intelligence in World War II* (New York, 1978), pp 193-94; Hinsley, *British Intelligence*, vol 2, pp 331, 361, 640; Lewin, *Ultra Goes to War*, pp 252-53; Kozaczuk, *Enigma*, p 171; Calvocoressi, *Top Secret Ultra*, pp 118-19.

48. SRH-230, Henry Schorreck, "The Role of COMINT in the Battle of Midway," pp 1-9; SRH 012, vol 1, pp 260-325, vol 2, pp 146-55; Layton, *"And I Was There,"* pp 453-56; Parrish, *Ultra Americans*, pp 97-98; Winterbotham, *Ultra Secret*, p 252.

49. SRH-016, pp 34-54; Clark, *Man Who Broke Purple*, pp 189-90; W. J. Holmes, *Double-Edged Secrets: U.S. Naval Intelligence Operations in the Pacific during World War II* (Annapolis, MD, 1979), p 108.

50. Howe, "American Signal Intelligence," pp 7, 175; Hinsley, *British Intelligence*, vol 2, pp 57-58.

51. SRH-349, p 15-16; SRH-037, "Reports Received by U.S. War Department on the Use of ULTRA in European Theater," pp 8-9; SRH-044, "War Department Regulations Governing the Dissemination and Security of Communications Intelligence," p 16; SRH-110, pp 39, 42.

52. SRH-110, p 39; Calvocoressi, *Top Secret Ultra*, p 122.

53. SRH-110, p 40.

54. SRH-349, pp 42-43; SRH-033, p 4; SRH-010, "History of Converter M-325 (SIGFOY)," p 12; SRH-359, "History of Converter M-134-C," pp 250-53; SRH-110, pp 40-41; Hinsley, *British Intelligence*, vol 2, p 631; Garlinski, *Enigma War*, p 123; Calvocoressi, *Top Secret Ultra*, p 23; Clark, *Man Who Broke Purple*, pp 140, 196; David Kahn, *Kahn on Codes* (New York, 1983), p 114. See also SRH-360, "History of Mark II ECM."

55. SRMA-003, "U.S. Army Converter M-228," p 8, RG 457, NA; SRH-349, pp 42-45. In March 1945, an Army unit completed work on an attachment device called TELABA, which automatically deciphered SIGABA traffic received on punched tape. See SRH-357, "History Signal Intelligence Division (ETO) June 1942-July 1945," pp 194-95. For discussion of the principal American enciphering machines for voice and picture communications see SRH-349, pp 40-49. The British did not have a machine similar to SIGCUM, but in July 1944 the Army was authorized to issue SIGCUM to British units "for use only in combined communications on facilities employed jointly by United States and British Armed Forces."

56. SRH-110, pp 40-41.

57. *Ibid.*

58. *Ibid*, p 4; Howe, "American Signal Intelligence," pp 172-73.

59. SRH-361, pp 251-52, 278-84; Good, "Early Work on Computers at Bletchley," p 72.

60. Howe, "American Signal Intelligence," p 128; SRH-110, p 12; SRH-061, "Allocation of Special Security Officers to Special Branch Military Intelligence Service, War Department, 1943-1945," pp 1-2; SRH-035, p 21.

61. SRH-185, p 11; SRH-110, pp 11-12, 37; Howe, "American Signal Intelligence," p 128.

62. SRH-110, pp 13-14, 19, 23, 37, 45-46; SRH-107, pp 36-38.

63. SRH-005, pp 6-9; SRH-143, "ULTRA in the Battle of Britain: The Real Key to Success?" pp 30-32.

64. SRH-349, p 35; SRH-146, "Handling of ULTRA within the Military Intelligence Service," p 1; SRH-005, pp 9-10, 14; SRH-035, pp 26-27, 55-60.

65. SRH-033, pp 2-3; SRH-107, pp 3-4; SRH-141, part 2, p 200; SRH-185, pp 10-11; SRH-061, pp 1, 2, 9.

66. SRH-119, "Military Intelligence Service War Department—Special Security Officer and Other Correspondence Relating to Special Intelligence in the Pacific Ocean Area," pp 1, 53-55; SRH-006, "Synthesis of Experiences in the Use of ULTRA Intelligence by the U.S. Army Field Commands in the European Theatre of Operations," pp 10-11; SRH-033, pp 1, 3.

67. SRH-026, "Marshall Letter to Eisenhower on the Use of ULTRA Intelligence."

68. SRH-023, "Reports by U.S. Army ULTRA Representatives with Army Field Commands in the European Theatre of Operations 1945," part 2, p 48; SRH-110, pp 2-4, 17; SRH-061, p 2; Calvocoressi, *Top Secret Ultra*, pp 66, 68, 71.

69. SRH-153, "MIS, War Department Liaison Activities in the UK, 1943-1945," pp 8-14; SRH-141, part 2, p 178, 192-95; SRH-110, p 2; SRH-061, pp 1-3.

70. Howe, "American Signal Intelligence," p 182; Parrish, *Ultra Americans*, pp 106, 163, 195-97; Hinsley, *British Intelligence*, vol 3, part 1, pp 460-61.

71. Bruce W. Bidwell, "History of the Military Intelligence Division Department of the Army General Staff," Office of the Chief of Military History Manuscript File, part 5, "World War II 8 December 1941-2 September 1945," p 14, RG 319, NA; SRH-185, pp 26-30, 45; "History of MID, 7 Dec 41-2 Sep 45," pp 33-59.

72. SRH-146, p 2; SRH-005, pp 10, 16; SRH-035, p 63; "History of MID, 7 Dec 42-2 Sep 45," pp 36-59.

73. SRH-125, p 29.

74. SRH-005, pp 10, 16-18, 24-25; SRH-146, pp 2, 4; SRH-185, pp 28, 33-46.

75. SRH-005, p 24; SRH-107, p 24; SRH-006, pp 19, 25; SRH-023, part 2, pp 34, 50-52.

76. SRH-185, pp 30-31; SRH-146, p 3.

77. SRH-109, "Organization and Operations of the German Specialists, MIS, War Department," pp 3,7; SRH-005, p 24.

78. SRH-117, p 10.

79. SRH-033, p 2; SRH-035, pp 22-23; SRH-061, p 20.

80. SRH-032, "Reports by U.S. Army ULTRA Representatives with Field Commands in the Southwest Pacific, Pacific Ocean and China Burma India Theaters of Operation, 1944-1945," p 13; SRH-044, p 27-B; SRH-127, "Use and Dissemination of ULTRA in the Southwest Pacific Area, 1943-1945," p 30. For information on MIS personnel with the JICPOA see Holmes, *Double-Edged Secrets*, pp 175-76.

81. SRH-349, p 12; SRH-032, pp 5-7; Holmes, *Double-Edged Secrets*, p 196; Horner, "Special Intelligence in the South-West Pacific Area," pp 313, 321, 324.

82. SRH-032, p 5; SRH-362, pp 139-47.

83. SRH-203, "General Headquarters Southwest Pacific Area, Military Intelligence Section, General Staff, Special Intelligence Bulletins," part 4; SRH-032, pp 6-7, 27; SRH-119, p 21; SRH-127, pp 30-33, 36, 39, 43-47, 89, 98, 122; SRH-034, "Marshall Letter to MacArthur on the Use of ULTRA Intelligence," p 2.

84. SRH-032, pp 6-10.

85. SRH-032, p 7; SRH-033, p 4; SRH-061, p 21; SRH-119, pp 1-2, 4; SRH-127, pp 41-42, 124, 132, 148. For the names of Special Security Officers and Representatives in the Pacific theater see SRH-119, pp 53-55; for Special Security Representatives in Europe see Howe, "American Signal Intelligence," p 129.

86. SRH-033, p 5.

87. Lewin, *American Magic*, pp 144-46.

88. SRH-023, part 1, p 58; SRH-219, "ULTRA Material in the Blamey Papers," p 20; SRH-006, p 24; SRH-033, p 6; Hinsley, *British Intelligence*, vol 2, p 648.

89. Hinsley, *British Intelligence*, vol 2, pp 647-48.

90. SRH-127, p 174; Wesley Frank Craven and James Lea Cate, eds. *The Army Air Forces In World War II*, 7 vols (Chicago, 1948-58; reprint Washington, 1983) Vol 4: *The Pacific: Guadalcanal to Saipan August 1942 to July 1944*, pp 213-14; Edward Van Der Rhoer, *Deadly Magic* (New York, 1978), pp 134-51; Winterbotham, *Ultra Secret*, p 252; Clark, *Man Who Broke Purple*, pp 190-91; Lewin, *American Magic*, pp 187-91.

91. SRH-023, part 2, p 97.

92. Parrish, *Ultra Americans*, pp 246-47.

93. *Ibid*, pp 233-50; Winterbotham, *Ultra Secret*, p 134.

94. Parrish, *Ultra Americans*, p 275; Alfred Friendly, "Confessions of a Code Breaker," *Washington Post*, October 27, 1974, pp C-1, C-3.

95. SRH-023, part 1, pp 25-26, 64; SRH-162, "History of Security Monitoring WWI to 1955," p 9; SRH-037, p 13; SRH-023, part 2, p 53.

96. SRH-116, pp 31-32; SRH-023, part 1, p 53, part 2, p 97.

97. SRH-119, p 39.

98. *Ibid.*

99. Holmes, *Double-Edged Secrets*, p 136; SRH-032, p 26.

100. SRH-032, pp 13, 26-28, 33.

101. SRH-359, pp 193-226; Clark, *Man Who Broke Purple*, pp 196-98.

102. SRH-043, "Statement for Record of Participation of Brig. Gen. Carter W. Clarke, GSC, in the Transmittal of Letters from Gen. George C. Marshall to Gov. Thomas E. Dewey," pp 1-14; SRH-125, pp 44-45. For newspaper and radio reports concerning the Pearl Harbor attack and communications intelligence see SRH-012, vol 2, pp 138-45.

103. SRH-125, pp 44-45; SRH-043, pp 1-4. For General Marshall's letters to Governor Dewey see *New York Times*, December 8, 1945, p 5.

104. SRH-349, p 28; Calvocoressi, *Top Secret Ultra*, p 55; Hinsley, *British Intelligence*, vol 1, p 144; vol 2, p 24; vol 3, part 1, p 481.

Bibliography

Government Sources

National Archives

Record Group 457, Records of the National Security Agency/Central Security Service

SRH-002. William F. Flicke, "War Secrets in the Ether."

SRH-005. "Use of (CX/MSS ULTRA) by the United States War Department 1943–1945."

SRH-006. "Synthesis of Experiences in the Use of ULTRA Intelligence by the U.S. Army Field Commands in the European Theatre of Operations."

SRH-010. "History of Converter M-325 (SIGFOY)."

SRH-012. "The Role of Radio Intelligence in the American-Japanese Naval War."

SRH-013. "Ultra History of U. S. Strategic Air Force[s] Europe vs. German Air Force."

SRH-016. "The Need for New Legislation Against Unauthorized Disclosure of Communication Intelligence Activities, 9 June 1944."

SRH-017. "Allied Strategic Air Force Target Planning."

SRH-023. "Reports by U.S. Army ULTRA Representatives with Army Field Commands in the European Theatre of Operations 1945."

SRH-026. "Marshall Letter to Eisenhower on the Use of ULTRA Intelligence."

SRH-031. "Trip Reports Concerning Use of ULTRA in the Mediterranean Theatre 1943–1944."

SRH-032. "Reports by U.S. Army ULTRA Representatives with Field Commands in the Southwest Pacific, Pacific Ocean and China Burma India Theaters of Operation, 1944–1945."

SRH-033. "History of the Operations of Special Security Officers Attached to Field Commands, 1943–1945."

SRH-034. "Marshall Letter to MacArthur on the Use of ULTRA Intelligence."

SRH-035. "History of the Special Branch, MIS, War Department."

SRH-037. "Reports Received by U.S. War Department on the Use of ULTRA in the European Theater."

SRH-043. "Statement for Record of Participation of Brig. Gen. Carter W. Clarke, GSC, in the Transmittal of Letters from Gen. George C. Marshall to Gov. Thomas E. Dewey."

SRH-044. "War Department Regulations Governing the Dissemination and Security of Communications Intelligence."
SRH-046. "Procedures for Handling ULTRA DEXTER Intelligence in the CBI, Rear Echelon, HQ U.S. Army Forces, China, Burma, India Theater."
SRH-061. "Allocation of Special Security Officers to Special Branch Military Intelligence Service."
SRH-107. "Problems of the SSO System World War II."
SRH-109. "Organization and Operations of the German Specialists, MIS, War Department."
SRH-110. "Operations of the Military Intelligence Service, War Department, London."
SRH-115. "U.S. Army Investigations Into the Handling of Certain Communications Prior to the Attack on Pearl Harbor, 1944-1945."
SRH-116. "Origin, Functions and Problems of the Special Branch, M.I.S."
SRH-117. "History of Special Branch M.I.S., June 1944-September 1945."
SRH-118. "Incidental Exhibits re Pearl Harbor Investigation (MIS WDGS)."
SRH-119. "Military Intelligence Service War Department—Special Security Officer and Other Correspondence Relating to Special Intelligence in the Pacific Ocean Area."
SRH-125. William F. Friedman, "Certain Aspects of 'Magic' in the Cryptologic Background of the Various Official Investigations into the Pearl Harbor Attack."
SRH-127. "Use and Dissemination of ULTRA in the Southwest Pacific Area, 1943-1945."
SRH-132. "History of the Special Distribution Branch, MIS, WDGS."
SRH-141. "Papers from the Personal Files of Alfred McCormack."
SRH-143. "ULTRA in the Battle of Britain: The Real Key to Success?"
SRH-146. "Handling of ULTRA Within the Military Intelligence Service."
SRH-153. "MIS, War Department Liaison Activities in the UK, 1943-1945."
SRH-159. "Preliminary Historical Report on the Solution of the 'B' Machine."
SRH-162. "History of Security Monitoring WWI to 1955."
SRH-185. "War Experience of Alfred McCormack."
SRH-203. "General Headquarters Southwest Pacific Area, Military Intelligence Section, General Staff, Special Intelligence Bulletins."
SRH-219. "ULTRA Material in the Blamey Papers."
SRH-230. "The Role of COMINT in the Battle of Midway."
SRH-269. Robert L. Benson, "U.S. Army COMINT Policy: Pearl Harbor to Summer 1942."
SRH-276. "Centralized Control of U.S. Army Signal Intelligence Activities, 30 January 1939-16 April 1945."
SRH-349. "The Achievements of the Signal Security Agency in World War II."
SRH-357. "History Signal Intelligence Division (ETO) June 1942-July 1945."
SRH-359. "History of Converter M-134-C."
SRH-360. "History of Mark II ECM."
SRH-361. "History of the Signal Security Agency."
SRH-362. "The Japanese Army Problems: Cryptanalysis, 1942-1945."
SRMA-003. "U.S. Army Converter M-228."
SRS-549. " 'MAGIC' Summaries, Asst. C/S, G-2, 20 March 1942-31 December 1942."

Record Group 319, Records of the Army Staff

Army Center for Military History. "A History of the Military Intelligence Division, 7 December 1941-2 September 1945."
Bidwell, Bruce W. "History of the Military Intelligence Division Department of the Army General Staff." Office of the Chief of Military History Manuscript File.

Congress

Senate. *Hearings before the Joint Committee on the Investigation of the Pearl Harbor Attack.*

39 parts. 79th Cong, 1st sess. Washington: Government Printing Office, 1946; reprint New York: AMS Press, 1972.

Books and Studies

Angell, Joseph W. "Historical Analysis of the 14-15 February 1945 Bombing of Dresden." USAF Historical Division, Research Studies Institute, Air University, 1953 in USAF Historical Research Center, Maxwell Air Force Base, AL.

Bell, William Gardner. *Secretaries of War and Secretaries of the Army*. Washington: United States Army Center of Military History, 1981; reprint, 1982.

Blumenson, Martin. *Breakout and Pursuit*. [United States Army in World War II: The European Theater of Operations]. Washington: Office of the Chief of Military History, 1961; reprint, 1970.

Cole, Hugh M. *The Ardennes: Battle of the Bulge*. [United States Army in World War II: The European Theater of Operations]. Washington: Office of the Chief of Military History, 1965.

Craven, Wesley F. and Cate, James L., eds. *The Army Air Forces In World War II*. 7 vols. Chicago: University of Chicago Press, 1948-1958; reprint, Office of Air Force History, 1983.

Department of Defense. *The "Magic" Background of Pearl Harbor*. 5 vols. and appendices. Washington: Government Printing Office, 1977.

Griess, Thomas E. *The Second World War: Europe and the Mediterranean*. West Point Military History Series. Wayne, NJ: Avery Publishing Group, 1984.

Hansell, Haywood S., Jr. *The Strategic Air War Against Germany and Japan: A Memoir*. USAF Warrior Studies. Washington: Office of Air Force History, 1986.

Howe, George F. et al. "American Signal Intelligence in Northwest Africa and Western Europe." World War II Series. Fort George Meade, MD: National Security Agency, 1980.

__________. *Northwest Africa: Seizing the Initiative in the West*. [United States Army in World War II: The Mediterranean Theater of Operations]. Washington: Office of the Chief of Military History, 1957; reprint, 1970.

Jones, Vincent C. *Manhattan: The Army and the Atomic Bomb*. [United States Army in World War II: Special Studies]. Washington: Office of the Chief of Military History, 1985.

Millett, John D., ed. *The Organization and Role of the Army Service Forces*. [United States Army in World War II: The Army Service Forces]. Washington: Office of the Chief of Military History, 1954.

Murray, Williamson. *Strategy for Defeat: The Luftwaffe, 1933-1945*. Maxwell Air Force Base, AL: Air University Press, 1983.

Schwabedissen, Generalleutnant a. D. Walter. *The Russian Air Force in the Eyes of German Commanders*. Introduction by Telford Taylor. USAF Historical Study 175. Maxwell Air Force Base, AL: USAF Historical Division, 1960; reprint, New York: Arno Press, 1968.

Thompson, Wayne, ed. *Air Leadership: Proceedings of a Conference at Bolling Air Force Base, April 13-14, 1984*. USAF Warrior Studies. Washington: Office of Air Force History, 1986.

Watson, Mark Skinner. *Chief of Staff: Prewar Plans and Preparations*. [United States Army in World War II]. Washington: Historical Division, Department of the Army, 1950.

Wolk, Herman S. *Planning and Organizing the Postwar Air Force, 1943-1947*. Washington: Office of Air Force History, 1984.

Non-Government Sources

Books

Ambrose, Stephen E. *Ike's Spies: Eisenhower and the Espionage Establishment*. New York: Doubleday, 1981.

Babington-Smith, Constance. *Evidence in Camera: The Story of Photographic Intelligence in World War II*. Foreword by Marshal of the Royal Air Force the Lord Tedder. London: Chatto and Windus, 1958.
Beesly, Patrick. *Very Special Intelligence: The Story of the Admiralty's Operational Intelligence Centre, 1939–1945*. Garden City, NY: Doubleday, 1978.
Bennett, Ralph. *Ultra in the West: The Normandy Campaign 1944–45*. New York: Charles Scribner's Sons, 1980.
Calvocoressi, Peter J. *Top Secret Ultra*. New York: Ballantine Books, 1981.
__________. and Wint, Guy. *Total War: The Story of World War II*. New York: Pantheon Books, 1972.
Carver, Field Marshal Sir Michael. *The War Lords: Military Commanders in the Twentieth Century*. Boston: Little, Brown, 1976.
Cave Brown, Anthony. *Bodyguard of Lies*. New York: Bantam, 1975.
__________. *Wild Bill Donovan: The Last Hero*. New York: New York Times Books, 1982.
Clark, Ronald. *The Man Who Broke Purple*. Boston: Little, Brown, 1977.
Clayton, Aileen. *The Enemy Is Listening*. Foreword by Air Chief Sir Frederick Rosier. New York: Ballantine Books, 1980.
Coffey, Thomas M. *Decision Over Schweinfurt*. New York: David McKay, 1977.
Copp, DeWitt S. *Forged in Fire: Strategy and Decisions in the Air War Over Europe 1940–45*. Garden City, NY: Doubleday, 1982.
Cruickshank, Charles. *Deception in World War II*. New York: Oxford University Press, 1980.
Erickson, John. *The Road to Stalingrad: Stalin's War with Germany*. London: Weidenfield and Nicolson, 1975; reprint, Boulder, CO: Westview Press, 1984.
Ethell, Jeffrey L. and Price, Alfred. *The German Jets in Combat*. London: Jane's Publishing, 1979.
Farago, Ladislas. *The Broken Seal*. New York: Random House, 1967.
Galbraith, John Kenneth. *A Life In Our Times: Memoirs*. Boston: Houghton Mifflin, 1981.
Garlinski, Jozef. *The Enigma War*. New York: Charles Scribner's Sons, 1979.
Hamilton, Nigel. *Master of the Battlefield: Monty's War Years 1942–1944*. New York: McGraw-Hill, 1983.
Hansell, Haywood S., Jr. *The Air Plan That Defeated Hitler*. Atlanta, GA: Higgins-McArthur, Longino and Porter, 1972.
Hinsley, F. H. et al. *British Intelligence in the Second World War: Its Influence on Strategy and Operations*, 3 vols. London: Her Majesty's Stationery Office, 1979–1984.
Hodges, Andrew. *Alan Turing: The Enigma*. New York: Simon and Schuster, 1983.
Holmes, W. J. *Double-Edged Secrets: U.S. Naval Intelligence Operations in the Pacific during World War II*. Annapolis, MD: Naval Institute Press, 1979.
Irving, David. *The Destruction of Dresden*. New York: Holt, Rinehart and Winston, 1964.
__________. *The Mare's Nest*. Boston: Little, Brown, 1965.
Jones, R. V. *The Wizard War: British Scientific Intelligence, 1939–1945*. New York: Coward, McCann, Geoghegan, 1978.
Kahn, David. *Hitler's Spies: German Military Intelligence in World War II*. New York: Macmillan, 1978.
__________. *Kahn on Codes: Secrets of the New Cryptology*. New York: Macmillan, 1983.
Kennedy, Gregory P. *Vengeance Weapon 2: The V-2 Guided Missile*. Washington: Smithsonian Institution Press, 1983.
Kimmel, Husband E. *Admiral Kimmel's Story*. Chicago: Henry Regnery, 1955.
Kozaczuk, Wladyslaw. *Enigma: How the German Machine Cipher Was Broken, and How It Was Read by the Allies in World War Two*. Trans. and ed. Christopher Kasparek. Frederick, MD: University Publications of America, 1984.
Laqueur, Walter, ed. *The Second World War: Essays in Military and Political History*. London: Sage, 1982.
Layton, Edwin T., Pineau, Roger and Costello, John. *"And I Was There": Pearl Harbor and Midway—Breaking the Secrets*. New York: William Morrow, 1985.
Lewin, Ronald. *Ultra Goes to War: The First Account of World War II's Greatest Secret Based on Official Documents*. New York: McGraw-Hill, 1978.

__________. *The American Magic: Codes, Ciphers and the Defeat of Japan*. New York: McGraw-Hill, 1978.

Lukas, Richard C. *Eagles East: The Army Air Forces and the Soviet Union, 1941–1945*. Tallahassee, FL: Florida State University Press, 1970.

__________. *The Strange Allies: The United States and Poland, 1941–1945*. Knoxville: University of Tennessee Press, 1978.

MacDonald, Charles B. *A Time for Trumpets: The Untold Story of the Battle of the Bulge*. New York: William Morrow, 1985.

MacIsaac, David. *Strategic Bombing in World War Two: The Story of the United States Strategic Bombing Survey*. New York: Garland Publishing, 1976.

Manchester, William. *The Arms of Krupp, 1587–1968*. Boston: Little, Brown, 1968.

Masterman, J. C. *The Double-Cross System in the War of 1939 to 1945*. New Haven: Yale University Press, 1972.

May, Ernest R., ed. *Knowing One's Enemies: Intelligence Assessment Before the Two World Wars*. Princeton: Princeton University Press, 1984.

Middlebrook, Martin. *The Schweinfurt-Regensburg Mission*. New York: Charles Scribner's Sons, 1983.

Montagu, Ewen. *Beyond Top Secret Ultra*. New York: Coward, McCann, and Geoghegan, 1978.

Montgomery of Alamein, Bernard L. Montgomery. *El Alamein to the River Sangro, Normandy to the Baltic*. New York: St. Martin's Press, 1974.

Overy, R. J. *The Air War, 1939–1945*. London: Europa Publications, 1981.

Parrish, Thomas. *The Ultra Americans: The U.S. Role in Breaking the Nazi Code*. New York: Stein and Day, 1986.

Parton, James. "*Air Force Spoken Here*": *General Ira Eaker and the Command of the Air*. Bethesda, MD: Adler and Adler, 1986.

Prange, Gordon W. *At Dawn We Slept: The Untold Story of Pearl Harbor*. New York: McGraw-Hill, 1981.

Rostow, W. W. *Pre-Invasion Bombing Strategy: General Eisenhower's Decision of 25 March 1944*. Austin, TX: University of Texas Press, 1981.

Schaffer, Ronald. *Wings of Judgment: American Bombing in World War II*. New York: Oxford University Press, 1985.

Smith, Melden E., Jr. "The Bombing of Dresden Reconsidered: A Study in Wartime Decision Making," Dissertation from Boston University Graduate School, 1971.

Speer, Albert. *Inside the Third Reich*. New York: Macmillan, 1970.

Stanley, Roy M. *World War II Photo Intelligence*. New York: Charles Scribner's Sons, 1981.

Strong, Major-General Sir Kenneth. *Intelligence at the Top: The Recollections of an Intelligence Officer*. Garden City, NY: Doubleday, 1969.

__________. *Men of Intelligence: A Study of Roles and Decisions of Chiefs of Intelligence from World War I to the Present Day*. London: Cassell, 1970.

Tedder, Arthur William. *With Prejudice: The War Memoirs of Marshal of the Royal Air Force Lord Tedder G.C.B.* Boston: Little, Brown, 1966.

Toland, John. *Infamy: Pearl Harbor and Its Aftermath*. Garden City NY: Doubleday, 1982.

U.S. Army Air Forces. *Ultra and the History of the United States Strategic Air Force(s) in Europe vs. the German Air Force*. Frederick MD: University Publications of America, 1980.

Van Der Rhoer, Edward. *Deadly Magic*. New York: Charles Scribner's Sons, 1978.

Webster, Charles and Frankland, Noble. *The Strategic Air Offensive Against Germany, 1939–1945*, 4 vols. London: Her Majesty's Stationery Office, 1961.

Whaley, Barton. *Codeword BARBAROSSA*. Cambridge, MA: MIT Press, 1974.

Winterbotham, F. W. *The Ultra Secret*. New York: Harper and Row, 1974; reprint, New York: Dell Publishing, 1982.

Wohlstetter, Roberta. *Pearl Harbor: Warning and Decision*. Stanford CA: Stanford University Press, 1962.

Articles

Ambrose, Stephen E. "Eisenhower and the Intelligence Community in World War II." *Journal of Contemporary History* 16 (1981): 153-66.

Ball, Desmond J. "Allied Intelligence Cooperation Involving Australia during World War II." *Australian Outlook: Journal of the Australian Institute of International Affairs* 32 (December 1978): 299-309.

Bennett, Ralph. "Ultra and Some Command Decisions." *Journal of Contemporary History* 16 (January 1981): 131-51.

Calvocoressi, Peter J. "The Secrets of Enigma." *The Listener,* January 20, 1977, pp 71-72.

__________. "When Enigma Yielded Ultra." *The Listener*, January 27, 1977, pp 112-14.

__________. "The Value of Enigma." *The Listener*, February 3, 1977, pp 135-37.

Clodfelter, Mark A. "Culmination Dresden: 1945." *Aerospace Historian* (September 1979): 134-47.

Deutsch, Harold C. "Clients of Ultra: American Captains." *Parameters, Journal of the U.S. Army War College* 15 (Summer 1985): 55-62.

__________. "The Historical Impact of Revealing the Ultra Secret." *Parameters, Journal of the U.S. Army War College* 7 (1977): 16-23.

__________. "The Influence of Ultra on World War II." *Parameters, Journal of the U.S. Army War College* 8 (December 1978): 2-15.

Galbraith, John Kenneth. "Albert Speer Was the man to See." *The New York Times Book Review*, January 10, 1971, pp 2-3, 30, 32.

Good, I. J. "Early Work on Computers at Bletchley," *Cryptologia* 3 (April 1979): 74.

Harris, Ruth R. "The 'Magic' Leak of 1941 and Japanese-American Relations." *Pacific Historical Review* 50 (February 1981): 77-96.

Horner, D. M. "Special Intelligence in the South-West Pacific Area in World War II." *Australian Outlook: Journal of the Australian Institute of International Affairs* 32 (December 1978), 310-13.

Kahn, David. "The International Conference on ULTRA." *Military Affairs* 43 (April 1979): 97-98.

__________. "The Significance of Codebreaking and Intelligence in Allied Strategy and Tactics." *Cryptologia* 1 (July 1977): 209-22.

Murray, Williamson. "Ultra: Some Thoughts on Its Impact on the Second World War." *Air University Review* 35 (July-August 1984): 52-64.

Randell, Brian. "Colossus: Godfather of the Computer." *New Scientist*, February 10, 1977, pp 346-48.

Rosengarten, Adolph G., Jr. "With Ultra from Omaha Beach to Weimar, Germany—A Personal View." *Military Affairs* 42 (October 1978): 129-30.

Syrett, David. "The Secret War and the Historians." *Armed Forces and Society* (Winter 1983): 293-328.

Woytak, Richard A. "The Origins of the Ultra-Secret in Poland, 1937-1938." *Polish Review* 23 (1978): 79-85.

Newspapers

Washington Post, October 27, 1974.

New York Times, December 8, 1945.

Appendix 1

Memorandum of Activities of Intelligence Section
319th Bomb Group
June 1942 - March 1943
by
Capt. Lewis F. Powell, Jr.
28 August 1943

Editor's Note: Captain Powell was assigned to the Intelligence Section, 319th Bomb Group and he describes in this memo how intelligence officers were trained in the United States during the summer of 1942 and then how they performed in combat in North Africa in late 1942 and 1943. For the original report see USAF Historical Research Collection, GP-319-HI, Roll BO239, Frame 1771 at Maxwell Air Force Base, Alabama.

28 August, 1943

MEMORANDUM OF ACTIVITIES OF INTELLIGENCE SECTION OF 319TH BOMB GROUP FROM JUNE, 1942 TO MARCH, 1943

. . . .

The 319th Bomb Group (B-26's) was activated the last week in June, 1942. Major J. R. Abbot, a Harrisburg graduate, became its S-2 early in July. He had no trained assistance until August 10th, when four more Harrisburg officers were assigned to the Group, each to act as a Squadron S-2.

The T.O. then called for four S-2 officers in each squadron and three in the Group headquarters. Graduates of O.C.S. were assigned to fill the T.O. requirements in each of the squadrons, and one to the group. Thus, we had a total of eighteen intelligence officers, only five of whom had been trained. The section maintained this strength until quite recently, when two officers transferred.

Intelligence training programs were begun separately by each of the squadrons about the middle of August. Although each program was set up on a squadron basis, there was a measure of coordination through the Group. In my Squadron (439th) a dual program was begun which involved (1) training my own section Appendix 1, page 2 (three officers and four men) in intelligence procedure and map work, and (2) training the combat crews in intelligence procedure (interrogations, observations, reporting, etc.) and aircraft recognition.

On August 27th, and before any real progress had been made, our advanced Air Echelon including all intelligence personnel left Harding Field for the staging area. We did not again see any of our combat crews (with the exception of a few crews for a few days only in England) until the latter part of November in North Africa.

Our group began combat operations almost immediately, and without our ever having an opportunity to do any substantial amount of training of combat crews. However, all of our intelligence officers attended the one week school conducted in England by the 8th Bomber Command and also visited RAF operational stations. This was invaluable to the ones who had not attended Harrisburg, and several developed into very competent intelligence officers.

Pursuant to a directive of III Air Force, all intelligence was pooled and conducted on Group (rather than Squadron) basis. This caused the awkward situation of eighteen intelligence officers and an equal number of men having to work together on a job that perhaps a half a dozen could have managed. This was especially true since our Group never had more than twenty-two aircraft at any one time, until after it was withdrawn from combat in late February 1943 and sent back to reform.

The 319th Bomb Group began operations against the enemy on 28 November, and continued "on operations" until the later part of February. It was the first medium group to operate in this theatre. During these operations, our intelligence section peformed the following functions:

1. Maps and target charts: We were the custodian of all maps and targets charts. Appropriate ones were issued the combat crews immediately following briefing, and collected after interrogations. To insure the return of maps and charts, it became necessary to have the navigator of each plane sign for whatever was issued. The S-2 section was responsible for keeping an adequate supply on hand at all times, which involved the frequent taking of inventory and requesting additional maps and charts from Bomber Command. Despite repeated instruction to the contrary, many navigators insisted on plotting their course on the maps in such a way as to disclose our base. This necessitated a constant checking of maps to prevent use of the marked ones.

2. Target Folders: A separate file or folder was kept on each target. Considerable data had been prepared by III Air Force on the more obvious targets before the campaign began. At the outset, this data was all we had for our folders. After operations began there was a constant flow of information on these and other targets, all of which was annotated and appropriately filed. All reports, such as the daily intelligence summaries were checked for additional information suitable for the target folders.

3. Photographs: No cameras were available for the B-26's until the early part of February. Hence, for two months the only photographs handled were those sent down from higher headquarters. During the early weeks, these were "few and far between" and were filed in our target folders. Later the volume of photographs disseminated became so great that separate photographic files had to be opened. It was found that a few of the original target charts required correction as a result of new information from more recent photographs; hence all target charts were carefully checked against photographs as the latter became available. After some cameras were provided for our aircraft, these were put in the custody of the intelligence section. One of our officers took charge of servicing the cameras, issuing them to crews, developing the negatives and doing the printing. Prints were not available before our mission report was submitted. Hence we undertook no first phase interpretation (except for our own information), but sent prints to both Wing and Bomber Command for interpretation.

4. Flak and Situation Maps: We maintained two principal maps, which were kept current by daily posting. One, scale 1/500,000, showed (a) the location of all enemy airfields (with annotations on the side giving latest information as to numbers and types of enemy a/c using such fields), (b) the location of friendly airfields or landing grounds which could be used for emergency landings, (c) the safe landing lines, and (d) the bombing line. The other map, scale 1/200,000, was primarily a flak map. On this we posted all flak positions, both heavy and light, and visually portrayed the effective range of fire of heavy flak batteries. This map, which also showed enemy airfields and the ground situation, was used in planning operations. As a matter of interest, we also maintained a land situation map on the Russian campaign.

5. Briefing: An intelligence officer, ususally the Group S-2, worked with the Group CO and S-3 on planning a mission, and then participated in the briefing. The planning stage involved the intelligence materials above listed, namely maps, target charts, target folders, photographs and the enemy situation map. At the briefing, the S-3 covered all operational matters such as target, route, formation, altitude, bombs and bombing run, fighter escort, evasive tactics, etc. The S-2 then talked briefly on the importance of the target, and enemy defenses (flak, airfields, aircraft, etc.). Colors of the day and other "communications" information were sometimes

given by the S-2 and sometimes by the Group communications officer. Weather was briefed by the Weather officer.

6. Interrogation: This was one of the most important of intelligence functions. We prepared our own interrogation form and revised it later as experience dictated. The names of the crew, target, bomb load, and take off time were typed in the form before the crew returned from the mission, and each crew was assigned in advance to a particular intelligence officer. Usually enough intelligence officers were available to assign only one crew to each officer. Even where this could not be done, we endeavored to interrogate each crew separately. This was not difficult since the crews rarely all came in at the same time. At first, there was some difficulty in obtaining all the necessary information from the crews. This resulted from the inexperience of the interrogators and the anxiety of the crews to get it "over with." Gradually this situation improved, especially as the crews began to see their bombing results and observations appear in reports. (Note: Some intelligence officers, in their anxiety to let the crews go, will tend to hurry through an interrogation. I am convinced that thoroughness is the prime attribute of worthwhile interrogation, and all crew members and interrogators must be instilled with this idea. It has been suggested that crews should be interrogated at their planes immediately upon landing. In my opinion, this would be a great mistake. It is impossible to do a thorough job out-of-doors, with the crew standing about. They must be seated indoors, or inside a tent, and maps and target charts must be available for reference.)

7. Reports: A "flash" report to the Wing and Bomber Command was made by telephone immediately of any important intelligence information (e.g., location of a convoy, or troop concentration). After the last crew was interrogated, we had a conference of the interrogating officers. The Group S-2 designated an officer each day (usually one of the Squadron S-2's) to be responsible for drafting the mission report. This officer and the Group S-2 usually conducted the conference, formulated the telephonic mission report, and later prepared the written mission report. The telephonic report was usually put in within thirty minutes after the interrogation; the written report was usually ready for delivery to the courier within two hours.

8. Intelligence Training: One of the major duties of our S-2 section was the training of combat crews in aircraft recognition, naval recognition, tank recognition, escape and capture security and intelligence procedure. Classes were held at regular hours on days when there were no operational missions.

9. Escape: The S-2 section had custody of, and distributed and collected, escape kits, money pouches and blood chits.

10. Airbase Security: Although perhaps not strictly an intelligence function, our S-2 section collaborated with the Base Group in planning and executing measures for air base security. This included a survey of the need for anti-aircraft guns, slittrenches, an alarm system, blackout precautions, and defenses against attack by paratroops and airborne troops. These matters should not be problems for a tactical unit to solve, because it lacks both the trained personnel and equipment. But where no other provision is made (as was true at our airfield for several weeks), it was necessary to improvise and our S-2 section took the initiative in doing this.

11. Censorship: All mail and packages were censored by S-2 officers.

12. Public Relations: One S-2 officer from each Squadron acted as a public relations officer,

in addition to his other duties. This consisted, chiefly, of writing up stories about news-worthy experiences and achievements of the combat crews.

The foregoing are the principal functions actually performed by the S–2 section of the 319th Bomb Group during this period of its operations in this theatre. However, Intelligence officers in our group had various duties at other times. For six weeks Major Abbot was Commanding Officer of the Advance Air Echelon, and the Squadron S–2's commanded the detachments of their squadrons. During this time we had the usual duties of Group and Squadron administration. In England for several weeks, one of our major duties was training ground personnel in the manual of arms, extended order drill, and on the rifle range.

In conclusion, I should like to emphasize that Intelligence worked very closely with Operations, and I think each section had respect for and confidence in the other. Also the relationship between the S–2 officers and combat crews was excellent.

Prepared by

LEWIS F. POWELL, JR.

Captain, A.C.

Appendix 2

Notes Taken at Bletchley Park
February - March 1944
by
Maj. Lewis F. Powell, Jr.

Editor's Note: In May 1944 Major Powell was the ULTRA Representative at Headquarters, United States Strategic Air Forces (USSTAF) in Europe. Responsible for providing ULTRA intelligence to Gen. Carl A. Spaatz and selected staff officers, Powell spent a few weeks in February and March 1944 in training at Bletchley Park, England, site of the top secret British ULTRA intelligence project. Powell's notes are a valuable and unique historical record, revealing the state of Allied intelligence on the German Air Force prior to the Normandy Invasion of June 6, 1944. Copies of the original notes are located in the USAF Historical Research Center, Maxwell AFB, Alabama. This appendix was prepared in the style of a typographical facsimile. Because Major Powell made these notes during briefings and meetings at Bletchley Park, he often used acronyms, abbreviations, and, of necessity, German Air Force terms. In transcribing these handwritten notes, the editors used brackets [ ] to add clarifying letters, words, or translations from the German to the English.

APPENDICES

Lewis F. Powell, Jr.

Bletchley Notes
Lewis F. Powell, Jr.
Maj. A.C.
0903679
Office of Military Attache
American Embassy
London

This address was a "cover" in the event these notes fell into enemy hands.

S.O. BOOK 135

Code 2872

MISCELLANEOUS NOTES

G R

SUPPLIED
for the
PUBLIC SERVICE

This contains my notes on the German Air Forces (GAF) on basis of working at Bletchley and in preparation for invasion of France. Notes were written in spring of 1944.

Lewis F. Powell

Notes taken at Bletchley, Feb/Mar 1944

GAF Bomber Force (S/L Jim Rose)	List of LRB units: (17) KG1 KG26 KG51 KG76 KG2 KG27 KG53 KG77 KG3 KG30 KG54 KG101 KG4 KG40 KG55 LG1 KG6

Mediterranean

KG30 - JU88s. (As of 25/3/44 - II & III KG30 were on W.F. [Western Front] operating vs. Eng. [England].

KG54 - JU88. Very poor. As of 25/3/44, I & II KG54 were on W.F. operating vs. Eng.

KG76 - JU88. Very poor unit. Two Gruppen in N. Italy in April 44.

KG26 - Only torpedo unit in GAF. I Gruppe still has HE111; others with JU88. Excellent unit. Lately has operated with KG100 (glider bomber unit), who go in first. KG26 (I & II) in S. France. IV Gruppe is on Baltic training. Plans call for [...].

LG1 - Only LG unit. Really a LRB unit. Based in Athens, but since Anzio has been in N.Italy. I & III Gruppen only are operational. II & IV are near Vienna at moment. This may indicate plan to move entire unit to the fields now being developed in that area.

KG100 - Originally experimental. Began bombing Eng. on beam. Later went to S. Russia. Then went to Med. Is now reequipped with [..] DO217 & radio bombs.

I KG100 recently reequipped with HE177s {ops. vs. London).
II KG100 } [...] DO217 glide bomb (HS293) units
III KG100 } Active off Italy. Were in Foggia. Now in S. France

Ed. note: KG was the GAF initialism for *Kampfgeschwader* or bomber unit. The generic term "Geschwader" designated the largest homogenous unit in the GAF with a specified table of organization and equipment. *Geschwader* consisted of three *Gruppen* with an assigned strength of 90 aircraft. In addition, the unit had a single *Stab* or headquarters squadron with four aircraft. Thus, a standard GAF unit, for instance the KG30, would have 94 aircraft assigned. Also, the Roman numerals I, II, and III designated the *Gruppen* in the standard combat unit.

Western Front

KG2 - Reequipping with JU188. Old Line, anti-Eng. LRB. One exception is V Gruppe, which has ME 410's and does intruder work. Ques. whether V KG2 is still on ops? Check & know main bomber bases.

KG6 - This is much like KG2. Old line anti-Eng. LRB.

KG40 (see the report [...] Jun [..]) - Famous anti-shipping unit under Fl F. [*Fliegerführer*] Atlantic, Bordeaux. Now changing from FW200 to HE177. 3 Staffel [Squadrons] of I Gruppe at Trondheim. Also has JU88 fighters report & JU290's. II KG40 now training on HE177s at Bordeaux; III KG40 has FW200s at Bordeaux; training for anti-invasion; 3 KG40 does sea recc [reconnaissance] with FW200's from Trondheim; one Staffel [Squadron] in N. Norway.

I KG66 - A special pathfinder Gruppen, now equipped with same navigational aids used by RAF pathfinders. Use JU188's & have priority on best crews.

I SKG10 - 190 Fighter-bombers used vs Eng. Sometimes operates as fighters.

Special Heavy Fighters:

I ZG1 - Heavy Fighters (JU88's). Patrol B.[Bay] of Biscay. Formerly V KG40. Over-strength - some 65 a/c.

II ZG1 - [...] In Germany. Will probably be assigned to FLK. [Fliegerkorps-numbered air force] II for invasion.

Ed. note: SKG designated the *Schnellkampfgeschwader* or hit-and-run unit.

Ed. note: ZG designated *Zerstoerergeschwader* or attack fighter units.

W. Front (Cont.)

KG30 - (See "Med") By 25 March II & III KG30 on W. Front ops. vs Eng.

KG50 - (See "Med") By 25/3, I & II on ops vs Eng.

Special Units

KG1 - Old Hindenburg unit. Once had great prestige. Now being reequipped — to (I & II) Gruppen with HE 177. III Gruppe is very special — will probably be used on the W. Front. It was originally eq. [equipped] with 75mm guns for anti-tank (panzer-schlacht) — this was a failure. Now III KG1 being reequipped with 50mm gun. Has been on both Med. and Russian Front. I & II KG1 & Stab # went in[to] Italy until Oct 43, when they withdrew to Germany (leaving a/c) to reequip with HE177.

KG51 - Was HE111 unit. Now being reequipped with 410's. Only one Gruppe to be used definitely as LRB; at least one Gruppe will be a TEF [twin-engine fighter] unit. III KG51 reported on ops. vs Eng. with 410s by 20 March.

KG55 - HE111 unit — Possibly going over to ME410.

One of the worst!

KG77 - JU88 LRB, now being converted to JU88 torpedo — thus, showing disposition of GAF to build up anti-shipping forces. May operate like KG26. Off ops very long time. Poor grade. Definitely training on Baltic. Probably will be used vs. Invasion. At least 2 Gruppen moved [to] S. France [in] April.

KG101 & 102 - Now operational. Do special training and experimental work. E.g. IV KG101 which trains formation leaders. (This has an operational Staffel [squadron] which sometimes participates in raids on London.

Ed. note: In the GAF these organizational symbols designated Group 1 & 2 (I & II) and Headquarters Squadron (*Stab*) of Bomber Unit (KG) One (1).

Russian Front (I needn't remember, except KG51 and 55, which probably will come to W. Front)

KG4 - HE111 - Nothing special

KG27 - HE111. For hist of KG27 see p. 36 of "GAF in Maps and Diagrams."

(KG51) - Old HE111. Now going over to ME410 } See preceding page

(KG55) -

KG3 - Only JU88 unit on R. Front; only few of units actually there now.

GAF Training & Training Units

(See S/L Cullingham's Chart)

Bomber training:

1. Boot School (Fliegerersatzabteilung) — (2-3 mos)

2. "A" School (Flugzeugfuehrerschule for pilots or equivalent for other crew members) — (9 mo).
   - About 30 schools
   A-1 — A-126, for single engine training
   (Formerely old A/B schools.)

3. "B" School (50 hrs.)
   Conversion to twin engine a/c [aircraft]. Formerly old "C" Schools. Some 22 of them, numbered B1 - B22.

4. Erganzung Gruppen (Replacement Gruppen) (3/6 Mos).
   After completion of "B" school, crews are posted to the IV Gruppen of the respective Gerschwader for R.T. [Replacement Training].

   (a) During R.T., some personnel are passed to blind flying school on detached basis, and

   (b) Others to "formation leader" school, which actually is IV KG101.

> Strength:
> Total of 17 R.T.U. [Replacement Training Units] Bomber Gruppen. Normal strength - 35/45 a/c [aircraft] per Gruppe, or a total of about 600 a/c [air crews]. About 50/75 crews per Gruppe, with 12/15 instructors. Each gruppe could raise an Einsatz Staffel (operational squadron) of 9 a/c, or a total of 17 x 9 = 153.

Note on IV KG76: From PW [prisoners of war] and other sources we have lots of "gen" [general intelligence] on this R.T. unit. Crews were orig required to have 100 hours with IV Gruppen. In Dec 43 this was raised to 120 hours. This Gruppe was supposed to graduate 25 crews per mo, but actually is turning out about 16. Total time of replacement training supposed to be 4 mos, but actually it has taken much longer to obtain necessary hrs.

Fighter Training:

1. Boot School (2/3 mo)

2. "A" School (9 mo)

3. School Geschwader

(a) The IV Gruppen of JG [*Jadggeschwader*-fighter] units are no longer R.T. [Replacement Training] units. Only LRB [Long Range Bombers] IV Gruppen remain R.T. units. IV Gruppen [of] all others are operational.

(b) School Geschwader (Schulgeschwader) have been organized to provide the equivalent replacement training for pilots.

(c) Total of eight — JG101 — JG108.

300 a/c 4. Three Fighter Pools (Erganzungsgruppen)
Pilots pass from school geschwadern to these pools, which are like replacement centers.

(a) Erg. Jagdgruppe West — provides pilots to W. Front, namely to JG1,2,3,5, and 26, (27 ?).

(b) Erg. Jagdgruppe Med. — provides pilots for Med. and S.E. [Southern Europe], namely JG4, 53, 77.

(c) Erg. Jagdgruppe Ost — pilots for the E. Front, namely JG51, 52, 54.

Note: All three fighter pools now in France, probably as an emergency reserve. Each Erg. Gruppe has four Staffeln [squadrons] of approx. 25 a/c each, i.e. 100 a/c per Gruppe = 300 a/c. Each Gruppe has one operational staffel of 10 a/c.

Confirmed

Traffic Analysis

Function of M I 8 (Y) is to study W/T [wireless telegraphy] networks of the enemy Army & Air Force. Try to reconstruct enemy networks on which the traffic passes.

Q-code is international code.

GAF Training (contd)

Other Combat Types: (SG, ZG, NJG, F, NAG)

Training follows same channels as fighters, eg.:
(1) Boot School (2) "A" School (3) School Geschwadern (SE101, SG151, SG152, ZG101, NJG101, 102, (F)101, NAG101). → (4.) Erg. [Erganzung — Operational Training] Gruppen or pool for particular type. (NJG101 and 102 have no pool)

special case: SG151 was formed from all of Fourth Gruppen of Schlacht [Ground Attack] units and may operate at times — has ops vs Balkan guerrillas.

Numbering of School or Training Units. All begin with "10" plus something — usually "101" — E.g. JG101, ZG101, SG101, NJG101, etc.

Note: See S/L Cullingham's chart

Ed. note: Abbreviations indicate: SG—*Schlachtgeschwader* (ground attack fighter-bombers); ZG—*Zerstoerergeschwader* (attack fighters); NJG—*Nachtjagdgeschwader* (night fighters); NAG *Nahaufklaerungsgeschwader* (short-range reconnaissance).

German Army

Before War

G. divided into 12 Military Districts — each supporting an A.[Army] Corps. Idea was that depots within districts were to supply A. Corps in field with reserves, equipment, supplies, etc. This was a tidy system, but has broken down, and beautiful system is now gone.

Since War

Only long term administrative parts of High Command remain in Berlin — the Supreme Command (OKW) is at a Battle Group Hq. near Koenigsburg (E. Front).

Kesselring is OKW head in Med., as well as CG of the [...] Army Group and Luftflotte 2.

Runstead [Field Marshal Gerd von Rundstedt] is OKW head on W. Front as well as CG of Army.

Policy is to have an OKW head in every area, who is supreme commander.

Army Group (2 or 3 Armies)
↓
Army (2 or 3 Army Corps, usually)
↓
Army Corps (2 or 3 divs, usually)
↓
Divisions (Inf Divis = 17,000 men)
3 Inf Regs

Mil. Districts have been retained with few additional ones. Since no. of Corps have been greatly expanded, each District now has several Corps to service. Military Districts are much like Luftgau [GAF administrative air zones].

Panzer Corps or Armies means only that top staff are "panzer" experts, and actually means that some (or all) of Divs. are Panzer.

Panzer Divs.:	1 Tank Reg 2 Motorized Inf. Regs.	Usual composition of Panz. Div.
Originally	400 tanks	

Now establishment calls for 200 (& units usually have less)

Hqs. and composition of Groups, Armies, and Corps level change frequently. But composition of Div. remains fairly constant. That is the regiments, etc, will remain in same Div. All units of a Div. (below the Regiment) bear the same number, Eg. if the Baking Co is No 115, this doesn't mean the Div. is 115, but it does mean all subordinate units (except Regs.) have same number — 115. This is very helpful in O.B. [Order of Battle] work. Numbering of regiments is more difficult — no system to this.

Numbering System:

Army Groups Herres Gruppen	Letters or Names	Div	Arabic
Army (Armee Gruppe - name, Eg. Narva)	Arabic	Reg	Arabic
		Batt	Roman
Corps	Roman	Co	Arabic

SS Divs. (total of 20)

Only 4 in 1940 — all motorized & very good.

(Ordinary inf. div. use horses for most of their transport).

Quality has been sacrificed as SS Divs. increased.

SS Corps were set up, but none (except one in Estonia) is actually operational. Conflict bet. [between] these and Army Corps under which SS Divs. are actually fighting.

Many of new SS Divs. are actually foreign "nordic," eg. SS Netherlands Div.

Waffen SS are simply the SS in the field.

G.A.F. Divs. (Goering's Private Army)

5 of these are Parachute Divs. Note: 1st Para. Div. now in Italy is quite good.

In add. to these, GAF planned 22 inf. divs. There were actually 22 at one time, but never up to full strength — very low grade. Several have now been merged. Probably only 11 or 12 now left, 4 or 5 which are in the West.

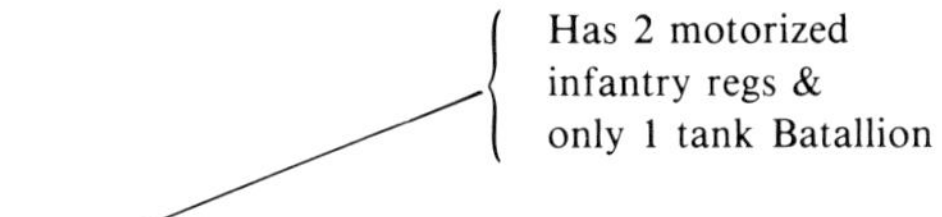

Note: Panzer Grenadiers Divs. are merely motorized. All infantry regiments are now Grenadier Regs.— altho the Div. is still called Infantry.

New Development:

Each Panzer Div. is now being given a new Panzer Abt. [detachment] of Tiger Tanks — 60 to 70 Tigers (very good).

Now only one Regt. of Panzer Div. is actually a Panzer Regt.

Disposition of G.[German] Army (As of approx. 10 March 44)

Total of about 400 Divs. of all kinds.

Russia

200 Divs. (170 of Ger. & rest Satellites)

Army Group A	Crimea 17th Army	3 Romanian Divs., 3 German Divs.)
	S. Russia 6th Army	8 to 10 Divs.
Army Group South (S. Russia to Pripet Marshes)	Nikopal-Uman 1st Panzer Army 4 Panzer Army 2 Panzer Army 8 Army	50 to 60 Divs., including 10 motorized Divs.)
Army Group Center	2 Army 4 Army 9 Army 3 Army	About 60 Divs.

Army Group North (Estonia & Latvia)	16 Army 18 Army	About 20 [Divisions]

Finland

	20th Mountain Army	7 Divs.

Norway

Army Norway		8 Divs.

Italy

Total of some 22 Divs.

Army Group C	10th Army Main Front	8 Divs.
	14th Army Beachhead	8 Divs.
	-------- N. Italy	6 Divs.

France

Is great training center for reforming & refitting Divs. withdrawn from Russian Front.

Total of 54–56 Divs. of varying quality, including 2 SS Panzer Divs. being formed and at least one ord. [ordinary] P. [Panzer] Div.

Army Group D (Rundstedt)	15 Army
	7th Army (Brittany)
Army Group B (Rommel)	1st Army (Bordeaux)
	19th Army (Avignon)

Balkans

23 Divs.

Germany

About 20 Divs. — but actually have no combat capabilities. Are Div. staffs engaged in administration, recruiting, training, etc.

GAF "Y" Service

GAF Y gets lots from our ALO's [Air Liaison Officers]. Here enemy tries to move the target before we can get planes up to bomb it.

Decentralization is employed. Each Luftflotte [Numbered Air Force] and Army Group has its own high as well as low level Y. Each Luftflotte has one or more Signals Regts, & the III Abtl. [Battalion] of each [...] Reg. is the Y Abtl. Eg. III/LN Reg 5 is the Y Abtl of Luftflotte 5. The 14th Co. (14/LN Reg) is the most imp [important]; [it] is Hq Co. of III Abtl; it does analysis and handles the intelligencing of Y material;works very closely with Ic [Intelligence Section] of the Luftflotte.

Fliegerkorps' "Y" Service is integrated with "Y" Service of Luftflotte.

Fliegerfuehrer has a listening station bearing his name.

Ed. note: The mission of the GAF "Y" Service was to locate and intercept enemy signals, principally radio and electronic.

Ed. note: *Fliegerkorps* were subordinate operational commands which operated within the *Luftflotte* command area. Each *Fliegerkorps* was a composite, highly mobile air command which operated under its own control.

Ed. note: *Fliegerführer* were special air commanders who led highly specialized operational flying units.

Luftgau

The original Luftgau have not moved, altho several have expanded and two have merged. In 1939 there were a total of 10. Numbers: I, III, IV, VI, VII, VIII, XI, XII, XIII, & XVII.

These numbers were based on Army Military Districts. This explains why some numbers are missing.

A Luftgau Stab. [Headquarters Staff] z.b.v. [zur besonderen Verwendung — for special purposes] is sent ahead with invasion. Job [is] to organize & set up for a Field Luftgau, ARC, etc.

All airfields in Germany had been given a number — 10/III which indicates it was Luftgau III ... but all this [is] now changed.

All ARCs [airdrome regional commands] and OACs [operational airdrome commands] have Roman numbers from I to XVII. But the field Luftgau have been given numbers from XXV up. Thus, Luftgau XXX may have under it an ARC which may be ARC 7/VIII (meaning that the Stab. [Hq Staffs] originate under [......] Luftgau VIII); and the ARC may have several airfields under it which in turn may be numbered E 5/IV, E 6/VII, etc. Note that the OACS have Roman numbers that relate back to the original Luftgau in [the] Reich and not to either the field Luftgau or ARC under which it may be subordinated. Sometimes fields are designated A 10/IV, B 10/IV, or C 10/IV. The "A" "B" or "C" are not clear. But all important operational airfields have the "E" before the number.

All GAF supply units are numbered in this way. See p. 72 (Appendix D) of Air Pub. 3038 for details of Ground Org [organization] in Tunisia, Eg Supply Co. 1/XII, Field Ammunition Depot 4/VII, etc.

The Roman number will never be higher than XVII because they all relate back to the one of [the] original Luftgau.

Ed. note: The GAF *Luftgau* (air zone or region) was a housekeeping subcommand of a *Luftflotte* designed to relieve the *Luftflotte* commander of routine administrative, supply, maintenance, signal communications, training, and air defense responsibilities. The *Luftflotte* commander concentrated on combat operations and drew support from these fixed regional *Luftgau* commands. Each *Luftgau* region was subdivided into approximately five airdrome regional commands (ARC), which in turn were subdivided into five or more operational airdrome commands (OAC).

Night Fighting Technical Problems
(F/L Robt Prior)

Radar
Radio
Fighter Control

At first Hun night fighters worked only with searchlights — but this didn't succeed, largely because of difficulty of returning planes in cone of lights.

Hun then went over to GCI [Ground Control Intercept] (radar).

Wuertzburg # — very effective up to 40/60 kilometers. (Normally Hun tries to put them about 30 kil. [kilometers] apart.)

Freya — has a much longer range (250 kilometers), but doesn't give height. Measures range and bearing only. Hence is used to pick up a/c first, then switch over to Wuertzburg for accuracy. [...] Modern Freya have add.[additional] eq. [equipment] which makes them more accurate at close range.

Lich[t]enstein — air borne radar, used by night fighter.

Typical Layout of GCI

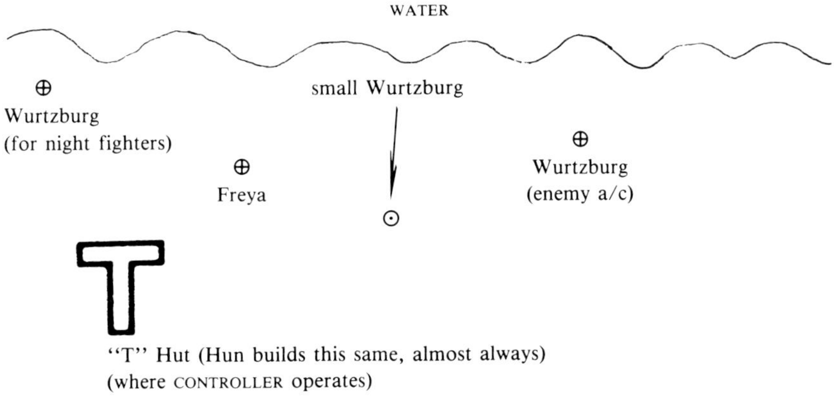

WATER

⊕ Wurtzburg (for night fighters)

small Wurtzburg

⊕ Freya

⊕ Wurtzburg (enemy a/c)

"T" Hut (Hun builds this same, almost always)
(where CONTROLLER operates)

Note: All of the above usually concentrated within radius of a few hundred yards.

Ed. note: Würzburg was the formal name for the GCI equipment used in the GAF by both offensive fighters and the air defense networks.

The inf. [information] from the radar stations was originally passed by telephone to "T" Hut Controller, who maintained plotting board, & who controlled fighters. Now, the information is passed mechanically to "T" Hut. Own planes with IFF [Identification Friend or Foe]. "Fuge" 25a is Hun name for IFF. [..]

Note: All GAF radio & radar eq. [equipment] is referred to as "Fuge" & such & such number. "FuGe" or "FuG".

In 1941 Hun decided searchlight system was a failure, & pumped in a big way for GCI. Searchlight belt was largely replaced by GCI stations. Must be a total of 300 GCI stations in Germany and on W. Front. One belt on west, with main belt back from coast, and special ones around imp.[important] targets. Complete line from Norway to Med. Some 200 men at each station - hence 60,000 men tied up. Each station is part of a group, all of which form a sector. The Sector Controller allots single e/a [engine aircraft] to each of the GCI stations in his sector. Night fighters have meanwhile been sent up & directed to orbit the radio beam of a particular station.

Obsolete: But in 1943 (July 26) window technique made all of the Wuertzburg GCI stations completely obsolete. Tried out in Hamburg raids, throwing GCI into utter confusion. GCI now practically valueless, except (a) for stragglers, and (b) picking up main stream (diversions) of a raid

---

Ed. note: Fuge was the German acronym for *Funkgerät* or radio apparatus.

Ed. note: "Window" was the British Royal Air Force code name for aluminum foil strips dumped in quantity from Allied bombers within range of Wuerzburg installations. Floating downward, they created havoc with German radar images and obscured the Allied bombers from the GAF air defense intercept stations. The Germans used a similar technique with metallic chaff given the code name *Dueppel*.

Night Fighting continued:

Running Commentary: GAF by July 43 was about to give up GCI anyway because of its relative impotence against great masses of bombers. [..] New system was the Running Commentary which was adopted shortly after windows were used. No individual vectors are given. A single controller follows general path of bombers, and actually predicted the target, and sent NJG [Night Fighter Units] to the target where they used their own a/c radar, plus flares & searchlights. Fighters are sent up to orbit some 21 beacons, pending determination of targets. More recent development is directing night fighters into stream of bombers at earliest possible moment - even over channel. Eng.[English] "spoofed" the voice control of Running Commentary; also jammed it. Hun then used music broadcasts, and now is using w/t [wireless telegraph] (very simple Morse Code).

Benito: (used for medium range night fighting) This is an extension of Wurtzburg. Most GCI stations now have Benito (they call it "Y"). The fighter a/c [aircraft commander] has an R/T [radio transmitter] set which sends out a continuous note which is D/F'ed [direction finder] (two stations always necessary to D/F), thus giving positions, and the quality of note gives altitude. Benito can't be jammed; hence controller can follow exact position of his own fighters. Hence can bring about interception whenever course of bombers can be plotted on GCI.

Note: Benito is used very extensively to control day fighters. It determined range & bearing of fighters.

The Day Benito control stations are usually separate from night GCI stations.

"Fuge 200" is ASV (anti-ship radio).

Two giant radar sets used by Hun - one called a Wasserman & the other .... Both are used mainly for a/c reporting & not for control. Usually found on coast — around the entire coast of Europe.

NB. Practically every radar station has a dummy.

All of the night fighter & signal org [organization] of N.W. Germany & low countries under Jagdkorps I.

Seeburg Interception: A system of plotting automatically the results observed by Wurtzburg and Freya by means of a Seeburg Plotting Table.

[..]Block F Work on GAF Defenses (F/L Fred Stacey * formerly in N.A. Miss Joy Parker)

I. Night Defense (F/L Chapman & Miss Joy Parker)
Mrs. Henn

A. Sources of Intelligence (almost altogether ground to air)

(1) R/T [radio traffic] is a principle source altho W/T [wireless telegraph] increasing as a result of jamming:

Control in this manner is referred to as "long range night fighting" (most of GAF night fighters are employed in this manner)

(a) Running Commentary from ground control stations. Each Jagd-division has one high powered, very long range station which gives running commentary for its area. Principally r/t but some w/t on HF [high frequency]. (Note: VHF is clearer but much shorter range). Free lance a/c from all six NJG [Night Fighter Units] are given running comment on raid; are given orders to assemble over certain beacons and then to fly to certain targets or into stream of bombers. Much like day control, except these a/c fly in formation.

Referred to as "short range night fighting."

(b) GCI Stations giving directions to R/T within its own area (HF & VHF). Close vectors on particular a/c. Call signs of both a/c and control stations, as well as frequencies, change daily. Not a very good source.

"medium range night fighting"

(c) Benito control and commentary is good source. Only one B.[Benito] control for each J.D. [Jagddivision-fighter division]. The re-radiation by the a/c repeats the R/T [radio transmission] of the Benito Control. Note: Benito also may work as part of GCI. Med. [medium] range fighting under Benito Control is now done only by 3JD within its area, and NJG [Night Fighter Unit] 1 and 2 are units employed.

* Note: Stacey's section does not propose to be "operational". This is handled directly from source, as well as from field units. His emphasis is long term analysis and reports, especially on tactics. Statistics on no. [number] of sorties is not accurate — purely arbitrary rule of thumb based on 10 a/c (per Staffel- [Squadron]) where one is identified.

(d) Airfield Flying Control — re: take-offs, landings, etc. Good source. Always R/T on HF. Especially valuable in O.B. [Order of Battle] work.

(e) Flying Safety Service — W/T [wireless telegraphy] only. (a/c always identify themselves on universal frequency by "factory markings") Lots of "gen" [general intelligence] on night raids.

Product of "Night" Section (F/L Chapman/ Mrs Henn)

1. BMP - night 2. Distac - night 3. Tac - night	Parallel day publications→

Miss Dorothy Gunn
(low level intercepts
source of intelligence
on GAF)

Reaction to Day Attacks (R/T & W/T)

Products of F/L Stacey's and Miss Gunn's department:

1. BMP [British Military Paper] — daily summary covering R/T and W/T reaction to all of our day missions, with general comments & maps on main raids.

2. DISTAC ("Distilled Tactics") — About 4 days after each maj raid. Play by play account of R/T set up according to pro forma.

3. TAC [Tactics] — About once a month (1 - 3 already out). Summary of tactics, etc, based on last 8 or 10 major raids.

4. Special reports — Occasionally.

Note: Stacey's section not operational. See note on preceeding page.

Miscl [Miscellaneous] notes on talk with Miss Gunn (22/3/44)

1. General. Until recently reaction to raids was obtained in great detail from R/T (chiefly ground to air by controller). This source has largely dried up in last month or so, except for few controls near coast and the controls for ZG [attack fighter] units (ZG26 & ZG76) which still use HF rather than VHF.

2. Jafue 3 (Holland/Ruhr area). Controller for this area used to be excellent source, but now has almost completely disappeared. Presumably units formerly in Jafue 3 have moved further east.

Ed. note: *Jafue*, an acronym for *Jagdfuehrer*, was the term applied to the commander of a specialized fighter unit. Later in the war it was the name given to a specialized fighter command organized for a specific task, such as the air defense of geographical area. By 1944, Jafue were being designated with either numbers - *Jafue* 7, or proper names - *Jafue* Holland.

3. Jafue 4 and 5 (France). These can still be heard, but since only few units are based here, the information is not great. Tactics: Units here are usually moved up into W. Germany for major raids. Really serve as a reserve for other areas. Will take off from their dispersed a/f's [air fields] at early hour (sometimes before our bombers cross coast) and move to some central a/f. They use 40.9KC which is a universal frequency; this facilitates the transfer of units from control by their home Jafue to another control.

4. Jafue 1 (Berlin and central Ger) Twin engine rocket fighters (ZG26) use HF and hence can be heard anywhere. Until recently ZG26 was based just E. [East] of Hanover in 2 J.D. [Jagddivision - fighter division], but evidence now indicates they have moved to a/f west of Hanover, and are now being controlled by 1 J.D. (Jafue 1). Excellent reception of heavy R/T [radio transmitted] traffic. (Presumably we get dope on ZG76 in JG7 in same way.)

5 W/T [Wireless Telegraphy]- Since SEF [single-engine fighters] didn't use W/T, this is not much of a source. Some inf. is however obtained from point to point traffic of ground units and from TEF [twin-engine fighters].

6. Shadower a/c; navigator a/c, etc. Miss Gunn admits ideas about these are still in a state of flux. It seems likely that GAF has some new devices for leading or directing [...] fighters to bombers which are believed related to shadows and navigators. However [there is] very little traffic from these special a/c.

7. Controllers. One per Jafue usually, though sometimes several voices at one hut controlling different groups.

8. D/F [Direction Finder]. Location of enemy fighters often checked by D/F fix on R/T or W/T traffic.

9. Beacons and Assembly Points. [....] Day fighters often use assembly points somewhat like night fighters. Radio beacons used when visibility poor.

Factory Markings (F.M. is abbreviation)

(a) About yr ago system of 4 letter (AFGP) markings begun at factories. Supposed to supercede old open markings.

(b) Each factory assigned a "trigram" of letters which it uses up by adding one letter to identify particular a/c.

(c) Trigram changed each time alphabet (excluding J) is run through ... ie, every 25 a/c. Thus if trigram for factory X is AFG, the first a/c mfg [manufactured] would be AFGA, AFGB, etc, etc; and then a new trigram would be assigned.

(d) These markings used in Safety Service in marking landings, etc. Gives types of a/c wherever we break the system, and helps identify unit.

Call Signs * (Night Fighters Only)

New system adopted with Running Commentary. Each NJG [night-fighter unit] now has a call sign (bird names, e.g. Eagle) which doesn't change. Each a/c also has a number, 1-10 reserved for the Stabb [Headquarters Flight], 11 to 20 for first Staffel [Squadron], 21 to 30 for 2d Staffel, etc. Eg. "Eagle 15" a/c identify themselves by R/T [radio transmission] in landings, etc.

* Referred to as Tactical Call Signs ("T.C.")

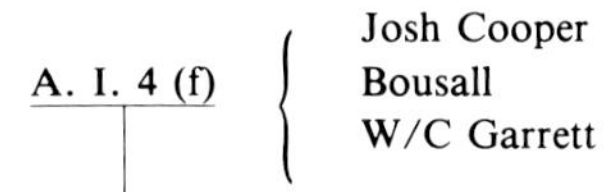

Broad gen [general] division between GAF Offensive activities and Defensive activities:

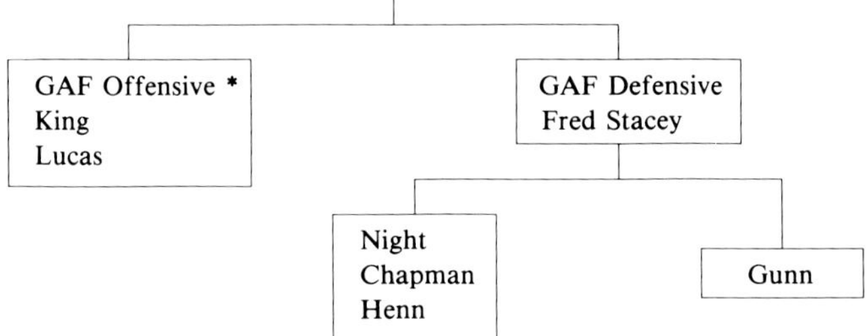

* Notes on "GAF Offensive" work of A.I.4(f):

1. Material largely from W/T { air to ground / ground to air } (Remember puzzle books)

2. Operational Watch (Miss ......) puts out:
   (a) Daily OPD on "GAF Recce and Off. OPs"
   (b) SALU [Special Air Liaison Unit] - weekly, statistical.

Note: Rem [remember] dope which Miss ... (Op Watch) showed me over the water.

Open Unit Markings

System of a/c markings once widely used, but now being abandoned for Factory Markings (see preceding page). Was as follows for Bombers:*

1. System consisted of four symbols (letters or letters and numbers), Eg. FI & ML.

2. First two symbols indicated unit, Eg. FI was for KG76.

3. The third indicated individual a/c.

4. The last symbol indicated Staffel [Squadron] (& of course, Gruppen).

	Code for last symbol:		
Symbols	HKL	MNP	RST
Staffel Nos.	123	456	789

Stabs. A= Gerschwader Stabb; B,C, & D = Gruppen Stabbs. [Hq Flights]

Example: FI & ML = a/c M of 3 KG76.

Some which have been identified:

C9 = NJG5
F8 = KG40
M8 = ZG76
S1 = SG3
IH = KG26
3E = KG6

* I think this system applies to all twin engine a/c such as ZG's, NJG's, F units, etc. Also it seems to apply to Schlacht [ground-attack] units — everything except SEF [single-engine fighters].

Western Front - Day Fighters
(F/L Peter Calvocoressi) (22/3/44)

Command Organization The Jagdkorps are equivalent of Fighter Commands, with Jagdivision and Jafue as subordinate commands. The JD are most imp. operational Hq, both for night and day, altho day defense is delegated to Jafues.

(Luft Reich)

Jadgkorps I (N. Ger., Holland, Denmark, and N. Belg.)

1JD - (Doeberitz/Berlin), NW Ger., esp. approaches to Berlin.
Jafue 1

2JD - (Stade - NW Ger and Denmark)
Jafue 2

3JD - (Denmark-Holland, N. Belg., Ruhr)
Jafue 3

Jagdkorps II (Luft 3) Hq

France
JD4 - (Metz, France; Belg. border to line S.E. from Abbeyville)

Jafue 4

Note: JD4 extends S.E. from as far as Alsace-Lorraine. No well defined "back door" to these JDs.

JD5 - (Hq ....France: Abbeyville to Brittany)
Jafue 5

Jafue Brittany - apparently in area of JD5, but probably subordinated directly to JK II [*Jagdkorps* II]. Controls a few day fighters, but rarely operates them.

JD6 - Never actually identified, but should be in S. France eventually.

Jafue S. France - has been reported. Has no operational a/c at this time. Fighters in S. France which protect area actually under Fl. Div. 2 [*Flieger* Division].

Jadgkorps III (Luft Reich - S. and E. Germany)

JD7 - S. Germany, Boundaries in state of flux.

JD8 - Not yet reported, altho its formation may be expected.

Jafue Ostmark (Vienna) does exist, and acts directly under J.K. III [*Jagdkorps* III]. Has A.O. [Air Operations] for day fighters & A.O. for night fighters.

JD9 - Not yet known to exist, but logical to expect formation.

Jafue Upper Silesia does exist in Poland and may become JD9 under either JK I [*Jadgkorps* I] or JK III [*Jadgkorps* III].

Jafue E. Prussia may became JD10. Neither of these eastern Jafues are now believed operational.

Importance of Commands: Until recently Jafues 2 & 3 (JD 2 & 3) were most important for day ops. Strong tendency for Jafue 1 to supercede in imp [importance].

Note on Diversions: France no longer defended except when [...] no attack in Ger. Hence diversion to France never works. Diversion vs. Germany is good when France is target.

SEF [Single-Engine Fighters] on Western Front
(F/L Peter Calvocoressi - 23/3/44)

Six Principal Geschwader: Only six SEF Geschwader have the responsibility for day defense on the W. Front. Most of these have full strength (4 Gruppen) disposed on this front. Odd Gruppen of two or three Geschwader are on other fronts, but their absence is compensated for by two or three odd Gruppen on W. Front.

The six principal JG's [*Jagdgeschwader* - Fighter Units], with their approximate disposition and Gruppen strength are:

JG1	JG2	JG3	JG11	JG26	JG27	
Holland, Belg,Ruhr	France	S.W.Ger, Ruhr	N.W.Ger, Den.	S.E.S.H. from Seine to Elbe	S.Germany	
(3JD)	(4&5JD)	(1JD)	(2JD)		(7JD)	
IJG1	*	IJG3	IJG11	IJG26	IJG27	
IIJG1	IIJG2	IIJG3	IIJG11	IIJG26	IIJG27	
IIIJG1	IIIJG2	IIIJG3**	IIIJG11	IIIJG26	IIIJG27	moved from Balkans 1/3/44
	IVJG2	IVJG3	IVJG11	IVJG26	IVJG27	

In addition:

IIIJG54 - odd Gruppe in N.W.Germany (2JD) brought back from Russ.
IIJG53 - odd Gruppe at Vienna Seyring

IJG300, I,II,IIIJG301, IIJG302 } SE [single engine] night fighters, which may be used in day

IVJG5 - Norway for convoy escort (Not used vs. raids on Germany)
ISKG10 - FW190 fighter bombers (NW France), sometimes used

* IJG2 sent to Italy to support attack on Anzio beachhead.
** IIIJG3 now believed to be in S. Ger. under 7JD

Note: Sturmstaffel formerly at Langenhagen, now believed to be at Salzwedel.

Notes on SEF Geschwader (W. Front)
(Peter)

JG1 - Principal unit of Jafue 3. Was in Holland for a long time, but now probably [...] W. Germany . II JG1 [*Jagdgeschwader*-Fighter Unit, Second Group] is now being fitted with mortars, & being trained for Jabo [*Jadgbomber*-fighter-bomber] operations.

JG2 - France, all the way from Brest to Belgium under Jafue 5 and 4, except I JG2 (Italy).

JG3 (Udet) - Formerly concentrated in Ruhr, except for III JG3 which is at Leipheim (near Frankfurt). Covers SW Germany. Other Gruppen now moving east, and II and IV definitely under Jafue 1.

JG11 - Formed from JG1; lies to E. of JG1 under Jafue 2. 10th and 11th Staffel [Squadrons] in Denmark doing ship escort work.

JG26 - Gruppen widely dispersed from Seine to Elbe. Has no definite area like JG1 and 11. We don't get much "gen" [general intelligence] on it. This Gesch. [*Geschwader*] was orig. on [...] Russ. Front.

JG27 - Dispersed in S. Ger. under Jafue 7. Operates vs both 8th and 15th A.F.

	GAF Defensive Tactics - W. Front	Stacey
Re-read →	(Excellent report [.............]	Guinn, 1/2/44.
	(Period covered by report 22/12/44-21/1/44)	

Because of: (a) our mass attacking force, (b) deeper penetrations, (c) relays of fighter escorts, (d) bad weather attacks, and (e) jamming of radar, etc, the GAF has had in recent months to evolve new methods of tactics and fighter control.

Basic answer of GAF seems to be that suitably equipped a/c would have advantage over ground controls in keeping in touch with details of an operation, provided ground controls gave them a general idea of course of events.

Old System: In days of summer offensive (1943) Jafue Holland/Ruhr controlled fighters on 4 or 5 VHF channels. Formation leaders were Benito controlled, & were vectored (by several orders from control) to within 5 kilom. [kilometers] of our formations. Intercepted R/T gave good picture of where every a/c came from, their route, point of interception, etc. Beginning in Oct system changed. Control became more interested in establishing contact with friendly SEF & very few other details were intercepted. Apparently enemy has abandoned old type control; now use special a/c:

Navigator a/c ("Lotse"). Probably work about as follows:
(1) The navigator a/c (either SE or TE) becomes airborne,
(2) He then collects the fighters round him. This may happen over the field,

or at an ''interception'' or an ''assembly'' point. May use D/F [direction finder] nodes for his ''rats'' to home on, but exact mechanics unknown;

(3) Once contact made bet. [between] navigator and his fighters, R/T dries up;

(4) Throughout whole process, navigator has received from control his own position (which control gets from Benito or ordinary D/F notes) and the position of our own raiders;

(5) When contact is made with our raiders, navigator has been known to issue detailed orders for attack.

Note: Above procedure is thought to be used for SEF in Holland/Ruhr areas and TEF in NW and SW Ger. Query what we [....] is used by SEF in NW Ger. In France, control of fighters have remained sub [substantially] unchanged.

Shadowers & Observers: Exact function of these special a/c (which may be the same) are not known. Presumably they have specialized duties - e.g. reporting the composition of our formations, height, course, effectiveness of AA fire, etc. These special a/c use the call sign DACKEL on their HF traffic over NW Germany. Reports of ''Dackel'' a/c not yet intercepted - channel unknown.

Day Assembly Points. These must not be confused with "Interception Areas," which are areas in which SEF of Jafue 3 (Holland/Ruhr) assemble; these interception areas are not fixed points but are chosen so as to lie on the expected route of bombers.

(1) When route approaches over Holland, enemy tends to use following fixed assembly points:

Wunstorf } (used if deep penetration is expected)
Diepholz }
Bielefeld.

(2) When route is north of Frisian Islands following:

Hoya
Diepholz

(3) When route crosses Danish coast, enemy tends to use same points as in (2).

GAF Hqs, Parks & Depots in the West

For detailed study of these, with maps, etc, see publication under above caption by W/C Russel of AM (A. 1. 3 (E)) dated 3 Jan 44, as since supplemented. (Russel is AM [Air Ministry] expert on GAF ground org and supply.)

German Aircraft Production
(AM estimates from "Fighting Value of GAF," 1/3/44)

Type	Dec 43	Jan 44
LR [Long Range] Bombers	315	315
Dive B [Bombers] and G [Ground] attack	85	65
SEF [Single-Engine Fighters]	600	650
TEF [Twin-Engine Fighters]	255	190
* Totals	1255	1220

Estimate Effect of Attacks on A/C Plants in February: *

	350	[revised figure]
SEF output reduced by 60% to appx.	260	per mo.
	100	[revised figure]
TEF " " " 75% " "	85	" "
LRB " " " 30% " "	225	" "
Miscl	a/c 125	
Revised Total	800	

Four factories: Gothaer at Gotha, M.I.A.G. at Brunswick, Messerschmitt at Regensburg, and Erla at Leipzig should be out of series production for some months; others severely curtailed. But increases can be expected at Wiener Neustadt & from N. Eastern areas.

Note: For detailed list & analysis of plants and damage done see AM's "Fighting Value of GAF" for 1/3/44, p 6, etc. Also see [..] annex thereto for detailed list of GAF repair facilities.

* See next page for more recent estimate.

* In addition some 25 coastal types (Arado 196 & BV 138 & 222) and 120 transport a/c (70 JU52, 5 DO24, & 45 Fi/156) are produced monthly.

German Aircraft Production (cont)

Sunsit No. 511 (26/4/44) contains revised estimates of effects of Feb. attacks. Reasons for revision are:

(1) Rate of Production prior to Feb attacks was higher than supposed:

SEF [Single-Engine Fighters]	725	Actual prod. for Feb. est. to be 1225 a/c
TEF [Twin-Engine Fighters]	225	
LRB [Long-Range Bombers]	330	
Miscl [Miscellaneous]	125	
	1405	

(2) PR [Production Records] of factory a/fs [airfields] showed a "substantially" greater no. of a/c available for salvage than at first estimated. Probably 140 SEF & 210 twin engine a/c so available on factory fields attacked.

(3) Germans using satellite sources of production, especially Hungarian prod. of ME210s.

Revised Estimates of Production for March, exclusive of 350 salvaged a/c above, follows:

SEF	350
TED	100
LRB	225
Miscl	125
	800

"Pipeline" Reserves: Estimated to have been as follows on 19 Feb 44:

SEF	300
TEF	175
LRB, Miscl	450
	925 a/c

This reserve believed reduced by 1 March by some 43.

250 to 675 a/c.

Repair a/c: By pressure on repair org & at the expense of training units, est. that some 325 a/c (including 100 SEF) will be made available during March for first line units from repair depots. This compares with 275 in Feb.

First Line I.E. [Initial Estimate] Strength on 1 March:
5330 a/c. This compares with 5400 on 1 Feb.

"Input" into first line units during March: (Estimated)

New production	800
From repairs	325
From salvage	300
From reserves	175
	1600

Gross Wastage:

Dec	1390
Jan	1785
Feb	1805

Thus, if March wastage equals average for Jan/Feb (1800 a/c), GAF first-line units will suffer deficit of some 200 a/c. Thus by 1 April, I.E. [Initial Estimate] strength should still be [..] above 5000 - although this strength will be unsupported by adequate prod. [production] or reserves.

Substantial Monthly Deficit after 1 April: Assuming no recuperation of production, prospects appear as follows:

New Production	800	a/c
Repair	325	
Salvage	50	
Reserve	000	*
Estimated total input →	1175	
〃 April deficit	625	a/c

* Estimated that April reserves will be down to "irreducible minimum of 500 a/c."

Production minimum: Present fighter production mainly centered in two complexes, FW190 plants in the East & Wiener Neustadt plants in Austria (250 a/c). Destruction of them would reduce total monthly prod. to 550 a/c - which is thought to be irreducible minimum.

Wastage may be reduced by GAF policy of conservation - thus reducing deficit.

Production, Repair, & Wastage
S/L Horne A. I. 3 (b) [......]

T/E [Twin Engine] Production:

Very well taped. Full details from F.M. [factory markings], W.N. [wing numbers], P.W.[prisoners of war], and Crash Intelligence. Some gen. [general intelligence] from PRU [photo reconnaissance units] - esp. of factory a/fs [air fields].

Rem. [remember] think daily and weekly reports from station "X" [Bletchley Park].

Almost every TE [twin engine] a/c is heard over W/T [wireless telegraphy] - usually at or very shortly after it leaves the factory.

HE 177 - some 50/55 per mo from 2 factories
JU 188 - only about 20 per mo since successful attacks on plants in Jan & Feb. Only a total of about 100 altogether.
DO 217 - out of prod.

S/E [Single Engine] Production:

Much more dif. to follow. But enough is obtained to give a rough idea. Wonderful gen. [general intelligence] from crash int. [intelligence] in Africa, Sicily, Italy. Now best source is W.S. [Wastage Statistics].

No really firm estimates possible. Rely in large part on expert analysis of photos & plans of factories (also some agents). Analysis of capacity, extent of damage, etc.

Repair:

Largely guesswork I think. Some clues, however, — such as ratio of new a/c to repaired a/c with certain units.

Also, our own experience.

Gross Wastage:

1. Estimate total no of sorties:
   a. On W. Front
      1) LRB, SEF, etc [Long-Range Bombers, Single-Engine Fighters]
      2) which are operational and which routine
      3) which involved contact with enemy.

   b. Same on each of other fronts.

   c. Sortie estimates kept up daily, based on consid. [consideration] of all evidence - e.g. our own missions, weather, reported reactions, known GAF strength in area affected, etc.

2. Assignment of loss ratio
   a. Different ratio for dif.[different] types of a/c, dif. fronts, dif type of ops, etc. Eg. - ratio of LRB on W.F. [Western Front] - is 1 to 10; on R.F. [Russian Front] - 1 to 30.

   b. Fighter ratio varies widely depending on combat. 1 to 10 if combat; 1 to 75 if no combat.

   c. Our own experience considered.

   d. Loss ratios reviewed & changed often.

New Equipment in GAF
(See AM [Air Ministry] Appreciation "Fighting Value of GAF" 1/3/44)

Jet Propelled A/C:

ME 262 - TE [Twin Engine], low wing monoplane. May be operational in small numbers during the next six months. Max speed reported to be 527 mph at 13,000′ (See paper on this at ACAS (I), 15 June (Ultra))

HE 280 - Parallel development to ME 262 & probably has about same capabilities.

ME 163 - Little known. Sometimes called the "Peenemünde 30" because it was photographed at Peenemünde. Shaped like a moth, with no tail unit. ?? Short range.

Arado 234 - Little known.

Heavy Bombers:

HE 274 - High altitude (36,000′), pressure cabin, heavily armed with turrets, speed 340 & 22,000 pound bomb load. First prototype has been delivered for testing.

JU 390 - Is a 6 engine 290 - still in experimental stage.

Ed. note: ACAS (I) was the British Royal Air Force designation for Assistant Chief of Air Staff (Intelligence).

Benito Running Commentary Control
(As of 27/11/43)

Benito is now used extensively (day & night) to enable ground controllers to identify & plot own (GAF) fighters. System can't be used to plot Allied a/c as it involves sending a radio signal to an a/c equipped with a device that re-radiates the signal to ground control. It is used at night to vector NJGs [Night Fighter Units] into stream of bombers.

Only one a/c can be plotted at any one time by a Benito reradiation. In order to adapt this to larger numbers, day fighters form on the a/c which is plotted and are led by such a/c to the Allied bombers.

There is evidence that as an a/c begins to re-radiate it also transmits a D/F [Direction Finder] note - enabling control to obtain a bearing as well as distance.

Indications are that NJG1 [Night Fighter Unit/ 1] (or presumably NJG2) based at Gilze, Venlo, St Trond, and possibly Deelen a/f [air fields] are Benito equipped.

Words & Phrases

"Zielflug" - used to describe technique of homing on D/F [Direction Finder] note from "navigator" a/c.

"Erganzung Gruppen" - Training units. E.g. all of IV Gruppen of LRB [Long Range Bombers] are reserve training units

"FR" - Radio controlled bombs

"Coy" - Company

"Schwarme" - 5 a/c
"Ketten" - 3 a/c
"Rotten" - 2 a/c

Ed. note: The smallest GAF operational fighter unit was the *Rotte* or cell of two fighters. Two *Rotten* made up a *Schwärme* or flight, with three *Schwärme* constituting a *Staffel* or squadron. The *Ketten* consisted of three fighters

Imp. Words, Phrases, & Abbreviations

"LN" - Air Signals (Luftnachrichten) - LN usually used to refer to Signal Units. e.g. LN Regt 3 (belongs to Luftflotte 3), LN Reg 31 (belongs to Fliegerkorps I), LN Comp. KG 54 (Signals Co with KG 54), etc.

"LGN" - Luftgau Signals Regiments. E.g. LGN [..] 17 is Sig. [Signal] Reg [Regiment] of Luftgau XVII.

"LN Stelle" - Signals Station. Each OAC (Operational Airfield Command) has its own LN Stelle manned by a platoon, & taking the same Luftgau number; e.g. LN Stelle 73/III would belong to OAC E 73/III.

"J.L.O." - Jaegerleitoffizer (Fighter Control Officer) with GAF GCI stations.

"FuGe" (FuG) - Prefix for designation of all GAF radio and radar equipment (e.g. "FuG200" is "Hohentwiel" used for spotting ships like ASV; "FuGe202" is Lichtenstein or night fighter radar like A1; "FuG25A" is "Erstling" or German IFF; "FuGe62" is Wuerzbus [sic] and FuGe65 is Wuerzburg Giant; "FuGe80" is Freya. Fu16 is VHF radio set.

GAF radio radar eq. see notes on GAF night fighters

FBK - Designation of ground echelons of geschwadern.

Knickerbein

(END OF BLETCHLEY NOTES)

Ed. note: FBK meant *Flughafenbereichkommandanteur* or Airfield Regional Commander.

Ed. note: *Knickebein* referred to a GAF system of intersecting unidirectional radio beams used in *Luftwaffe* bombing operations.

Appendix 3

Excerpt: Recommendations Section from Report on Visit to Operational Air Commands in Mediterranean Theater (4 April - 10 May 1944) by Maj. Lewis F. Powell, Jr. 14 May 1944

Editor's Note: When Major Powell completed his ULTRA training at Bletchley Park, England, in March 1944, he was sent to the Mediterranean Theater for a month to see firsthand how ULTRA intelligence was being used by operational air commands. His trip report recounted his schedule, people and air commands visited, and the intelligence procedures he observed. Concluding with six recommendations, Powell's report illustrates his grasp of the important relationship between Special Branch and the Military Intelligence Service in receiving and disseminating ULTRA. For the entire report see SHR-031, "Trip Reports Concerning Use of ULTRA in the Mediterranean Theater," RG 457, National Archives.

14 May 1944

Subject: Report on Visit to Operational Air Commands in Mediterranean Theater (4 April - 10 May 1944)

To: Lt. Col. Samuel McKee, MID, WD, Station London

1. The subject report is attached hereto in quadruplicate.

Lewis F. Powell, Jr.
Major, Air Corps

X. RECOMMENDATIONS. The following recommendations as to Special Intelligence in the Air Forces and the personnel engaged in handling it are based primarily on observations made on this trip. It is appreciated that Special Branch is not in a position at this time to act on certain of these recommendations, but it is believed that they merit consideration in organizing and planning for future operations, especially in the Pacific.

a. Special Branch Should Be Made a Joint Ground-Air Force Agency.

Discussion: The idea of controlling and coordinating Special Intelligence by a single centralized agency at the War Department level is sound. Special Branch admirably meets the need for such an agency so far as the Ground Forces are concerned, but as a section of G-2, M.I.S., it is too essentially a Ground Forces organization to be fully effective with the Air Forces. It is appreciated, of course, that the Air Forces are a part of the Army and that Special Branch is an Army organization with jurisdiction over both Ground and Air Forces. However, the Air Forces have already obtained a large measure of practical autonomy, and in actual fact the attitude of Air Forces personnel, especially in the field, is considerably more independent than the de jure status might justify. Moreover, on the subject of Special Intelligence the Air Forces in England and the Mediterranean are able to say, with much truth, that they have made their own arrangements independently of Washington and the Ground Forces. Finally, it must be recognized that any significant problem of air intelligence, including the disposition of air intelligence officers, should normally be handled by experienced Air Force officers. In view of the foregoing considerations, it is believed that the effectiveness of Special Branch in its relationship with the Air Forces would be improved materially if it were established as a truly joint Ground-Air Forces agency.

b. Each Operational Air Command Where Special Intelligence Is Required Should Have an American Officer Whose Primary Duty is Special Intelligence.

Discussion: This recommendation involves two main points:

(1) The handling of Special Intelligence should be the primary duty of at least one carefully selected and highly qualified officer at each command. (This officer will be referred to hereafter as the "Special Intelligence Officer"). He should, of course, be available for other intelligence duties, but these always should be secondary to his responsibility for all Special Intelligence matters. In certain commands, the Assistant Chief of Staff, A-2, may wish to be his own Special Intelligence Officer. While this may prove satisfactory in certain of the smaller commands (such as Twelfth Tactical Air Command), the senior A-2 on the

staff is usually too preoccupied with other urgent affairs to give Special Intelligence the detailed and primary attention which it requires.

(2) Since the creation of NAAF in February 1943, there have been several joint American-British Air Commands. (Examples: NAAF, Tactical Air Force (Caserta), MACAF, AEAF). The senior commanders who require Ultra service customarily include both American and British officers. In some instances in the past, as was natural under circumstances then existing, there was no American Special Intelligence Officer. Now that qualified American officers are available, it is felt that each such Joint Command should have at least one American specialist in Ultra. The present situation at NAAF in this respect is discussed above under general comment (f.1.).

c. The Special Intelligence Officers at the Various Commands Should as a General Rule Be Members of Special Branch.

Discussion: It is assumed, in view of General Marshall's recent letter, that in ETOUSA, at least, the policy has been established of having members of Special Branch attached to the various operational commands as the officers primarily responsible for Ultra intelligence. It is not clear whether this policy will be applied to NATOUSA as well, or whether intelligence officers already indoctrinated but not members of Special Branch will be transferred to it. Circumstances within the commands vary to such an extent that it would probably be unwise to attempt to apply any rule universally. However, it is strongly believed that it would be desirable for the Special Intelligence Officer at every operational air command (as defined above under b.) to be a member of Special Branch. Accordingly, it is felt that the policy enunciated in General Marshall's letter should be applied to other theaters and to existing Special Intelligence Officers wherever practicable. The full success of such policy would certainly be implemented if Special Branch is meanwhile given a joint Ground-Air Forces status, as contrasted with its present position as a section of G-2.

d. Close Liaison Should Be Maintained By Special Branch and Bletchley Park with the Commands in the Field.

Discussion: A close relationship between those who produce and process the material at the source and those who use it in the field is highly desirable. The RAF has recognized the necessity for this and officers from Air Ministry and Bletchley Park have made frequent visits to field recipients. Also, there has been some actual interchange of RAF personnel. It is recommended that Special Branch follow this precedent, and particularly that officers who are familiar with the work at Bletchley Park be sent periodically to visit the various operational commands. It is equally important, although perhaps more difficult to arrange, for Special Intelligence recipients to visit Bletchley Park. Even those who have had training there would benefit by brief refresher visits.

e. The Role of American Army in the Special Intelligence Field Should Be Brought to the Attention of the Proper Officers in the Operational Commands.

Discussion: It was found that comparatively few officers at the commands visited had any real appreciation of the part now being played by the American Army in this field. The impression still prevails that Special Intelligence is purely a British product in the most exclusive sense. It is not generally known, even by senior air commanders, that American personnel assist the British at Bletchley Park in the various steps involved in producing and processing Special Intelligence. Nor is it known that the American Army has assumed the major responsibility for developing this intelligence for the Pacific theater. In short, very little is known by Air Forces officers of the work of Special Branch and the Signal Corps, or of the extent to which cooperation now exists between the British and American Forces in this entire field. It is believed that officers engaged in handling Special Intelligence in the field, and especially the commanders, should be familiarized with the scope and general aspects of this cooperation.* One means of accomplishing this is the establishment of closer liaison between Special Branch and the field as suggested in d. above. The visit of Colonel McKee to the Mediterranean in February, which did much to inform the commands on this subject, is an example of the type of liaison needed.

f. In the Training of Special Intelligence Officers Greater Emphasis Should Be Placed on the Development of a Sound Knowledge of All Sources of Air Intelligence.

Discussion: The importance of other sources of intelligence must never be minimized. The most valuable Special Intelligence officer is one who also thoroughly understands and appreciates the value of intelligence derived from ordinary radio intercept, prisoners of war, "crash" or technical intelligence, photographic reconnaissance, reports and observations of combat crews, and reports of agents. While the importance of those other sources will usually be conceded, there seems to be a tendency in practice to rely too heavily upon Ultra to the exclusion of all else. Officers trained by Special Branch must avoid this tendency, and this can best be accomplished by greater emphasis during the training period on what may be described as general combat intelligence. This is particularly necessary for officers who may not have had prior experience with Air Force intelligence. The course of lectures at Bletchley Park is fairly comprehensive and lays a good general background. Perhaps a week instead of two or three days should be spent in Block "F". If possible, there should be a visit to Kingsdown for observation of the tactical employment of "Y". The real emphasis on other sources should come during the visit to operational commands, where special study should be made of the technique of correlating, evaluating and using all intelligence. It is specifically recommended (1) that considerable time be spent with officers at the commands who work primarily on other sources; (2) that the photographic reconnaissance wing (MAPRW) be visited; (3) that one or more of the tactical radio intercept stations (276 Wing) be visited; and (4) that several days be spent with tactical air units actually engaged in combat operations.

---

* Of course, care must be exercised not to minimize the magnificent efforts of the British, both past and present, or to exaggerate our present role.

Lewis F. Powell, Jr.
Major, Air Corps

Appendix 4

Memorandum on the Operational Intelligence Section of USSTAF by Maj. Lewis F. Powell, Jr. 1 June 1944

Editor's Note: Major Powell arrived at Headquarters, USSTAF located at Bushey Park, England, in May 1944. He was the only ULTRA Representative from the Military Intelligence Service at the headquarters, and it was his responsiblity to receive, safeguard, and brief ULTRA personally to the Commanding General, Carl A. Spaatz. Powell worked in the Operational Intelligence Section, commanded by Lt. Col. Julian B. Allen. This section was part of the Office of the Director of Intelligence, USSTAF, commanded by Brigadier General George C. McDonald. This memorandum, written just prior to the Normandy Invasion, summarizes Powell's initial view of the intelligence operation. Three months later he assumed command of the section.

HEADQUARTERS
UNITED STATES STRATEGIC AIR FORCES IN EUROPE
Office of the Director of Intelligence

AAF Sta. 586,
APO 633, U.S. Army
1 June, 1944

MEMORANDUM:

TO : Lt. Col. Julian B. Allen
OPERATIONAL INTELLIGENCE SECTION OF USSTAF

1. The functional organization of the Operational Intelligence Section, summarized very generally, appears now to be as follows:

a. German Air Force Intelligence.

(1) Personnel: Lt. Col. Haines, Capt. Reed and Capt. Dow.

(2) Functions: All Intelligence on the German Air Force, including Order of Battle, dispositions, strength, capabilities, production and wastage. Col. Haines, working primarily at Air Ministry, is concerned with the broad picture of all these subjects. Capt. Reed follows Order of Battle in detail, maintains card records and the top secret Order of Battle map at this Headquarters; passes Order of Battle changes of importance to subordinate Commands; prepares the Order of Battle section for the Weekly Intelligence Summary; and maintains the records on Special Intelligence.

b. Combat Intelligence.

(1) Personnel. Major Simone, Capt. Fellowes and Capt. Bodtke.

(2) Functions: Generally speaking, these officers are responsible for following closely and in detail current Intelligence from all sources, and for supervising the maintenance of proper records on such Intelligence. Major Simone receives and routes all Intelligence material except Special Intelligence, prepares special memoranda and reports for Col. Allen and supervises the other officers in this sub-section, including the War Room. Capt. Fellowes is principally concerned with G.A.F. Intelligence from all sources other than Special Intelligence and for maintaining in convenient form the latest available information on enemy airfields. He supervises the maintenance of the G.A.F. charts and graphs in the War Room, based upon information obtained from Col. Haines. Capt. Bodtke's primary interest is enemy fighter reaction. He prepares a daily reaction report, with copies to General Anderson, SHAEF, Air Ministry and Col. Allen. At the present time, he also writes the Eighth Air Force section of the Daily Intelligence Summary and the "Recent Tactics" section of the Weekly Intelligence Summary.

c. Technical Intelligence.

(1) Personnel: Lt. Col. O'Mara and Capt. Compton.

(2) Functions: This subsection is responsible for all Technical Intelligence, providing information to the Commanding General and Staff at this Headquarters through Col. Allen, and disseminating information to subordinate Commands and units through Weekly Intelligence Summary and Special Reports. A special duty at the present time is the acquisition and maintenance of all possible information on "Crossbow" targets.

d. Publications.

(1) Personnel: Capt. Benson and Lt. Handsfield on the Weekly Inelligence Summary; Capt. Thompson and Lt. D'Urbal on the Daily Intelligence Summary; and Major Coffin and Capt. Davies on Special Reports.

(2) Functions: Production of the publications as above mentioned. The Weekly and Daily Intelligence Summaries are normal Intelligence publications. The three reports under the supervision of Major Coffin, the semi-monthly "Record of Results," the monthly "Summary of Operations," and quarter-annual report on "Results of Operations" are essentially statistical and operational in character. At the present time there is little coordination between these various publications, all being produced more or less independently under Col. Allen's supervision.

e. Photo Intelligence.

(1) Personnel: Capt. Campbell and Capt. Bell.

(2) Functions: This sub-section is primarily concerned with results of bombing as shown by strike and reconnaissance photographs. Strike photographs are obtained daily for the preceding day's missions, are interpreted and brief reports written for presentation by Col. Allen to the afternoon Staff Meeting. Damage files are maintained on each important attack, with photographs and all damage assessment reports. Daily cables are prepared for AGWAR [Adjutant General, War Department] and Fifteenth Air Force, summarizing damage to targets based on photographic evidence. Suitable photographs are also selected for Major Coffin's reports.

f. War Room.

(1) Personnel: Major Simone and Lt. Key.

(2) Functions: Maintenance of all Intelligence maps and displays in the War Room, as well as the physical condition of such room. Lt. Key is immediately in charge under the general supervision of Major Simone. (In addition to his War Room duties, Lt. Key also assists in the preparation of the Daily Intelligence Summary). All target folders are filed in the War Room. Target information is received here from Air Ministry, copies are retained for our files, and distribution made by Courier to the Eighth Air Force. Lt. Key is specially charged with maintaining the ground situation on the Italian Front, and later the "Second" Front. The Operational teleprinters are physically located in the War Room block and are believed to be an Intelligence rather than an Operational responsibility.

2. The Operational Intelligence Section is, on the whole, functioning most efficiently and no major improvements have occurred to me. However, the following comments and suggestions are submitted for consideration and discussion:

a. It seems desirable for the officers indoctrinated on Special Intelligence to work in closer cooperation with each other. I have in mind particularly Major Simone and Captains Fellowes, Bodtke, and Reed. Now that the first three of these officers are indoctrinated it should be more feasible to tie together and coordinate Intelligence from all sources. It is understood that you plan to move all four of these officers into a room together next to your own. This will facilitate this coordination and should be accomplished as soon as possible.

b. The records now being maintained on the G.A.F. and enemy airfields are rather elaborate and, in some cases, involve considerable duplication. It is suggested that there be a consolidation of these records wherever possible. For example, the Order of Battle records now being maintained separately by Capt. Reed and Capt. Fellowes could well be merged so that one master file of important Intelligence on G.A.F. units would be maintained. The same thing might be achieved by consolidation of airfield records.

c. Capt. Reed possibly needs some assistance in tabulating and filing of Special Intelligence. If Major Simone, Capt. Fellowes, Capt. Bodtke and Capt. Reed are all in the same office, adjacent to yours, the four of them together should be in a position to share this responsibility and expand the indexing of Special Intelligence.

d. Analysis and reporting of enemy reaction is an Intelligence function which is now being performed very efficiently by Capt. Bodtke as to "yesterday's" missions. The Operations Section, on the basis of "flash Y" information, frequently reports enemy reaction to to-day's missions at the afternoon conference. I do not think Operations should report on reaction from "Y" sources and it is suggested that we arrange to obtain this information through Intelligence channels which can be reported on the day of the mission. It is appreciated that some information of this type is now being received from Capt. McClintock, but it may be desirable for Capt. Bodtke to obtain a fuller report either from Eighth Air Force or directly from Kingsdown.

e. The "Kingsdown Digest," used by Capt. Bodtke for his report, is apparently greatly delayed as a result of going through Air Ministry. I should like to see arrangements made for a more direct transmission of all "Y" Intelligence. During Overlord it seems probable that the volume of "Y" information will greatly increase, as will the importance of following such information closely.

f. The scope of Special Intelligence now being sent us should be expanded to include full coverage of the Balkans and Russian front. While much of this is now furnished by telephone from Air Ministry, this, in my opinion, is not nearly as satisfactory as receiving it direct through normal channels. Likewise, our direct ground coverage on the Italian front should be expanded. In short, I feel that we should receive all Special Intelligence required by this Command through prescribed channels rather than have some of it relayed by telephone. This would save much time, both of officers here and at Air Ministry; it would reduce the possibility of mistake in handling the material; and would probably be more secure.

g. On the subject of security, I feel that all of us are inclined to be a bit lax at times. With un-indoctrinated personnel having free access to our offices, the problem is particularly difficult. I know you have in mind the necessity of re-arranging the offices on our corridor. In view of the "tissuepaper" walls, this is a rather urgent project.

h. The daily "Operations Intelligence Summary" is an excellent publication, but appears to me to be predominantly operational in character with very little real Intelligence information. This is doubtless a poor time for any radical innovation, but I do think the Operations Section of this Headquarters should produce the part of the summary detailing our operations, leaving to us the production of a strictly Intelligence section dealing with the enemy situation.

i. The principal function of our Section is to keep the Commanding General and his Senior Staff members fully advised on the enemy situation. This, I think, is being admirably performed. A secondary function is to assist and service subordinate Commands. I am not equally sure we are doing everything possible on this score. I appreciate that the opportunities for such service are rather limited in this theater because of the volume of Intelligence available to all Commands from Air Ministry, and also because of the full Intelligence Sections maintained by our subordinate Commands. In any event, I feel that all of us should keep this in mind with the view to expanding our service wherever there is a real need. The Weekly Intelligence Summary is an excellent example of one very useful kind of assistance to subordinate as well as collateral Commands.

j. It is believed a regular weekly meeting of the officer personnel of the Section would be desirable. At such a meeting, held in the War Room at a regular time, the personnel of this Section could be kept informed as to the broad picture. Such a meeting would afford an opportunity for an exchange of views, and would enable the members of each sub-section to keep abreast of what is being done in other sub-sections. It would tend to eliminate the natural tendency for a group of this size to divide itself into more or less isolated cells of separate activity.

k. It is important, I think, for members of the Section to visit from time to time subordinate and collateral Commands, and also all important sources of intelligence.

l. As soon as practicable, the Section (and especially the Combat Intelligence Subsection personnel) should be apprised of the part this Headquarters will play in Overlord in so far as this might affect the functions and responsibilities of this Section. We should review our present sources of intelligence and consider the extent to which Overlord will affect these sources or create new sources.

3. In considering the manner in which I can be of greatest value to you as your Assistant, I suggest the gradual delegation to me of the following duties:

a. Presentation at Daily Conference of information generally within sphere of Fifteenth Air Force (including Mediterranean, S. France, Italy, Balkans and Russia).

b. Presentation of all information when you are absent.

c. Preparation of a preliminary draft of your special weekly summary for General McDonald.

d. Report to Air Ministry the daily intentions of Fifteenth Air Force.

e. Receive the late afternoon report from Capt. Wheeler.

f. Work with the Combat Intelligence Sub-section and Capt. Reed on the coordination of intelligence from all sources.

g. Handle such administrative and routine matters within the Section as you can delegate.

h. In general, learn to "pinch-hit" for you on all matters whenever you are away, and at all times endeavour to relieve you of as much detail as possible.

4. In conclusion, I should like to say that I have been greatly impressed by the personnel, including officers, enlisted men and civilians, of your Section. They are able, diligent and very enthusiastic about their work. I am happy to be the freshman member of your excellent organization.

LEWIS F. POWELL, JR.,
Major, Air Corps

Appendix 5

Notes on Operational Intelligence Division
of
Directorate of Intelligence, USSTAF
by
Lt. Col. Lewis F. Powell, Jr.
9 June 1945

Editor's Note: When the war ended in Europe in May 1945, General Carl A. Spaatz, Commanding General of USSTAF, directed that each of the headquarters directorates prepare a history of its activities from January 1944 to May 1945. Brigadier General George C. McDonald, Director of Intelligence asked each division, including Lt. Col. Powell's, to write chapters. Powell wrote the chapter for the Operational Intelligence Division and it was incorporated into the final history unchanged. For the complete history of the intelligence directorate see Carl Spaatz Papers, USSTAF, Box 290, USSTAF Historical Section, History of Directorate of Intelligence, Manuscript Division, Library of Congress.

HEADQUARTERS
UNITED STATES STRATEGIC AIR FORCES IN EUROPE
Office of the Assistant Chief of Staff, A - 2

APO 413, U.S. Army
9 June 1945

SUBJECT: Notes on Operational Intelligence Division of Directorate of Intelligence, USSTAF.

TO: Brigadier General George C. McDonald, AC of S, A–2

Preliminary Note: This will not purport to be a draft in definitive form of a history of Operational Intelligence. It is proposed merely to set forth here enough information on the functions, responsibilities and accomplishments of Operational Intelligence to assist in the preparation of the official history of the Directorate of Intelligence, USSTAF. The period of time involved is from the inception of USSTAF on 5 January 1944 to the present. During such time there was only one major reorganization of Operational Intelligence, namely that which occurred early in 1945 when the Directorate of Intelligence was reorganized in its entirety along divisional lines and the Target and Flak Sections were integrated with Operational Intelligence. This draft will not undertake to list all the personnel who have worked in Operational Intelligence at various times, it being assumed that the complete history will incorporate appropriate personnel appendices naming the officer and enlisted personnel who have worked with the Directorate of Intelligence, together with their duty assignments.

1. The work of Operational Intelligence of the Directorate of Intelligence, USSTAF, can be discussed conveniently on the basis of three periods, the first from the inception of USSTAF in January 1944 to the establishment of the Advanced Headquarters on the Continent on 30 August 1944; secondly from that date until the reorganization of the Directorate of Intelligence during the first week of January 1945; and thirdly, from the date of such reorganization to the present time.

2. During the first period the Chief of Section was Colonel Julian S. Allen. The functions performed were as follows:

a. War Room. Maintained a War Room adequate and appropriate for daily briefing of the Commanding General and Senior Staff Members. Various personnel of the Section contributed evaluated Intelligence for display in the War Room, and for use in the daily briefings.

b. Enemy Order of Battle. Collected, analyzed and maintained Intelligence from all sources on the strength, composition, disposition, capabilities and fighting value of the German Air Force; and particularly after D-Day, collected, analyzed and maintained Intelligence on the strength, disposition and general capabilities of the German Army.

c. Enemy Airfields. Collected and maintained Intelligence on enemy airfields including their location, use, occupation, servicability and the facilities thereon.

d. "Y" Intelligence. Collected and analyzed all "Y" Intelligence for the principal purpose of ascertaining scope and character of enemy air reaction. Such Intelligence was collated with combat reports and crew sightings, and with other order of battle information.

e. PW Intelligence. Collected, analyzed and maintained Intelligence obtained from the interrogation of PW's and the examination of captured documents, collating such Intelligence with information from other sources.

f. Photographic Intelligence. Collected, analyzed and maintained Photographic Intelligence, including prints and reports; prepared daily strike assessment reports for use in briefing the Commanding General; collaborated with the Target Section in bomb damage assessments; and maintained an adequate photographic library.

g. Intelligence Reports and Publications. Prepared and disseminated appropriate regular and special Intelligence reports and publications. Regular publications included the Daily Intelligence/Operations Summary, the Weekly Air Intelligence Summary, and the Semi-Monthly and Monthly Intelligence Reports to Headquarters Army Air Forces. Special Reports were prepared from time to time on various subjects, usually of current operational interest.

3. Most of the foregoing functions were assumed by USSTAF from Eighth Air Force. However, General McDonald initiated certain changes both in substance and in procedure. Perhaps the most significant of these related to the Intelligence briefing of the Commanding General and Senior Staff Officers. Previously daily briefings in the War Room had been on a "secret" basis, with comparatively few restrictions as to personnel permitted to attend. Such briefings were essentially general in character and designed primarily to keep the entire staff informed on the progress of the war in this and other Theaters. Top secret Intelligence of an important operational nature was usually not presented in these briefings, but privately to the Commanding General as requested. General McDonald eliminated the general open briefing, and substituted what in effect was a daily conference attended only by the Commanding General and a small number of Senior Staff Officers. At such conference, after briefings on the weather and on current operations, Operational Intelligence presented orally a comprehensive summary of the enemy ground and air situation. This presentation included a blending of pertinent and selected Intelligence from all sources, and was designed to provide the Commanding General and Deputy Commanding General for Operations with adequate Intelligence upon which to predicate operational decisions. It is fair to say that at this time this was the major responsibility of Operational Intelligence. While it disseminated Intelligence to subordinate and lateral commands as well as to Headquarters Army Air Forces, its paramount duty was to keep the Commanding General, the Deputy Commanding General for Operations and Senior Staff Members of this Headquarters fully and adequately advised on the enemy situation, including the strength, disposition and fighting value of the German Air Force and the German Army. This was accomplished through means of the daily briefing and from time to time by written reports and appreciations; it was also accomplished, to a very great extent, by keeping General McDonald fully advised, who in turn spent many hours with the Commanding General.

4. Another change of importance inaugurated by General McDonald related to the form and content of the Weekly Air Intelligence Summary. Under policies promulgated by him, the contents of this summary were limited strictly to Air Intelligence as distinct from general information and current events. The Weekly Intelligence Summary was the primary medium through

which Intelligence was disseminated by USSTAF to subordinate and collateral commands. Its presentation of the strength, disposition and capabilities of the German Air Force was the official Intelligence on this important subject for the operating units in this Theater. The Summary also disseminated vital Operational Intelligence on flak, enemy technical developments and the results of our own operations. The demand for the Summary increased steadily, until on VE Day its circulation aggregated ______ copies per week.

5. One of the really important tasks of Operational Intelligence was to follow the German Air Force. After all this was the "enemy" which our Air Force was actually fighting. Until it was defeated, the planned attacks on strategic targets could never be carried out with maximum effort; nor could the long awaited invasion of the Continent be effected until defeat of the German Air Force assured our aerial supremacy. Even after the major battles with the GAF were fought and won, it was always the first duty of Air Intelligence to know accurately the strength, disposition and capabilities of the GAF. This was a field in which R.A.F. Intelligence had made great progress before we entered the war. Literally several thousand persons and substantial facilities were already employed by the R.A.F. towards collecting Intelligence on the GAF from all sources, analyzing, evaluating and disseminating such Intelligence. General Spaatz, on the recommendation of General McDonald, wisely decided not to duplicate or compete with this successful going concern, but to merge and cooperate with it. The manner in which this was accomplished has been briefly set forth in the section on our liaison with British Air Ministry. At the Air Ministry level, as well as at many of the working levels below, American Air Force personnel took their place beside the R.A.F. Those at Air Ministry were staff members of the Directorate of Intelligence, USSTAF, and as much a part of that Directorate as personnel who worked at Widewing. It was early agreed that there would be no public competition on the burning question of the strength and disposition of the GAF. USSTAF personnel at Air Ministry collaborated in the estimates of strength and disposition which were accepted as official by all Anglo-American commands.

6. In view of the foregoing the GAF Sub-Section of Operational Intelligence did not undertake to make its own estimates of strength and disposition. It did, however, have access to substantially all of the same sources of raw Intelligence as Air Ministry. Such Intelligence was received, correlated, evaluated, and recorded and was used as the basis for our own appreciations of the day to day capabilities of the GAF. It was necessary for Intelligence at USSTAF to be able to provide immediately answers to questions as to over-all GAF strength, the strength of particular units or commands, dispositions of particular units or commands, fighting value and capabilities. Air Ministry estimates and appreciations came out periodically. It was necessary at USSTAF to have these answers on a day to day basis. Accordingly, while the GAF specialists of Operational Intelligence worked in the closest harmony with the British and USSTAF officers at Air Ministry, they did their own independent thinking and analysis and provided the indispensable full time service on the GAF required by the Senior American Air Force Headquarters in this Theater. Information on the GAF was passed to the Commanding General and Senior Staff Officers at the daily briefing and from time to time by special written appreciations. In the interest of protecting certain of the sources from which some of our Intelligence was received, a large majority of these appreciations have a classification which prevents their incorporation in a history of this character. Suffice it to say, however, that it is believed that our Intelligence on the GAF was exceptionally good, and that we were able to assess and appreciate with very substantial accuracy the strength, disposition and capabilities of the GAF. It is a matter of record that our Air Commanders were never surprised in a strategic sense. They were kept advised by General McDonald and his Staff of major trends of the GAF, including the shifting of the weight of forces to and from the various fronts and the tactical

employment likely to be made under various circumstances. Likewise, we were able to anticipate the great majority of Germany's technical developments.

7. One of the most important aspects of work on the GAF was assessing its actual reaction to our strategic missions, and estimating its probable future reactions to such missions. This of course involved an intimate knowledge of strength, disposition and capabilities of the enemy day fighters. The principal source of Intelligence as to the actual reaction itself was wireless interception ("Y"), including instructions from ground controllers, reports of the very elaborate German air raid warning and plotting system, and air to air and air to ground traffic involving the fighters put up for interception. Initially we relied primarily on the very elaborate and efficient "Y" service already developed by the R.A.F. for the interception of the traffic and for the basic traffic analysis. In the spring of 1944, as deep penetrations became the rule rather than the exception, it was necessary to inaugurate airborne "Y" interception, which gradually became the principal source of raw material. The basic traffic analysis continued to be done by A.I.4(f) of Air Ministry. However, Operational Intelligence at USSTAF made its own independent study of the reaction to each major mission. Such study was predicated upon the information derived from "Y," both ground and airborne, upon a detailed scrutiny of the combat reports and sightings of our air crews, and upon a correlation of all of this with latest Intelligence on order of battle. A special reaction report was prepared on each major mission, such report being presented orally to the Commanding General, and sent to Eighth and Fifteenth Air Forces, and subsequently to Headquarters Army Air Forces. This report was of particular value in passing to the Fifteenth Air Force the experience of the Eighth Air Force in territory within their mutual range.

8. Following enemy ground order of battle was another major task of Operational Intelligence. USSTAF was subject to the operational control of SHAEF from April to September 1944. During this time, and thereafter upon request, USSTAF was called upon to cooperate more or less directly with the Ground Forces on numerous occasions. While "strategic" bombing always remained the essential basic commitment of USSTAF it was neither possible nor desirable to draw a sharp line between strategic and tactical operations. It is clear that the attack against Leuna in May 1944 was strategic in character, and the carpet bombing at St. Lo in July was purely tactical. But months later when the flow of German oil had become a trickle, and today's production might well be the fuel for next week's battle, an attack on this same synthetic oil plant could hardly be disassociated from its immediate and direct bearing upon the tide of battle at the front. Thus, for obvious reasons, it was essential for the Commanding General and his staff to know the ground situation intimately. They had to know the general ground situation in order to exercise sound judgment in the employment of Strategic Air Power; even more clearly they had to know a great deal about the detailed ground situation to act upon a request for a carpet bombing attack, or the interdiction of bridges across the Seine or Loire to prevent movement of reinforcing divisions. In critical operations such as the Ardennes Offensive the location and movement of German formations was essential Intelligence to any plan of operation. Our Senior Air Commanders likewise were obligated to follow the ground situation on the Eastern, Balkan and Mediterranean Fronts. Nothing illustrates so well the breadth and flexibility of air power as this. An Army or Army Group Commander on the Western Front was concerned alone with this Front. Not so with our Air Forces, which time and again cooperated directly in support of the Russian Armies, Tito's Jugoslavs and of course our own forces in Italy and Southern France. The establishment of Russian bases and the inauguration of shuttle bombing in the summer of 1944 accented this need for comprehensive Intelligence of our entire enemy ground forces.

9. It is customary in most Air Force Commands for one or more Ground Liaison Officers, especially trained in ground order of battle, to be attached for the purpose of providing the necessary ground Intelligence. The Commanding General of USSTAF preferred, however, to have his own staff provide this Intelligence and accordingly this was done under General McDonald's direction. German ground order of battle on all fronts was followed down to the divisional level, in so far as Intelligence was available. On the Western and Mediterranean Fronts sources were excellent, and it was possible to know with fair assurance the disposition of an overwhelming majority of German divisions virtually all of the time. Likewise, information on strength, equipment and fighting value, as well as upon command organization, supply and movement was all fairly satisfactory. In accomplishing this task of following the strength, disposition and capabilities of the German Ground Forces, Operational Intelligence was not able to rely upon assistance from the Air Ministry as in the case of following the German Air Force. However, indispensable assistance was obtained from SHAEF, British War Office and to a lesser extent from the Army Groups.

10. Operational Intelligence also had the responsibility of maintaining information and briefing daily on the dispositions and intentions of our own Ground Forces. This was not strictly an Intelligence function, but as it was so closely related to the capabilities of the German Army it was logical that we should follow the friendly as well as the enemy ground situation. This was accomplished by establishing and maintaining at all times the closest, friendliest liaison with SHAEF, to whom we are much indebted for making available detailed G-3 information several times daily.

11. The success of Operational Intelligence depends in final analysis upon the sources of Intelligence. Unless these are good the best collation, analysis and evaluation are likely to be futile. The principal sources of Intelligence are well known, and although techniques in the exploitation of these sources made great progress, few more sources were developed in the war. The overwhelming majority of our Intelligence came from photographic reconnaissance; PW interrogation; captured documents and captured equipment; "Y" intercept; ground reports from agents, collaborators, expatriates and friendly neutrals; visual reports and observations of crew members and tactical reconnaissance pilots. This is not the appropriate place for a discussion in any detail of these various sources. As indicated above, most of these were highly developed by the British when we entered the war. Our policy of collaboration and cooperation, as distinct from duplication and competition, resulted in the injection of American personnel into the exploitation of all of these sources. For example General McDonald with the full support of General Spaatz played a conspicuous part in the establishment of a strong American Reconnaissance Force in England early in 1944. But obtaining the photography is only half of the job. The British at Medmenham possessed perhaps the world's most efficient photographic interpretation and analysis center. We gradually built up at Medmenham, and eventually in an associate unit at Pinetree, a staff of American photo intelligence officers which in numbers approximately equalled the R.A.F. Staff. The photo interpretation reports which were the product of this combined effort were the most prolific as well as one of the most fruitful sources of Air Intelligence. American PW interrogators likewise teamed with the British at the Combined Services Detailed Interrogation Center (C.S.D.I.C.) where Air Officers worked with the Air Section (A.D.I.(K)) of British Air Ministry. After our forces were established on the Continent, advanced interrogation teams operated independently with the various Armies and Army Groups in the preliminary interrogation of PW's and screening of documents. USSTAF had its own Technical Intelligence Field Teams who followed closely behind our Ground Forces, preparing appropriate preliminary reports, and sending captured equipment back to Air Ministry and Wright Field for detailed study. The role of wireless interception in assessing enemy air reaction and in assisting

in order of battle Intelligence has been mentioned above. In the tactical employment of escort fighters "Y" also played a prominent role, and in the day to day operations of our Tactical Air Forces on the Continent "Y" and the associated radar MEW units were indispensable to the operations of tactical fighters and fighter bombers. We relied heavily on the Office of Strategic Services for Ground Intelligence reports of all kinds, but were also greatly aided by Ground Intelligence from British, French and other Allied sources.

12. Much of the foregoing Intelligence was received at Widewing in relatively raw form. Operational Intelligence had the task of processing this for use in the daily briefings, in the preparation of appreciations, the maintenance of proper records and the dissemination of Intelligence to other commands. A majority of the raw Intelligence was processed in whole or in part by the various specialists in the appropriate sections of Air Ministry, at War Office, at C.S.D.I.C. (A.D.I.(K)), Medmenham, Ministry of Economic Warfare, American Enemy Objectives Unit, SHAEF, etc. The processed product, in the form of special and periodic reports of various kinds, were received, studied and utilized by USSTAF Operational Intelligence in the accomplishment of the tasks above described. All of this Intelligence was likewise used for the very important work of the Target Section which at a subsequent date became a part of the Operational Intelligence Division.

13. The dissemination of Operational Air Intelligence to subordinate and adjacent commands and to Headquarters Army Air Forces was also a responsibility of Operational Intelligence. USSTAF exercised operational control over Eighth Air Force and Fifteenth Air Force; it exercised only administrative control over Ninth Air Force and First Tactical Air Force (Prov). The lines of responsibility were further blurred by the measure of tactical operational control exercised by MAAF over Fifteenth Air Force. In actuality, therefore, our principal operational responsibility was Eighth Air Force. Since it had operated in this Theater prior to the establishment of USSTAF its own channels of Intelligence were fairly well established. It was decided by General McDonald, in the interest of expediting the flow of Intelligence, that USSTAF should not intervene between the source itself and Eighth Air Force except where some useful purpose could be served. Accordingly the great majority of processed, semi-processed and raw Intelligence above described was passed directly and as expeditiously as possible to Eighth Air Force. Much of it was actually disseminated through USSTAF Intelligence personnel at Air Ministry. Operational Intelligence at Widewing did serve Eighth Air Force and its subordinate units in several important ways. The Weekly Air Intelligence Summary, mentioned above, was conspicuous as a medium for the dissemination of processed Intelligence. The Air Order of Battle information and the weekly appreciation of the GAF contained in this Summary were relied upon by the Eighth Air Force and its subordinate commands. In order to expedite delivery of essential order of battle information we teleprinted latest German fighter strength and disposition estimates to the Eighth Air Force each Saturday.

14. A Daily Operations/Intelligence Summary was prepared and disseminated by Operational Intelligence. This contained a summary of all air and ground operations in this and other Theaters. It was established shortly after the activation of Eighth Air Force, covers every operation of that Air Force, and is believed to be the only American Air Intelligence publication which was published daily without a break from the beginning of our operations in this Theater until the end of the German war.

15. In addition to the Daily and Weekly Intelligence Summaries, the special reaction report on each major mission (described above) was sent to Eighth Air Force and Fifteenth Air Force.

From time to time other special appreciations, usually involving high level Intelligence, were passed to Eighth Air Force, and there was of course a free exchange of information and thinking by scrambler telephone and personal conference. The Daily and Weekly Summaries, and occasionally special appreciations, were disseminated to the other American Air Forces in this Theater, although such Air Forces relied in major part on SHAEF for their Operational Intelligence. On the important subject of flak, which towards the end of the war assumed ever increasing importance, Intelligence was collected, processed and disseminated largely at the MI 15 Section of British War Office, where USSTAF Operational Intelligence Officers worked with British Army personnel. Flak information was likewise disseminated through the Weekly Intelligence Summary, and from time to time by special reports and studies.

16. As the top American Air Force Headquarters in this Theater, USSTAF was responsible for providing Washington with detailed reports on the progress of the Air War. Assessment of damage to the enemy is an Intelligence function. The spade work of such assessment was done primarily by photo interpretors at Medmenham and experts in the various pertinent target systems at Air Ministry, E.O.U. [Enemy Objective Unit] and E.W.D. [Economic Warfare Division.] It was the function of Operational Intelligence at USSTAF to assemble, evaluate and report to Headquarters Army Air Forces the results of our operations. This was accomplished through a regular report known as the Semi-Monthly Record of Results, prepared especially for General Arnold, with copies to General Spaatz and to the Assistant Chief of Air Staff, Intelligence, Headquarters Army Air Forces. This report summarized in convenient form Intelligence on the results of our strategic operations, and is believed to be one of the most important and constructive documentations of the accomplishments of American Air Power. There was also a regular monthly report on results of operations, with major emphasis upon photographic demonstration of such results. In this connection, the Photographic Intelligence Sub-Section of Operational Intelligence (as appears more fully from its own history) prepared a number of special photographic reports indicating the success of our operations.

17. The activities and responsibilities of Operational Intelligence as discussed above covered the period from 5 January 1944 to 30 August 1944, during which time all of USSTAF was located at Widewing, Bushey Park, England. On 30 August 1944 USSTAF Advanced Headquarters (for a brief period described actually as Main Headquarters) were established in France, first at Granville and later at St. Germain and Reims. It was necessary therefore to provide Operational Intelligence for General Spaatz at his advanced Headquarters. General McDonald, based on his experience in Africa, appreciated the significance of a highly mobile set up for Advanced, and accordingly an appropriate trailer was obtained and adequately equipped to serve the detailed requirements of the Commanding General. Colonel Allen, with two officers, two WACs and several enlisted men, took charge of this Mobile Operational Intelligence Unit.* General Spaatz was so well served by the Mobile Intelligence Unit that at all times thereafter he insisted on having it located at his personal residence, first at Granville, later at St. Germain and Reims. This unit had the responsibility of keeping General Spaatz fully advised on the enemy situation in all of its ramifications. This it achieved in a conspicuous way.

* At the time of the move on 30 August 1944 it was initially contemplated that the Main Headquarters would go to Granville. Accordingly the original staff taken by Colonel Allen was substantially larger than above described. The excess personnel were returned to Widewing after a brief stay at Granville.

18. The major portion of the personnel of Operational Intelligence remained for time being at Widewing, Bushey Park, and Lieutenant Colonel Lewis F. Powell, Jr., became the Chief of the Section. This continued to be the Main Headquarters of USSTAF until 1 December 1944, when the move to St. Germain occurred. Throughout the months of September, October and November Operational Intelligence at Widewing, Bushey Park, continued to function in substantially the manner described above.

19. When the Main Headquarters were moved to St. Germain we were faced with a difficult decision. The desirability of having a staff section fully integrated and located at one place is manifest. However, the entire structure of USSTAF Intelligence had been predicated upon cooperation with Air Ministry and other British agencies. These agencies were all located in England, chiefly in the London area, and accordingly it was finally deemed necessary to retain at USSTAF Rear in London a substantial part of the Directorate of Intelligence. This necessarily included certain portions of Operational Intelligence, such as the Reports and Publications Sub-Sections, the Enemy Air Reaction Sub-Section, most of the Target Section and all of Flak. However, as a policy it was decided to move all personnel not absolutely essential at Rear to the Main Headquarters in France. This was accomplished gradually to afford a minimum of dislocation in the flow of Intelligence from established channels, and by mid-January the readjustment of personnel, functions and channels had become fairly well settled. Colonel Powell spent the major part of his time at Main Headquarters and accordingly Lt Col Stewart McClintic was made Deputy to Powell and placed in charge of Operational Intelligence at Rear Headquarters.

20. Early in January, upon the initiation of General McDonald, his Deputy, Colonel Weicker, initiated an overall study of the functions and responsibilities of the Directorate of Intelligence with the objective of effecting a thorough-going reorganization. One of the desired purposes of such reorganization was to centralize the responsibility into a limited number of Divisions, pulling together under such Divisions all related functions. Colonel Powell collaborated with Colonel Weicker in the reorganization of the old Operational Intelligence Section into a divisional status. Brought together under this Division were the sections on Targets, Current Intelligence, Photographic Intelligence and Flak Intelligence, all dealing directly with operational aspects of USSTAF responsibilities. Reference should be made to the official function chart of the Directorate of Intelligence dated 16 January 1945 for a detailed statement of the functions and responsibilities of the Operational Intelligence Division and its four branches. It will be noted from such chart that the Target Branch was jointly under Operational Intelligence and the Special Intelligence Division at Air Ministry under Colonel Douglass. The apparent illogical division of responsibility was justified and indeed made necessary by the interrelation between the activities of Colonel Douglass' Division and those of Operational Intelligence. In practice this arrangement proved to be entirely satisfactory and efficient.

21. The history of the Target Section as such, including its highly important work on the various strategic target committees, has been prepared independently of this paper. Perhaps only one aspect of Target Intelligence under the reorganization structure requires additional comment. That pertains to the work on Tactical Targets which was initiated shortly following the reorganization, with the formation of a sub-section to specialize on such targets, particularly communications.* It was realized that we were then entering the final phases of the war and

* See memorandum Colonel Powell to General McDonald dated [.]

strategic bombing, in its original long range sense, had almost concluded its task. It was appreciated that from then on the weight of our strategic effort would be increasingly committed to close cooperation with the Ground Forces. While it was not the function of USSTAF to select strictly ground cooperation targets, it was deemed to be a proper function of our Intelligence to provide such information on these targets as would be of assistance to the Commanding General and the Deputy Commanding General for Operations in the making of their decisions. The Tactical Target Sub-Section cooperated closely with the target authorities of SHAEF, as well as with the appropriate target committees in London.

22. Following the reorganization the daily briefings were expanded to include considerable Target Intelligence. An effort was made to keep our Staff fully informed on the status of the principal target systems, and the condition of individual targets of special importance. This was accomplished through regular weekly briefings in the War Room, accompanied by appropriate charts and maps, and by special briefings and exhibits from time to time. This was particularly interesting in connection with certain communications programs such as the interdiction of the Ruhr.

23. A further bi-product of the reorganization was the plan for a greatly expanded Flak Intelligence and analysis service. The first step in the implementation of such a plan was the procuring from Headquarters Army Air Forces in January 1945 of Lieutenant Colonel Richard Devereaux, one of our outstanding Flak Intelligence officers. In the past flak work at United States Strategic Air Forces had consisted largely of coordination with the British War Office (MI 15) in the collection, processing and disseminating of Intelligence on the strength, disposition and capabilities of enemy flak, including the issuance of flak maps and detailed information on the location of guns. USSTAF maintained two officers and five enlisted men in MI 15, who assisted in the production of this Intelligence. From January 1945 onward the Flak Branch assumed materially increased functions, including the coordination of exchange of flak information and experience among the Air Forces and Commands in this Theater; it arranged for several inter-Air Force conferences on flak, at which methods of minimizing flak losses and damage were studied and recommendations made; it coordinated flak studies prepared by operational research sections and agencies with Flak Intelligence and the studies of radar countermeasures; and it also prepared several special studies on Flak Intelligence and problems which were of exceptional value. Specific recommendations were made for counter flak battery air action. Following VE Day, officers of this Branch went into Germany and studied the flak defenses of several of the more important targets (such as Leuna) and are now engaged in the preparation of a report which should contain Intelligence of operational value in the war against Japan.

24. Operational Intelligence was frequently called upon to prepare, or to participate in the preparation of, special reports and appreciations bearing upon the operational employment of our forces. As indicated elsewhere, most of these reports were too highly classified to be chronicled in a paper of this character. As the tempo of the war increased during these concluding months, with a consequent increase in the demands upon American air power as well as constant change in the character of such demands, the responsibilities of Operational Intelligence became greater and more exacting. The day to day flow of Intelligence had to be accelerated, and particularly during the critical months of January, February and March 1945 the situation required a number of carefully prepared appreciations on enemy capabilities, on the effectiveness of our air operations and on our target policies. Early in January 1945 the Directorate of Intelligence made a detailed analysis of probable enemy capabilities during the year 1945, with Operational Intelligence making a substantial contribution. This study assessed

the capacity of the enemy to interfere with the mission of American Air Power through the efforts of the GAF, particularly its new jet and rocket aircraft, through improved German flak and radar techniques, and the like. Assessment of these capabilities was deemed necessary to assist the Commanding General in planning for the employment of our air power throughout the year, including the determination of his needs for aircraft, personnel and equipment. Other highly significant studies during this period of time included a special appreciation entitled the "Impact of American Air Power on the German War Machine," which surveyed the effectiveness to that date of basic concepts of our air operations. It was of course necessary, particularly during such a period of action and change to keep target policy and priorities under constant surveillance and study. While the principal part of this task was borne by the Combined Strategic Targets Committee (with Operational Intelligence representatives on it and the working sub-committees), the Commanding General and his staff desired certain special studies. The most significant of these proposed a program for the "Employment of Strategic Air Power from 15 March 1945 to VE Day." This study, prepared jointly by Operational Intelligence and the Air Ministry Liaison Division, recommended the target policies and priorities which were approved by the Commanding General and subsequently by the Combined Strategic Targets Committee. The quality and usefulness of this study were of such character as to cause the Commanding General to commend the Directorate of Intelligence. When the plan to isolate the Ruhr by a bridge interdiction program was proposed in February 1945, Operational Intelligence prepared an analysis and estimate of the situation, and recommended that USSTAF support such interdiction program. The ultimate success of interdicting the Ruhr by air power is now a matter of history, being one of the major contributing factors to the crossing of the Rhine by our Ground Forces. Other studies and appreciations of less importance included one on the airborne operation of March 24th, in connection with crossing the Rhine; a thorough study of the results of Operation CLARION (against German communications), with recommendations; and several studies involving proposed operations against POL dumps, ammunition dumps and depots, and ordnance depots.

25. At the request of the Commanding General a special report was prepared by Operational Intelligence on the part played by Air Power in the Ardennes Offensive. This was no casual report, based on superficial study. A determined effort was made to gather all available evidence on air operations for the period 16 December 1944 until the German defeat was manifest on 15 January 1945. The report resulting from this study demonstrates beyond doubt the conspicuous achievements of air power in this epic battle. Conclusions and recommendations in such report may well be useful in the determination of the proper role of air power under comparable circumstances in the future. The report and the officer chiefly responsible for its production (Lieutenant Colonel Caleb Coffin) were the subject of special commendation by the Commanding General. In addition, the Commanding General has requested that a similar comprehensive study be made covering the entire period from 1 January 1944 to the end of the war. Some sixteen officers of Operational Intelligence Division are presently engaged in the preparation of such report.

26. It was of course necessary for the Directorate of Intelligence to maintain at all times the closest liaison with G-2 and A-2 of SHAEF. The importance of this increased with the development of the ground campaign, so that from September 1944 to the end of the war General McDonald, his Deputy, or one or more representatives from Operational Intelligence attended daily the briefing and air planning meeting at SHAEF Headquarters. Colonel Allen as Chief of the Mobile Intelligence Division assumed this duty in September, and from then on attended these meetings regularly. Colonel Powell likewise attended such meetings, representing General McDonald, from the 1st of January until SHAEF Headquarters were moved to Reims in March

1945. General McDonald also participated in the deliberations of the SHAEF Joint Intelligence Committee, and at various times Colonels Allen and Powell represented General McDonald and USSTAF at such J.I.C. meetings. Of great operational significance was the Weekly Air Commanders Meeting held at SHAEF, at which all of the Anglo-American Air Commanders met to discuss the past week's operations and to plan for the future. General McDonald himself usually attended these meetings, but in addition the Chiefs of the Operational Intelligence and Mobile Intelligence Divisions also represented USSTAF Directorate of Intelligence.

27. It would be gratifying to be able to summarize precisely the accomplishments of Operational Intelligence in terms of momentous operational decisions. This is not possible for reasons which are obvious upon reflection. Intelligence itself makes no decisions. Its function is to provide the Commanding General with adequate information on the enemy to enable him to make the decisions, in the light of this Intelligence and all other pertinent considerations. The essential elements of information provided by Air Intelligence relate to the targets to be hit and the enemy defenses, air and ground, which may interfere with hitting them. The Directorate of Intelligence, USSTAF, with its Operational Intelligence Division, its Air Ministry Division and its Mobile Division, endeavored always to provide the best obtainable Intelligence on both targets and enemy defences. It is believed that the conspicuous success of our Air Forces bears witness that by and large we succeeded in this endeavor.

28. In concluding, if a personal word may be permitted, I would like to pay tribute to the extra-ordinary group of people with whom I have worked. First, to General McDonald and his Deputy, Colonel Weicker, who more than any others have been responsible for the over-all excellence of American Air Intelligence in this Theater. They were sound in their judgments and decisions, generous in their delegation of authority, constantly zealous in their support of subordinates, inspiring at all times the utmost respect and loyalty. Then, to the officers and enlisted personnel of the Operational Intelligence Division who actually did the work, must of course go the real credit for whatever has been accomplished. Included among them were many persons of conspicuous ability and talent; all were intelligent, diligent, loyal, aware of the importance of their task, and above all keenly anxious to serve General Spaatz, General McDonald and the cause to which we were all dedicated.

LEWIS F. POWELL, JR.
Lieutenant Colonel, AC
Chief, Oper Intel Div

Appendix 6

Citation for Legion of Merit
for
Lt. Col. Lewis F. Powell, Jr.

WAR DEPARTMENT
THE ADJUTANT GENERAL'S OFFICE
WASHINGTON 25, D.C.

CITATION FOR LEGION OF MERIT

Lieutenant Colonel Lewis F. Powell, Jr., serving as Chief of the Operational Intelligence Division in the Directorate of Intelligence, Headquarters, United States Strategic Air Forces in Europe, from August 1944 to February 1945, contributed materially to the success of the Air Force Operations by furnishing the Strategic Air Force Commanding General and his Deputy Commander, full information on the strength, dispositions, and capabilities of the enemy during a period when maximum effectiveness of our air operations was essential to the overall success of the Allied Armies in the West. He reorganized his Division to include within it the Target, Flak, and Photo Intelligence Sections and formed a Tactical Target Sub-Section to analyze and evaluate the ever increasing mass of intelligence on enemy communications and movements. Through his preparation of top secret special intelligence appreciations, Colonel Powell was of direct assistance to the Commanding General in the formulation of immediate and long-range operational plans for the defeat of the enemy.

Index

Aerial reconnaissance: 9, 28, 41, 49
Air Index: 20, 77–78
Alexander, Henry C.: 58
Allen, Julian B.: 29, 31, 32, 34
Allen, Robert S.: 94
American Bar Association: 1
Anderson, Frederick L., Jr.: 31, 34, 38, 55–56, 59
Ardennes: 39–40
Area bombing: 42
Arlington Hall. *See* Signal Intelligence Service
Army Air Forces Intelligence School: 14
Arnheim: 39
Arnold, Henry H. "Hap": 89
Atkin, S. B.: 90
Atomic weapons: 55

Ballard, William F.: 13
Battle of Midway: 80–81
Battle of the Falaise Gap: 28, 40
Becker, Loftus E.: 16
Beeson, John K.: 60
Big Week: 40
Bismarck: 54
Bissell, Clayton L.: 86–87
Bletchley Park
- American integration at: 25, 84–86
- description of: 12, 26–27, 75–76
- operations: 19, 20, 26–27, 52, 76–78;
- Powell experience: 12, 19–27, 33
- U.S. delegation to: 74–75

BOMBE: 26, 77, 84
Bowers, Harry G.: 13
Bradley, Omar N.: 73
Bratton, Rufus S.: 66, 67
British Air Ministry: 60–63
British Bomber Command: 56
Buzz bombs: 49, 50

Calvocoressi, Peter J.: 21, 25, 34
Cannon, John K.: 7, 9, 10
Central Bureau, Brisbane: 90–92
Churchill, Sarah: 41
Churchill, Winston S.: 46–47, 56, 78, 92–93
Citation for Legion of Merit: 207
Clarke, Carter W.: 15, 69, 71, 72, 78, 87–89, 97
Coffin Project: 62–63
COLOSSUS: 77
Combat Intelligence Center: 91, 92
Cook, Everett R.: 18
Corderman, W. Preston: 81
Corning, Leavitt, Jr.: 13
Counter Intelligence Corps: 73
Curtis, Edward P., Sr.: 18

Darlan, Jean François: 4
Daylight bombing: 37
D-Day. *See* Normandy invasion
Dewey, Thomas E.: 96–97
Direction Finding (DF-ing): 28, 82
Directorate of Intelligence: 33, 87–89
D'Olier, Franklin: 58
Double-cross system: 50–51
Douglass, Kingman, Sr.: 60
Dresden bombings: 55–58

Eaker, Ira C.: 37n, 38, 56
Eighth Air Force: 33, 38
Eisenhower, Dwight D.: 32, 42-43, 73, 96
Elmhirst, Thomas W.: 62
England
Dresden bombings: 56
German agents in: 50-51
German rockets and: 49-50
intelligence sharing: 25, 74-78, 80-83
North African front: 9-10, 29
Powell experience in: 3-4, 19-27, 33
security incidents: 92-93
Soviet Union and: 46-47. *See also* Bletchley Park; ULTRA
ENIGMA: 52, 80, 82, 97
decoding operation: 26, 76-77
German Air Force code: 27-28
operation of: 76

Falaise: 28, 40
Far East Air Forces (FEAF): 94-95
Far East Section: 66, 68, 70, 71
Fellers, Bonner F.: 80
Fellers, James D.: 20, 22, 24, 27
Fifteenth Air Force: 33, 38
Forrestal, James V.: 1
France: 4, 47, 96
Friedman, William F.: 74, 84
Friendly, Alfred: 22, 24, 53

German Air Force (GAF)
Allied efforts against: 35-37
code use by British: 27-28, 77
Powell notes on: 116-67
U.S. intelligence on: 89
Germany
agents in England: 50-51
atomic weapons: 55
bombing of: 35-38, 40-42, 55-58
Eastern front: 44, 47
intelligence: 50-52
jet plane development: 47-48
naval intelligence on: 54
Normandy invasion and: 43
North African front: 5, 9, 11, 80
post-Normandy intelligence and: 39-40
signal system: 76-77
Soviet Air Force specialists: 61-62
Government Code and Cipher School. *See* Bletchley Park

Graham, Philip L.: 16
Ground force intelligence: 27, 28, 38

Haines, William W.: 59-61
Haines Report: 60-61
Hastings, Edward D.: 78
Hitchcock, Edward C.: 22, 24, 27
Huddleson, Edwin H.: 91
Humphreys, Robert H.: 9, 12, 21
Hut 3, Bletchley Park: 12, 20, 77, 86
Hut 6, Bletchley Park: 12, 19, 77
Hut 8, Bletchley Park: 77

Inglis, Francis F.: 62
Intelligence Branch: 66
Intelligence Group: 74
Intercept stations: 25-26, 52, 71, 76
Italy: 10, 24, 27
Ivelaw-Chapman, Ronald: 93

Japan
attack on U.S. bases: 65-66
ENIGMA machine use: 80
intelligence on: 66, 74-75
Pearl Harbor-related activities: 67-68
signal system: 17, 80-81, 93, 97
Joint Intelligence Center, Pacific Ocean Area (JICPOA): 90

Kasserine Pass: 6
Kimmel, Husband E.: 68
Koenig, Egmont F.: 2

Lanphier, T. G.: 89
Lathrop, William R.: 13
Layton, Edwin: 91
Lee, Raymond E.: 69
Legion of Merit citation: 207
Lovett, Robert A.: 56
Luard, James C.: 24

MacArthur, Douglas: 90
MAGIC: 17, 66-69, 74, 87, 96
Marshall, George C.: 66, 85, 97
McClintic, Stewart: 60
McCloy, John J.: 56, 69
McCormack, Alfred
Bletchley Park visit: 74, 75, 84
Directorate of Intelligence duty: 87-89
intelligence operations study: 69-71

Powell recruitment: 15-18
Special Branch duty: 15-18, 71-73, 94
Special Security Officer recruitment: 85
McDonald, George C.: 7-10, 17, 18, 29, 32-34, 50, 61, 62
McKee, Samuel: 84
ME-262 development: 47-48
Midway: 80-81
Miles, Sherman: 66, 68
Military Intelligence Division (MID)
MIS reorganization: 87
post-Pearl Harbor changes: 69-71
pre-Pearl Harbor operations: 65-68
reorganization: 70
Military Intelligence (G-2): 66, 71, 73
Military Intelligence Service, War Department, London Branch (MIS, WD, London): 84-86
Military Intelligence Service (MIS): 65
establishment of: 70-71
Pacific operations: 90-92
reorganization: 86-89
security incidents: 92-97
Signal Intelligence Service and: 71-72
Montgomery, Bernard L.: 9, 29

Naval intelligence: 54-55
News media, 53-54: 80-81
Nimitz, Chester W.: 92
Normandy invasion: 36, 37, 41-42
Norstad, Lauris: 12, 13
North Africa: 4-13, 25, 29, 80
Northwest African Air Forces (NWAAF): 8-13

Operational Intelligence Section: 12-13, 31, 33-34, 172-89
Oranienburg: 55
Oshima, Hiroshi: 75
Osmun, Russ: 87

Pacific operations: 90-92, 94
Peabody, Paul E.: 87
Pearl Harbor: 17, 65-68
Peenemünde: 49
Poland: 44-45, 77
Poore, Walter H.: 2
Powell, Lewis F., Jr.
Bletchley Park experience: 12, 19-27, 33
British Air Ministry duty: 60-63
defensive use of ULTRA comments: 47-51
entry into service: 1-2
Germans' code breaking effort comments: 51-52
Haines Report preparation: 60-61
intelligence work choice: 4-5
Italian ULTRA mission: 24, 27
Legion of Merit citation: 207
North African experience: 4-13, 29
Northwest African Air Forces duty: 8-13
notes from Bletchley Park: 116-67
operational effects of ULTRA comments: 35-41
Operational Intelligence Section operations memorandum: 33-34, 172-89
secrecy of ULTRA comments: 52-55
Soviet air force manual work: 61-62
Special Branch entry: 15-18
Strategic Bombing Survey views: 58-59
319th Bomb Group duty: 2-7, 111-15
training: 2, 4, 15, 18-22, 25-27
Twelfth Air Force duty: 7
U.S.-based duty: 13-15
U.S. Strategic Air Forces duty: 29-34, 38-50, 52, 55-56, 58, 59
ULTRA recommendations: 27-29, 168-71
Yalta views: 59
Priestley, Herbert: 2n
PROJECT YELLOW: 84
PURPLE: 66, 69, 75

Quesada, Elwood R. "Pete": 19-20, 93

Rail communications targets: 43
Rapid analytical machines (RAM): 80
RED machine: 66
Ribbentrop-Molotov Pact: 47
Roberts, Owen J.: 68
Roberts Commission: 68
Rockets: 48-50
Rommel, Erwin: 11, 80
Roosevelt, Franklin D.: 59, 68, 70
Rose, E.J.B. "Jim": 21, 33, 34
Rosengarten, Adolph G.: 22, 24, 27
Royal Air Force (RAF): 9, 10, 37, 38, 43, 49, 62

Section C: 85
Security incidents: 80, 92-97
Short, Walter C.: 68
Shuttle bombing: 43-45
Sicily invasion: 9
SIGABA: 52, 82, 91, 96
SIGCUM: 82
Signal Corps: 71
Signal Intelligence Service (SIS): 66, 67, 71-72, 74, 80, 84; *See also* Signal Security Agency
Signal Security Agency: 84, 86
6813th Signal Security Detachment: 86
Skip bombing: 6
Southwest Pacific Area (SWPA): 90-92
Soviet Union
  air forces of: 61-62
  Dresden bombings and: 56-58
  shuttle bombing operation: 44-46
  ULTRA use for: 46-47
Spaatz, Carl A. "Tooey"
  Northwest African Air Forces duty: 9, 10, 12
  Powell impressions of: 29, 59
  separate Air Force activity: 64
  Twelfth Air Force duty: 7
  U.S. Strategic Air Forces duty: 17-19, 25, 29, 31, 32, 38, 42-43, 59, 61, 63
Special Branch
  establishment of: 71-72
  European theater information: 74, 78, 84
  operations: 73-74
  organization of: 85;
  Pacific operations: 17, 91
  Powell experience: 15-17, 32, 62, 63
  reorganization: 87, 89
  Special Security Officer recruitment: 85
  staffing: 72-73
Special Communications Unit (SCU): 78
Specialists: 88-89
Special Liaison Units (SLU): 10, 32, 78, 90
Special Security Officers: 85, 86, 88, 89, 90-92, 94-96
Speer, Albert: 36, 41
Stalin, Joseph: 47
Stimson, Henry L.: 68-69
Storey, Robert G.: 24
Strategic air forces: 36-37
Strategic bombing: 43, 58-59
Strategic Bombing Survey: 58-59
Strong, George V.: 70, 71, 73, 84
Strong, Kenneth W.: 25
Synthetic oil plant targets: 35, 38, 40-41

Tactical bombing: 43
Target systems: 35-38, 40-43
Taylor, Telford: 21-22, 74, 84
Tedder, Arthur W.: 9, 12
319th Bomb Group: 2-7, 111-15
3-US unit: 86
TORCH operation: 4n
Training: 2, 4, 15, 18-22, 25-27, 112
Travis, Edward W.: 81
Turing, Alan M.: 26
Twelfth Air Force: 5-7
TYPEX: 52, 82

U.S. Navy: 68, 91-92, 95-96
U.S. Navy Op-20-G: 66
U.S. Strategic Air Forces (USSTAF): 18, 19n, 25, 29-34
  Dresden bombings: 55-56;
  Haines Report: 60-61
  history of operations: 62-63
  intelligence use: 38-42
  Oranienburg bombing: 55
  pre-Normandy transportation campaign: 42-43
  shuttle bombing operation: 44-46
  Soviet air force manual: 61-62
ULTRA
  American field dissemination: 85-86, 88
  American integration into: 24-25, 28
  Bletchley Park operation: 12, 19, 20, 26-27
  France and: 47
  German jet development information: 47-48
  history report: 60-61
  Military Intelligence Service use: 87, 88
  North African front and: 10-11
  Pacific operations: 90-92, 94-96
  personnel: 21-22, 26, 60
  Powell Italian mission: 24, 27
  Powell recommendations for: 27-29, 168-71;
  Powell selection for: 15-16
  pre-Normandy transportation campaign and: 42
  processing of: 77-78, 86

rocket information: 48–50
secrecy of: 11, 52–55, 92, 93
security incidents: 92–97
shuttle bombing operation and: 43–45
Soviet Union and: 46–47
operations effects: 35–41
transmission of: 52
U.S. Strategic Air Forces use: 29, 31–34

Vanaman, Arthur W.: 93
V-weapons: 49–50

War Department
Bletchley Park delegation: 74–75
intelligence operations study: 69–71
intelligence sharing negotiations: 78, 80–83
reorganization: 70
security incidents: 80
ULTRA security regulations: 85–86
Weicker, Lowell P., Sr.: 33, 34, 61
Winchell, Walter: 81
Winterbotham, Frederick W.: 22, 78
Women's Army Corps: 73

Yalta Conference: 59
Yamamoto, Isoroku: 93
Y intelligence: 82
"Y" service intercept: 10